BILL WINSTON

FAITH&
THE MARKETPLACE

II

Cover design by: Optmedia Creative Studio, Inc.

Literary consultation services provided by: Dr. Dennis J. Woods
Published by: Bill Winston Ministries

CONTENTS

PREFACE

*F*aith and the Marketplace is a result of a revelation from God given to me when I was enrolled in seminary back in 1986. After a time of seeking the Lord to better understand my purpose and calling in this life, I heard this, "Take the straps off." The Lord was taking me to a greater understanding of His Truth...one that would allow me to see a ministry as any enterprise where Jesus is Lord. People would then recognize a ministry as a manufacturing company, or a publishing company, or ABC Distribution Company. He revealed to me that there will be godly men and women with great integrity managing these companies. They will be God's anointed ministers in the marketplace. They will operate these businesses using the principles of faith along with their basic business skills.

Along with this revelation I was led to this scripture in Isaiah 48:17: *"Thus saith the Lord, thy Redeemer, the Holy One of Israel; I am the Lord thy God which teacheth thee to profit, which leadeth thee by the way that thou shouldest go."*

As I read these words I saw them like I had never seen them before. The word *profit* stood out like light in the darkness. From this revelation came the Joseph Business School (JBS), founded in 1998 and now a nationally accredited business school, training students using practical and biblical principles to be successful entrepreneurs and business leaders. The wealth created from the graduates' businesses will help establish God's kingdom in every place and eradicate poverty wherever it is found.

As the world's economic system continues to fail, those trained on how to do "Business by the Book" (a course I teach at JBS) will prevail. In fact, the church institution will become the most successful and wealthiest in the world, no longer living on leftovers after paying its bills or pastors struggling to raise money to move forward with the vision the Lord has placed in their hearts. It will destroy poverty at its roots as well as fulfill the prophecy that says, *"...the earth shall be full of the knowledge of the LORD, as the waters cover the sea"* (Isaiah 11:9). The Church is now moving into an end-time season when the wealth of nations is coming into the hands of the righteous. Why? So that *"this gospel of the kingdom shall be preached in all the world for a witness...and then shall the end come"* (Matthew 24:14). One man said, "Believers will experience a 'no budget' anointing."

Here is a biblical prophecy that must be fulfilled, and it will take finances to help accomplish it:

> The desolate land will be cultivated instead of lying desolate in the sight of all who pass through it. They will say, "This land that was laid waste has become like the garden of Eden; the cities that were lying in ruins, desolate and destroyed, are now fortified and inhabited"...I the LORD have spoken, and I will do it. Ezekiel 36:34–36 NIV

For the past seventeen years, I have been teaching and preaching, demonstrating and documenting that one Word given to me that day while in seminary, which I am now writing about in this book. Even though I taught and practiced it, this book clearly confirms that faith and the marketplace were never meant to be separated, and now it's time for the people of God (the Church) to bring them back together.

When Adam and Eve sinned and were put out of the garden of Eden, they began to produce another culture, a culture that was built outside the presence of the One True God. This was a culture originating from the mind of its architect, satan, and not from our Creator. Soon, laws were made to support this culture and to legalize its destructive influence.

For example, in the United States, some have legally challenged the phrase "under God" in our country's Pledge of Allegiance, and the U.S. Supreme Court's *Abington Township School District v. Schempp* decision in 1963 prohibits teachers and school officials from organizing or leading prayers or devotional Bible reading in public schools.[1] Decades later we are seeing the effects of this decision in the deterioration and destruction of much of our public school system, from safety to academic achievement to morality.

Knowledge alone will not exalt a nation. You must combine natural knowledge with revealed knowledge of the principles of the kingdom, such as integrity, love, holiness, and compassion. If you combine natural learning along with faith or spiritual knowledge and wisdom, you can see the full aspects of any problem, and can determine the best and sure approach to solving them.

Today, in almost every nation, crime, corruption, and cyber-terrorism have been on the increase, not to mention the rise in global poverty, which is now estimated to affect about 702 million people.[2] What happened? Faith left the marketplace. These problems remind me of the story of the mythical character Hercules fighting the giant Hydra, a dragon-type monster with many heads. As soon as Hercules would cut off one head, two more would grow back in its place.

What is happening here? Without God a society is stuck with inferior principles getting inferior results. In six of the seven pillars shaping our society—government, business, education, media, the family, and arts and entertainment[3]—there is a conspicuous absence of the government of God and faith in God.

Without faith in God and the wisdom of God to make divinely directed decisions, the world remains on a course of self-destruction. In the book of Proverbs it says, *"There is a way which seemeth right unto a man, but the end thereof are the ways of death"* (Proverbs 14:12). This is why the "ministers" who were spoken about when I heard that life-changing prophetic word in 1986 must receive their "calling" and take their rightful place as marketplace shapers of destiny. As Jesus points out in the gospel of Mark 10:27, *"...With men it is impossible, but not with God: for with God all things are possible."*

In this book, **Faith and the Marketplace**, I also discuss, in-depth, the restoration of the Old Testament model called "Kings and Priests." A reuniting of this biblical "dream team" of the prophet and the king. Today, that's the pulpit and the pew—clergy and laymen—working together for the good of the kingdom. Both kings and priests are anointed by God to win every battle and, by faith, literally transform the worst places on Earth into a garden of Eden. Looking back in biblical history, to ensure the continued success of a nation, every Abraham needed a Melchizedek...every King David needed a prophet Nathan...every Pharaoh needed a Joseph (a seer). And in the history of our United States Armed Forces...every General Patton needed the prayer of his army chaplain. And to solve the problems we face today, which are more than physical, we need the return of this divinely created unbeatable team.

I am convinced that through the reintroduction of faith into the marketplace and the partnership of kings and priests, our societies will not only be preserved but transformed to reflect the peace and prosperity God originally planned... *"Thy kingdom come thy will be done on earth as it is in Heaven."*

Mark Twain, the famous American writer, said, "The two most important days in your life are the day you are born and the day you find out why." I pray this book will help you discover your purpose here on Earth and the role you are to play as a king or priest in restoring faith to the marketplace once again.

Bill Winston

INTRODUCTION

As a young lad growing up in the small southern town of Tuskegee, Alabama, I always dreamed of going places and seeing the world. In my vivid imagination, I saw myself being a physician, a firefighter, a cowboy, even an action hero like Superman.

The occupation that eventually captured my interest the most was that of being a pilot. In our community, I had the privilege of knowing many of the legendary Tuskegee Airmen in my youth and they were all larger-than-life heroes who worked, worshipped, and lived in my hometown. Their sons and daughters were my classmates in elementary school. We all lived, learned, and dreamed together in Tuskegee.

One unforgettable occasion was when I had my first airplane ride with the man who was an instructor for the Tuskegee Airmen, Mr. Charles A. Anderson, affectionately known as Chief Anderson. After that experience, I knew I was destined to fly. Years later, I graduated from Tuskegee Institute (now Tuskegee University) and served in the United States Air Force where I became a fighter pilot. Military service took me around the globe, from the confines of a small, close-knit African American community in Alabama to Southeast Asia, Korea, and various parts of the United States.

Unbeknownst to me at the time, I was being prepared for my destiny. While in the military, there were some key leadership lessons that I learned, like the importance of discipline in an assignment, how authority works, mission planning and execution along with the importance of precision and excellence. I also learned what it means to have courage in the face of threat or opposition, the importance of "no one left behind," and the art of decision making and delegation.

After being honorably discharged at the end of my military service, I was hired in sales at one of the major international computer corporations, IBM. It was with this company that my life drastically changed. The first major change was in the area of business, where I learned the art of selling, how to handle rejection, the importance of profit, and the importance of providing quality service. The company was big on excellence in customer service and respect for the individual.

I also developed the art of servant leadership and how to tap into the hidden potential of others. Many of the sales representatives who joined my marketing team in the beginning were not the highest performers. However, with coaching, encouragement, and guidance, they became among the best. Some turned out to be the region's highest revenue producers and finest marketers. Needless to say, while helping the team to discover their greatness, I also discovered some interesting things about myself. I learned that part of my gifting was that of a motivator and teacher, with an ability to inspire and draw out the best in people.

The second major change was that I met my wife, Veronica, who has now been my partner in our adventures in faith for more than 30 years. She was also working at the company on the more technical side of the business, as a computer systems engineer.

The third and most important thing that took place was when I received Christ into my life. To merely say that "my life changed" would be an understatement. I began to see everything differently, including my purpose for being on this Earth. The Bible became more than a bunch of dos and don'ts—that's religion. Now it became heaven's constitution, a success book, that when its laws and principles are believed or applied, will "supernaturally" produce phenomenal results regardless of the environmental circumstances or market conditions.

Once born again into the kingdom of God, I began listening to anointed Bible teachers who gave me understanding that God offers me an opportunity to start over...that this old life I had messed up can be rewritten, every chapter of it. I also learned that this new kingdom I was born into is heaven's government brought to Earth and has a way of doing things that require almost a complete mental reversal from the way I had been taught to think.

The Bible says, *"...seek ye first the kingdom of God, and his righteousness; and all these things shall be added unto you."* This simply means to "seek God's way of doing things." I quickly began to learn how to apply biblical laws and principles to produce predictable sales results, not just one month but every month, consistently. Also, I soon learned how to access God's wisdom in solving every problem.

I became excited about making sales presentations, closing business deals, and working with my customers in helping to solve their problems. You see, when the wisdom of God is available, you'll climb to the top of the performance chart without a sweat. It was phenomenal! The scriptures tell us, *"He layeth up sound wisdom for the righteous...."* Not from the righteous...but "for the righteous." This is all based on the fact that God is omniscient, which means "all knowing." He knows the end from the beginning, and has seen your need and has already provided. No longer did I see problems as an obstacle or something sent to sabotage my success. No, now every problem became an opportunity to manifest this new kingdom and, oh yes, to bring home bigger commission checks!

Needless to say, because of my performance (and the grace of God, of course) I was promoted to management where I continued working the higher laws and principles of the kingdom. This application of "Faith and the Marketplace" created a platform of credibility that caused many of my coworkers and friends to become very inquisitive about how all this was happening to me. It reminds me of Pharaoh in Egypt, who never inquired about Joseph's father until Joseph, through the wisdom of God, solved his problems.

Here is something worth remembering, **Christianity was never meant to be dictated; it was meant to be demonstrated.** Your job becomes your pulpit, your performance becomes your platform, and the marketplace becomes your parish. Jesus said it like this, *"Let your light so shine before men, that they may see your good works, and glorify your Father which is in heaven."*

This is why I wrote **Faith and the Marketplace.** So many believers have seen their Christianity as separate from their job or business, something for only Sunday morning. And many have a difficult time reconciling their Christian faith with their desire for profit and business success. Let me assure you, the two were never meant to be separated.

A great illustration of this is a testimony I read about David M. Browne, the former CEO and president of LensCrafters, which he also cofounded. While growing up in church, Browne somehow received the belief that faith and business did not mix, and "he fell into the habit of applying one ethical system in his personal life and a completely different ethical system at work. But through an intimate encounter with God, Browne began to realize that there might be a way to bridge the two worlds after all."[1]

Browne bridged those two worlds by bringing "the servant leadership model of Jesus Christ"[2] to his management of LensCrafters. After changing his leadership style and eventually the culture of the entire company, the company's phenomenal business success over the next ten years speaks for itself. Company revenues grew to $2 billion; the number of company stores grew from 50 to 1,200; the company was considered the most profitable retailer at the time, with close to a 20% profit margin; the last 7 years of growth were funded by their cash flow and not debt; and LensCrafters was the first for-profit company to receive the Volunteer Action Award from the White House for its Gift of Sight program.[3]

As Matthew 11:19 says, *"God's wisdom...is shown to be true by its results" (Good News Translation)*. God strategically positions us in the marketplace to not only bring His compassion, but also, through our work performance, demonstrate His wisdom and ultimately His influence.

In these last of the "Last Days," according to the Scriptures, we will experience an outpouring of God's wisdom and witness explosive inventions that can only be compared with God's original Creation. And this outpouring will come through the Church, the Body of Christ. It will not be the intellectual, technological, or scientific wisdom taught at universities. It will be the wisdom that only the Holy Spirit teaches. It's the wisdom that established Daniel to counsel the Babylonian government, and Joseph to bring forth the most powerful economy the world had ever seen, which brought them both to prominence and marketplace leadership.

My desire is that through this book you will learn how to apply your faith in the marketplace to achieve "ten times better" results or performance in whatever your field or endeavor. This success can happen in the life of every believer once they find their place of grace (purpose) and understand kingdom principles. For me, this kingdom understanding first came through the teachings of a Bible teacher, who I listened to each morning on the way to work on a Christian radio station. For you, this kingdom understanding might be through your pastor or a "teaching priest," or through books and tapes.

My point is that every Christian serving in the marketplace needs a teacher, someone to bring understanding of "how to" apply the Scriptures in their everyday situations. In this book, you will see clearly that this "divine partnership"[4] of kings (those working in the marketplace) and priests (clergy and five-fold ministry) in these last days is not an option. If the Church is to preserve humanity, destroy poverty at its roots, and turn society from its path of self-destruction this partnership is a requirement. Revelation 1:6 states, *"And hath made us* (the church) *kings and priests unto God...."*

As one man wrote, "When you confine true ministry to (only) the fivefold (or pulpit) ministries, you make 95 percent of the church irrelevant."[5] Why? Because all of the people in the Church are "ministers" who are called to serve God whether in religion, media, business, government, arts and entertainment, education, or the family. As God prophetically spoke to me in 1986, it is time to "take the straps off"; that is, recalibrate our thinking so that every person in the Body of Christ understands their purpose and responsibility and fulfills their kingdom assignment.

Today, nations are threatening default because of their country's excessive debt obligations; cities are unable to meet their municipal budgets without voting in higher and higher taxes on its citizens; the threat of terrorism is worldwide; and drugs, poverty, violence, and joblessness are trying to destroy the urban communities. Well, it is time for the Church to take the stage. There is no other institution on Earth equipped to solve problems of this complexity and on this magnitude.

So, whether you are called to the pulpit or the pew, you have a calling. You are no longer ordinary. And you are born with much more potential and for a greater work than where you are right now. Like the Elijahs or Esthers, who decided the destinies of nations, the fulfillment of your kingdom assignment is extremely important. As a clergyman or on the city council, as an educator or evangelist, as an economic rainmaker or homemaker, or a missionary, you are anointed to render exceptional service. And through this divine partnership of kings and priests and, of course, Almighty God, you can effectively change the destiny of millions, if not billions, in cities and countries all over the world.

Finally, as you read this book, may you not only confirm your own unique place and purpose in the kingdom, but also put to work your faith in the marketplace to bring forth heaven on Earth wherever you are sent.

God bless you on your journey...enjoy!

PART 1
THE FOUNDATION

CHAPTER 1

KINGS & PRIESTS
A REVELATION

I n order to completely understand the concept of kings and priests and the connection between faith and the marketplace, one first has to understand the roles of Old Testament kings and priests and modern-day kings and priests.

THE OLD TESTAMENT KING

Two of the primary purposes of the Old Testament king were to rule over God's people and lead them into battle against the enemy. Whenever He had a faithful king, God would go with him into battle, and assure his victory. After he conquered the enemy, a faithful king would bring back the spoils of war, placing them in his own treasury but excluding the portion given back to God through the priest. The "tithe" would ensure that Israel could continue in "THE BLESSING" of the Lord.

Kings were the land and business owners. The kings also oversaw all of the commerce and trade. They managed the nation's economy by imposing taxes and fees, and regulating weights and measures. A king also had the responsibility of assuring that farmers left provisions for the poor and needy in the corners of their land. The system used to accomplish this was called *gleaning*, an ancient version of welfare. To preserve their dignity and work ethic, the Lord had them glean.

THE OLD TESTAMENT PRIEST

Among the twelve tribes of Israel was an entire tribe called "Levites" who were solely dedicated to the priesthood. Though the Levites had numerous functions, their primary role was to offer up prayers and sacrifices to God. They also took care of the temple, providing maintenance and other day-to-day liturgical functions. They were emissaries of mercy and took care of the orphans, widows, and strangers at the gates. They were the ones who interceded on behalf of the people, offered up sacrifices for sin and atonement, and pronounced blessings over the people (Numbers 6:22–27; Deuteronomy 20:1–4).

In the Old Testament, the priest would also bless the king and his army before proceeding into battle. To *bless* means "to say (or declare) something good, and by faith, empower it to come to pass." This is not just speaking; THE BLESSING, which is the scriptural name of the power that created all matter, also empowers goodness, favor, and supernatural victory to come to pass. With the blessing of the prophet (the priest), the power of God would go out before the army and the Lord would fight the battle and deliver the enemy into the king's hand.

> TO BLESS EMPOWERS GOODNESS, FAVOR, AND SUPERNATURAL VICTORY.

There also were times when the Lord would tell the priest exactly what the king and his army needed to do to defeat the enemy. An amazing example of this is found in 2 Chronicles, chapter 20, when, through a prophet, the word of the Lord came to King Jehoshaphat when he was surrounded by three hostile armies poised to attack, *"...Jehoshaphat stood and said, Hear me, O Judah, and ye inhabitants of Jerusalem; Believe in the* LORD *your God, so shall ye be established; believe his prophets, so shall ye prosper...And when they began to sing and to praise, the* LORD *set ambushments against the children of Ammon, Moab, and mount Seir,...and they were smitten...they were dead bodies fallen to the earth, and none escaped"* (verses 20, 22, and 24).

In summary, the Old Testament priest took care of all the ceremonial and ecclesiastical affairs, whereas the Old

Testament king took care of the secular, civil, and govern-
mental affairs. Both offices were important in people's lives,
and it was absolutely essential that they worked together.
Now let's look at these roles in modern day.

MODERN-DAY KINGS

As mentioned earlier, throughout history kings were assigned the responsibility for waging war and taking ground
for their kingdoms. In the Bible, we read that the Lord told
Abraham, *"For all the land which thou seest, to thee will I give
it, and to thy seed for ever"* (Genesis 13:15). He told Joshua,
*"Every place the sole of your foot shall tread upon, that have
I given unto you, as I said unto Moses"* (Joshua 1:3). And, in
the book of Psalms it says, *"Ask of me and I shall give thee
the heathen for thine inheritance, and the uttermost parts of
the earth for thy possession"* (Psalm 2:8).

Today, we have this same principle with the modern-day
kings, the anointed marketplace ministers. God is still very
much interested in His people possessing the land, and every
inch of ground that is to be taken now, as in the past, has
to be fought for. Unfortunately, today's kings are not completely aware of their purpose and calling. They are "attending church," fund-raising, giving money here and there, and
serving in what I refer to as "part-time kingdom purpose."
They do not fully understand their calling, and are not fully
engaged in their responsibilities or roles.

Their responsibility is the same as God gave Adam, to
have dominion over this planet and over all of its resources
and revenues. From economics and business to education
and politics, the kingdom is to rule over everything, including the judiciary system and the laws of the land. We are the
King's representatives to enforce the kingdom culture.

The earth is part of the territory that belongs to the kingdom of God and, again, *"...His kingdom rules over all"*...ev-
erything. Psalm 24:1 says, *"The earth is the LORD's...."* The
Church's job is to bring the government of heaven to bear
upon the earth wherever we are.

Revelation, chapter 1, verse 6, says, *"And hath made
us kings and priests unto God and his Father; to him be*

glory and dominion for ever and ever. Amen." This passage is speaking about the end-time Church. The modern-day kings are responsible for securing the *provision* of God; they are the "ministers of the marketplace" and it is critical that the modern-day priests "bless" the kings as they gather this provision. In this day and time, kings could be people from any walk of life. They could be people from the entertainment industry, social services, or medical fields. They could be the skilled laborers, like carpenters and electricians, or even stay-at-home parents. Occupation makes no difference, because whoever is not a priest is automatically a king.

MODERN-DAY PRIESTS

Priests in the New Testament are those who are in the five-fold ministry, full-time. They are the apostles, prophets, evangelists, pastors, and teachers, referred to as *ministry gifts* given to the Body of Christ (Ephesians 4:11–13). Similar to the Old Testament priests, today's priests still have the responsibility for caring for the house of God, for receiving the tithes (Malachi 3:8–11), and for warning and informing the people of God of what is coming or what God is saying. In Amos 3:7, the Word of God says, *"Surely the LORD God will do nothing, but he revealeth his secret unto his servants the prophets* (the priests).*"* Today's priests are also anointed to teach the Body of Christ and provide interpretation for correct understanding of the Word of God (2 Chronicles 15:3; Acts 8:30–31).

> **PRIESTS HAVE INSIGHT INTO KNOWING THE MOVE AND TIMING OF GOD.**

Priests have an unction that gives them insight into knowing the move and the timing of God (1 Kings 18). Oftentimes they receive instructions on how to defeat the enemy and win in battle whether in the marketplace or in people's personal lives (see 2 Chronicles 20).

I recall once when a member of our church came and placed a demand on the priestly anointing that is on my life by asking how to get some taxes paid that were overdue. I gave him what to do strictly by the unction of the Holy Ghost. He followed my instructions, the IRS reduced his taxes to a few hundred dollars, and he paid the amount off immediately. Today's priests also have a responsibility to remind kings about their stewardship obligations, just as Melchizedek did when he met Abraham after his victory in battle *"...And he gave him tithes of all"* (Genesis 14:20).

REVEREND BILLY GRAHAM AND PRESIDENT GEORGE H. W. BUSH

In the Bible, priests, on occasion, became involved in government affairs as advisors, like Daniel and Joseph. Perhaps the best contemporary example of a "priest" providing spiritual guidance and support to government leaders is the highly respected Reverend Billy Graham. On the Billy Graham Evangelistic Association's website in the article "Billy Graham: Pastor to Presidents" is the quote, "Every U.S. President since World War II (through Barack Obama) has met with Billy Graham."[1] The relationship between Rev. Graham and President George H. W. Bush demonstrates the importance of modern-day kings and priests. "Billy Graham has been an inspiration in my life," said Bush. "It is my firm belief that no one can be President...without understanding the power of prayer, (and) without faith. And Billy Graham helped me understand that."[2] Rev. Graham was with the President and Barbara Bush at the White House in 1991 on the night that the Gulf War began. The President invited him to stay at the White House to pray for the troops. As the President, Rev. Graham and Mrs. Bush watched the war begin, President Bush would later say that Reverend Graham's visit that evening gave him great strength.[3]

President Bush told his staff that he "wanted an approach that left no room for defeat. He was determined to provide the military with whatever they needed to win quickly and decisively."[4] As a result, the war lasted only 42 days.[5]

ADVISING A FORTUNE 500 CEO

I was once asked to meet with the CEO of a Fortune 500 company about what he, in his position of corporate influence, could do to help black male youth in Chicago. I met with him and told him, "I'm not sure what you can do today, but give me seven days and I'll be back with the answer."

You might ask, "How could you be so sure?" My answer is in the scriptures, which say that the Lord *"...layeth up sound wisdom for the righteous..."* and all we need to do is ask for it (see Proverbs 2:7 and James 1:5). That's how I knew I would be back with the answer, and *"...God cannot lie"* (Hebrews 6:18 GNT).

So, I asked God for wisdom and expected an answer that week, because wisdom is part of my inheritance. I put a demand on the supply of wisdom that was placed in inventory for me from the foundation of the world. Wisdom "downloaded" a presentation of the solution that I presented to the CEO the following week. When we met again I shared with him my answer, and he shouted, "THAT'S IT REVEREND! THAT'S IT!" The result was that he approved funding (money from a special chairman's fund) for a youth program to teach young black men business and entrepreneurship. I implemented the idea and today, from that same idea, we have the Joseph Business School, a Christian school of business and entrepreneurship that has locations on five continents.

POWER, PROTECTION AND WISDOM RESULT WHEN KINGS AND PRIESTS COME TOGETHER AS GOD INTENDED.

These examples of Old Testament and modern-day kings and priests illustrate the power, protection, and wisdom that can result when these two roles function together as God intended. In this book, I lay out the roles and responsibilities of each "calling." When kings and priests come together on one accord, I identify that as a **kingdom partnership**. It is what I call a perfect **covenant alignment**.

This "dream team" of the kingdom, if understood and properly functioning, will cause the power, performance, and progress of the Body of Christ to rise to an extraordinary level and bring much-needed solutions to the marketplace. We will righteously move into managing all that was previously ruled by ungodliness. This divine partnership forms the basis and model for faith and the marketplace to work together for the betterment of the world. This will not only change the way people view "the Church," but will also draw the movers and shakers and marketplace leaders of the world into the kingdom at a phenomenal rate.

CHAPTER 2

KINGS & PRIESTS
THE KINGDOM

To fully understand the divine partnership of kings and priests, one must first understand the order of the kingdom of God. When Jesus' preaching ministry began, His message was on the kingdom. So what is the kingdom of God? And why is it the most important news ever delivered to the human race?

The kingdom of God is a message not only about salvation and "going to heaven when you die." The kingdom of God has a bigger target than that. It's a gospel that includes salvation, but it's also about heaven being brought to Earth. It's about a new government or sovereign kingdom where God rules; a self-contained kingdom being first established on Earth in people's hearts.

It operates by superior principles from a superior position, and is a new order of living by faith where you don't need to look to other governments or anything else in this world to take care of you. You don't even have to try to meet your own needs. You are to *"...seek ye first the kingdom of God...and all these things shall be added unto you"* (Matthew 6:33).

In this kingdom, the King is obligated to care for and protect all of His citizens, and their welfare is a reflection on the King Himself. The word that most describes this is *commonwealth,* which is "an economic system of a kingdom which guarantees each citizen equal access to financial security,"[1] not to be confused with communism or socialism. Once a person is born again, they become a citizen of this kingdom and partakers of the benefits and privileges of the kingdom.

All the rights of citizenship are at the citizen's pleasure: power, wisdom, honor, riches, strength, glory, and blessing.

The number one goal of each citizen in this kingdom is to submit to the King, seeking only to remain in right standing with Him. Jesus' "kingdom" message was all about humanity rediscovering this self-contained government, and having it established on Earth by and through its representatives or "ambassadors." The message was about regaining our place of dominion and position of leadership in the earth as God originally intended.

Unfortunately, we have preached about going to heaven rather than ruling here on Earth. We have preached "church" instead of kingdom. That's why a fellow Christian will tell you, "My church is better than your church or my pastor is more anointed than yours." It is not possible to possess our inheritance or influence the nations with this mindset. Revelation of the kingdom, and totally submitting to the King, results in the power (John 14:21) it takes to "subdue kingdoms."

When we understand the order of the kingdom, we will better understand specific parts of the kingdom like the ministry of angels (they are the army of the kingdom of God), and the anointed offices of kings and priests. Jesus teaches, *"And this gospel of the kingdom shall be preached in all the world for a witness unto all nations; and then shall the end come"* (Matthew 24:14).

Why haven't we heard more about the kingdom being demonstrated, preached, and established in the world? I believe it's because of tradition, *"Thus have ye made the commandment* (Word) *of God of none effect by your tradition"* (Matthew 15:6), and because of many pastors' failure to embrace the greater revelation of the Holy Spirit by choosing instead to stay with their denominational dogma. This is largely the product of the Church leadership and their traditional ways of thinking.

Because many churches or denominations have not been taught about the kingdom, many of the children of God have taken their *"light of the world"* no further than the four walls of a church building. Talented and gifted marketplace leaders have found few or limited opportunities for their gifts in the local church. And, consequently, the kings have shown no strong sense of duty to support the kingdom's mission and programs.

However, God is training up leaders (priests) that will fully embrace their kingdom authority and properly empower and educate the kings for marketplace influence to effectively rule and reign over this Earth through the King, our Lord Jesus Christ.

Without the gospel of the kingdom, we are left with insufficient truth to advance heaven's government or overcome the enemy of humanity. Fifty years ago, one of the major religions of the world was dominant in only certain parts of the world. However, today, it is controlling a substantial percentage of global economies. "Kings" in that religion see it as their duty or obligation to support the spreading of their religion to all nations.

They pour into the nations with the financial backing to spread their faith and beliefs. They are not organized into many denominations as the Christian faith has been, but they act as "one nation." Jesus teaches us, "A house divided cannot stand." Their religion has never separated their faith from their everyday lives: Their businesses, their politics, their dress codes, their eating and spending habits, and, of course, their money. Their work and their worship go together.

WITHOUT THE GOSPEL OF THE KINGDOM, WE HAVE INSUFFICIENT TRUTH TO OVERCOME THE ENEMY.

Thank God, Jesus is our Savior and Redeemer; even so, to get all the benefits, we must make sure He's our King and our Lord. Lord denotes ownership. The gospel of the kingdom teaches that Jesus should be Lord of our lives, and the Bible should be the guide or constitution for every kingdom citizen.

Again, without the gospel of the kingdom and a proper understanding of the word "Church," we are left with insufficient truth to fulfill our heavenly mandate to evangelize the nations and bring the government of God to bear upon the earth wherever we are sent. The Church is just one part of the kingdom of God. This planet, the heavens, and angels are all a part of the kingdom of God. So, as kings and priests, we are part of the kingdom of God and understanding of this kingdom is necessary to "fully function" in these two offices and to fulfill the call or mandate that is on our lives for this generation.

KINGS AND PRIESTS: A KINGDOM PARADIGM

The revelation of kings and priests is a fundamental principle in the kingdom of God. God wants His kingdom to be established in every nation to influence every sphere and realm of society...the marketplace. Many people who currently control the "high places," which we call spheres of influence, are under spiritual influences they are not aware are affecting them. They think they are making their own decisions. But satan gives high place access to whom he will (Matthew 4:8–9), and picks kings and priests whose thinking and ideology are most susceptible to being manipulated and managed. This is true whether or not they are a banker, judge, politician, media mogul, educator, or some other authority figure. The enemy picks them and puts them up front to control the mountains of society.

The kingdom of God, which Jesus preached, ushers in a new lifestyle of living by faith. This means that God and His kingdom should be our only Source and Supply. One of satan's strategies to destroy the Church's power and influence is to get Christians to trust in everything else but God. His goal is to annihilate the Word of God and bring people of faith into unbelief. Jeremiah 17:5–6 says, *"...Cursed be the man that trusteth in man, and maketh flesh his arm, and whose heart departeth from the Lord. For he shall be like the heath in the desert, and shall not see when good cometh...."*

Satan, working through his system, subtly tries to seduce the Church to be more humanistic than kingdom, to get believers to lose their faith in God. Figure 1 provides characteristics of the kingdom of God and the kingdom of darkness. The latter kingdom is a fear-based system where people trust in their own efforts and other people, instead of trusting in God. In God's kingdom, as I mentioned earlier, it is a new order of living by faith, where we trust in God as our Source and Supply for everything. When a person lives by faith, he or she is able to see and do things beyond his or her natural ability. Faith elevates a person to the realm of believing the unbelievable and doing the impossible.

Figure 1: Characteristics of Two Kingdoms

Kingdom of God	**Kingdom of Darkness**
• God Ruled	• Satan Ruled
• Revelation knowledge (comes out of the Spirit)	• Sense knowledge (gained through the senses, human reason)
• Operates by faith	
• Trust in God as your Source	• Operates by fear (a fear-based system)
• God adds to you through grace and THE BLESSING	• Trust in your own efforts and other people
• Citizens are born again through Jesus Christ	• People try to meet their own needs or add to themselves without God
• Brings rest and peace	
• Operates by the spiritual laws of heaven	• Unsaved mankind; still separated from God
• Key Laws: 　1. Law of Spirit of Life in Christ Jesus 　2. Sowing and Reaping (Seedtime & Harvest)	• Brings fatigue, stress, and worry
	• Operates by the natural laws of the earth-cursed system of the world
	• Key Laws: 　1. Law of Sin and Death 　2. Buying and Selling

Every one of us must have the right paradigm, mental map, or belief to operate successfully in the kingdom of God. The first correction in most people's thinking, as it was in mine, is that the kingdom of God is not a democracy, nor a denomination, but a theocracy governed by a King, the King of kings and the Lord of lords. This is a sovereign rulership. There is no voting and there are no protests. Yet, there is still freedom (Gordon 1990). Only in the kingdom can you find liberty without voting. The kingdom is not bondage; it is protection.

To experience the fullness of being kings and priests, we must understand how kingdom authority operates. A good understanding of this authority is found in the story of the centurion in Matthew 8:5–10. A centurion came to Jesus to ask Him to heal his servant, *"And Jesus saith unto him, I will come and heal him. The centurion answered and said, Lord, I am not worthy that thou shouldest come under my roof: but speak the word only, and my servant shall be healed. For I am a man under authority, having soldiers under me..."* (verses 7–9).

THE KINGDOM IS NOT BONDAGE; IT'S PROTECTION.

The centurion had authority because he was under authority. If you want authority in the kingdom, you must be submitted to authority. Again, the kingdom of God is not a democracy, and kingdom living is not a religion; it is the life of God. We don't vote on what the kingdom agenda will be. In the kingdom, one accepts the rule of God in their lives and enters into the realm of His BLESSING here on Earth.

At the heart of submitting to kingdom authority is whether or not a person is truly surrendered to the Lordship of Jesus Christ. A person may be born again, but is Jesus Lord? If Jesus is your Lord, then you come under His authority to do the things that He says. Luke 6:46 (NASB) illustrates this when Jesus asks, *"'Why do you call Me 'Lord, Lord' and do not what I say.'"*

KINGDOM LIVING IS NOT A RELIGION.

As a former Air Force fighter pilot, my military training was extremely valuable in helping me understand this principle and how to live in the kingdom of God. In the United States, there is one military, although it has different branches: Army, Navy, Air Force, Marines, and Coast Guard. Our commanding officer gave the orders and we were expected to carry them out. Soldiers didn't vote on where they were assigned or who was in their unit. Soldiers looked after each other as a band of brothers, working as one team, knowing that their lives could depend on it. The Lord, as our spiritual Commander, has deployed troops in either the clergy or priestly ministry and the marketplace (kings) to work as soldiers, "agents of change," united to regain our place of dominion and reestablish His kingdom.

Scripture speaks about binding the strong man (Mark 3:27), and spoiling his house. Well, if you want to do this, you must go into his house. Many times those in the Church world do not think they should aspire to be an artist or physician, an athlete or a politician. They say, "No! No! That world is wicked, stay away from it." But Jesus said, *"I pray not that thou shouldest take them out of the world, but that thou shouldest keep them from the evil"* (John 17:15). It was never meant that we just speak from the platform of the Church to the entertainment field, or to the politicians in government. But we are to train up godly entertainers and politicians in the Church to go into Hollywood, the music industry, or to the Senate, being deployed into the various occupations and pillars of society to be the greatest influence in that industry, area, or profession. You'll find that God's way is to deliberately plant the righteous among the unrighteous. In darkness is where light shines brightest.

As we, children of God, return to our position as leaders on this planet, as God originally intended, He will use us to establish His government or kingdom and restore the whole Earth "back to Eden."

TWO CALLINGS AND TWO ANOINTINGS

It is important to understand the relationship between kings and priests. Again, kings and priests are two separate and distinct callings and anointings, although a person may serve in both roles on a personal or private level. For example, you may be the king and the priest in your own home or business. You may run your business and lead a Bible study for your employees. Or you could be the one who leads prayer in your home and also goes to work each day to provide for your family. In this scenario, each of us could be a king and a priest.

But on a larger scale, in the local church and the Church at large, kings and priests are separate offices that serve as partners to one another, balancing and assisting each other in finishing the work we were commissioned to do—advancing and establishing the kingdom of God. We have no greater priority than proclaiming His kingdom throughout every nation.

AN UNBEATABLE TEAM

We see these two offices working together when the prophet Elijah said to King Ahab, *"...Get thee up, eat and drink; for there is a sound of abundance of rain"* (1 Kings 18:41). Notice that the direction and timing of the move of God came through the prophet (priest). Since the king believed the prophet and followed his instruction, there was a tremendous benefit. This is the "kingdom model" that would cause Israel to win battles and conquer territories that the enemy previously possessed.

We also see these two anointings working together in 1 Kings, chapter 20. Ben-Hadad, king of Syria, made war against Ahab, king of Israel, saying, *"Your silver and gold are mine, and the best of your wives and children are mine"* (verse 3 NIV). King Ahab didn't fight back and consented. His enemy then demanded even more saying; *"I am going to send my officials to search your palace and the houses of your officials. They* (Ben-Hadad's servants) *will seize everything you value and carry it away"* (verse 6 NIV). This time King Ahab stood his ground and refused. Then, *"Meanwhile a prophet came to Ahab king of Israel and announced, 'This is what the LORD says: Do you see this vast army? I will give it into your hand today, and then you will know that I am the LORD.'"* (verse 13 NIV). God performed exactly what He said, and gave Israel the victory.

> THE "KINGDOM MODEL" HELPS US TO WIN BATTLES AND CONQUER TERRITORIES.

Another example of this unbeatable team of kings and priests is found in 2 Kings, chapter 19. The Word of the Lord was given to King Hezekiah through the prophet Isaiah when Israel was attacked by Rabshakeh, king of Assyria. Isaiah said, *"...Thus saith the LORD, Be not afraid of the words which thou hast heard, with which the servants of the king of Assyria have blasphemed me. Behold, I will send a blast upon him, and he shall hear a rumour, and shall return to his own land; and I will cause him to fall by the sword in his own land"* (verses 6–7) and *"...that night, that the angel of the LORD went out, and smote in the camp of the Assyrians an hundred fourscore and five thousand: and when they arose early in the morning, behold, they were all dead corpses"* (verse 35). Could it be that the reason our fight against terrorism or our war on poverty is taking so long is because this unbeatable team is not working together? The scriptures tell us, *"He* (God) *stops wars all over the world..."* (Psalm 46:9 GNT).

COUNTERFEIT PATTERN OF KINGS AND PRIESTS

In the Bible, worldly (secular) governments also replicated this kings and priests model. An example of this is the relationship between Pharaoh, king of Egypt, and his mystic cabinet of wise men, sorcerers, and magicians. When contending with Moses and Aaron, Pharaoh called for his priests to respond to Aaron's turning his rod into a serpent. When Pharaoh's priests threw down their rods, their rods also became serpents but were devoured by Moses' serpent... the more powerful partnership established by God. The godly king and priest, Moses and Aaron, won the contest.

Like Egypt, the government of Babylon, one of the greatest Old Testament kingdoms, also followed a kings and priests model. Babylon's political system was supported by occult powers like wizards, witches, and astrologers. From these occult, unseen powers came Babylon's strength. We find an example of this in the book of Daniel, where King Nebuchadnezzar of Babylon had a disturbing dream and was desperate for an interpretation. He called for his priests—the astrologers, sorcerers, and Chaldeans—but they were impotent because only God is the true interpreter of dreams. Therefore, the king only received the interpretation of the dream once he sought counsel from Daniel.

As we can see, the kings and priests pattern has both godly and worldly versions; however, the worldly version is a counterfeit of God's true pattern and is always inferior. Even though Pharaoh and Nebuchadnezzar were both powerful kings and formidable rulers, they knew there was a realm in which they were not graced to function. This is an important revelation. Understanding their own limitations, they had spiritualists advise them on things pertaining to the intangible and invisible spiritual realm.

The principle of kings and priests is still in active operation today. For example, many tribes still maintain ancient tradition where the king or tribal leader routinely consults their priests, who are called the witchdoctors or soothsayers (sorcerers). They are in partnership to rule over the personal and corporate affairs of the tribe or marketplace ventures. Even today, a common practice is for people to employ the soothsayers and spiritualists to consult "the spirits" for answers about their businesses, political matters, marriages, families, and whatever problem they may have. Lots of money is paid for their consultation services.

Again, this is the worldly version of kings and priests. But, it illustrates my point that there is power that results from this union. Most tribal nations recognize the advantages and authority of this kings and priests relationship and see results, even if limited.

We can also see such partnerships within the business arena in other countries that have become major players in the rapidly expanding global economy. These nations, small and great, have talented individuals who contribute greatly to their nation's phenomenal growth. A local newspaper in one of those nations had an article that stated that students at one of the major universities can earn a degree in astrology and land prestigious jobs with well-known multinational corporations and financial astrology websites. They are being hired as consultants, financial astrologers, and prediction experts "to make predictions on the stock market, the success of business ventures, and offer astro-tips on financial management."[2] I am not endorsing these spiritual practices in any way. I only discuss them to illustrate once again that the kings and priests principle is alive and being used in the twenty-first century.

From the Judeo-Christian perspective, any wisdom outside of God's wisdom is counterfeit wisdom in today's society. This counterfeit wisdom is inferior, and consulting any witch, medium, soothsayer, or diviner is forbidden by the Lord as it was the very thing used to tempt mankind in the garden of

Eden (Genesis 3:6). As I said earlier, there are limitations to this counterfeit wisdom. Pharaoh's magicians and soothsayers were only able to go so far in executing spiritism (occultism) in their efforts to duplicate the power of God through Moses. As scripture states, no enchantment can compare (or compete) with *"the finger of God"* (Exodus 8:19).

Additionally, Pharaoh's astrologers during the time of Joseph could not predict or prepare them for the seven-year famine that struck Egypt (Genesis 41), nor could the intelligence or cleverness of any Egyptian avert it. Only through Joseph, functioning as a godly priest, was Pharaoh (the king) properly instructed on how to manage and not just survive but thrive during a natural disaster of that magnitude.

BIBLICAL KINGS AND PRIESTS

With individuals who practice astrology or enchantments of various kinds, the need for a true biblical kings and priests partnership becomes evident. Kings need priests (prophets of the Lord), who hear from God, to speak into their lives the timings and directions of the move of God. Priests also teach those in the marketplace the superior principles of the kingdom that will enable them as marketplace ministers to take the lead in their sphere of influence.

One current example of this is in Sacramento, California, where the marketplace ministers are police officers. Recognizing the value of partnering with local clergy to strengthen positive community relationships, the Sacramento police department's newly appointed police chief established a "cops and clergy" outreach program.[3] Police officers team with local pastors and ministers to speak and counsel at-risk youth and adults in an attempt to change behaviors that could lead to arrests or incarceration. The program seeks to strengthen trust and improve communication between the police and community residents, ultimately making Sacramento a safer and more desirable place to live.

This partnership between clergy and police officers was also seen following the highly publicized riots in Baltimore, Maryland, after the death of Freddie Gray, a 25-year-old African American man, while in police custody. The violence and destruction of the riots made news around the world, but very few media outlets reported on the police department's partnership with local religious leaders to stop the violence and to restore the peace in a community broken by decades of hopelessness and despair. The Baltimore police department reached out to local church and faith leaders to "help calm tensions on the street" and "called their contributions 'instrumental.'"[4] As one local pastor said, "'Community policing is the officer on the beat joined together with the pastor on the corner.'"[5]

Priests also need kings. In the business or economic arena, these anointed marketplace ministers are kingdom change agents and the financial rainmakers whom God shall prosper economically, intellectually, and practically for the building or advancing of the kingdom. In the gospel of Luke, Jesus stood up in the synagogue and when He had opened the book, He found the place where it was written, *"The Spirit of the Lord is upon me, because he hath anointed me to preach...."* (chapter 4, verse 18). Notice, He didn't say, "to fund-raise." The Church has done everything from playing bingo, to just plain begging, in attempts to raise money for building projects, and so on. These practices come mostly from a wrong interpretation of scripture and traditional theological concepts.

For example, I heard a theologian give his interpretation of the account of Jesus' discourse with the rich young ruler in Mark, chapter 10. This certain professor said that what this story means is, "You can't go to heaven if you are rich. You must first give it all away." The commentator interviewing the theologian quickly replied, "Then we are all going to hell," speaking sarcastically. This theologian had no revelation of what the Scriptures meant. This wrong thinking has trickled down into the Body of Christ. Jesus referred to them as *"blind, leaders of the blind"* (Matthew 15:14).

The Church is meant to be the wealthiest, the most benevolent, and the most powerful institution in the world, ever! I call it..."The Benevolent Empire." We should have enough financial strength to lift the curse off any city our Lord would send us to...not to beg, but to bless!

For the first time since the days of King David, provision will be generated faster than the vision it is intended to support. If you recall, David, a king, acquired and stored all the materials and wealth necessary to build the temple years before his son Solomon built it.

THE CHURCH IS MEANT TO BE THE WEALTHIEST, MOST BENEVOLENT, AND MOST POWERFUL INSTITUTION IN THE WORLD, EVER!

Likewise, when kings and priests operate in their God-given assignments, they are sure to fulfill the plan of God, and money will be no object. They will tap into new information that will cause business, educational, and scientific breakthroughs, lifting curses such as poverty, premature death, and destruction off entire cities, while at the same time, claiming new territory and new converts for the kingdom until every community becomes like "heaven on earth."

CHAPTER 3

KINGS & PRIESTS
A DIVINE PARTNERSHIP

W e are in a time where the partnership of kings and priests is no longer an option but a require-ment for us to reach and fulfill our God-planned destinies. Priests need the ministry gift of kings. Kings need the minis-try gift of priests.

KINGS: A MINISTRY GIFT TO PRIESTS

Economic innovation is a major way to provide capital to advance the kingdom of God. Let's take entrepreneurship as an example. The "ministry" of an entrepreneur is to find a cure (healing) for the business world the same way a physi-cian is trained to heal the body. They are apostles of healing, both meeting the needs of humanity through good gifts and services. And this ministry gift of the entrepreneur needs to be understood and embraced by the priests.

As one author wrote,

> Instead of praising the entrepreneur as a person of ideas, an economic innovator, or provider of capital, the average priest or minister thinks of people in business as carrying extra guilt. Why? For owning, controlling, or manipulating a disproportionate per-centage of "society's wealth".... The time has come for religious institutions and leaders to treat entre-preneurship as a worthy vocation, indeed, a sacred calling.[1]

Business and entrepreneurship (as well as any market-place ministry) is a God-given calling, the same as pastoring a church. Entrepreneurs, through their gifts and passion, tap into their creative capacity to create new products and services that bring solutions to make life more enjoyable, improve health, and harness the earth's natural resources and more. They expand the "economic pie" by creating new markets and opportunities, instead of fighting with competitors over the same slice (Sirico 2010).

CREATIVITY AND INNOVATION ARE DIVINE EXPRESSIONS OF GOD.

We are made in the image of God, the Creator: *"So God created man in his own image, in the image of God created he him; male and female created he them,"* (Genesis 1:27). As one author wrote, "The entrepreneur's creativity is akin to God's creative ability in the first chapter of Genesis. In this sense, the entrepreneur participates in the original cultural mandate to replenish and subdue the earth that God gave to Adam and Eve."[2] The creative power (ability) that created all matter is "THE BLESSING."

Creativity and innovation are divine expressions of God, and should be encouraged, not stifled or rejected. As one priest said, "Religious leaders generally display very little understanding of the entrepreneurial vocation, of what it requires, and of what it contributes to society."[3] When kings are not accepted as true partners with the priest, the relationship can become adversarial, and tension and strife can hinder or dampen the creative process.

Instead of the priest praying, covering, and blessing the kings for battle (Deuteronomy 20:1–4; Numbers 6:22–26), they remain non-responsive, not understanding the importance of the divine relationship between them, and not adding their voice for the victory. As a result, the Body of Christ has continued to struggle and many financially cannot afford to miss one day of work. We should be thinking, acting, and living like God lives. I personally believe that abundance is a shared responsibility between kings and priests, because we, not the government, are scripturally mandated to care for the poor, the widows, and the orphans (Leviticus 23:22;

James 1:27 AMP). Because these two callings have not been working together as they should to obtain greater victories in the marketplace, where there should have been a flood of provision because of the "spoils of war," we have seen only a trickle flowing into the kingdom of God. **I decree great increase in the Body of Christ starting now.**

Running any successful endeavor—a film production company, medical center, college, daycare, home, or family takes time and energy. Every marketplace vocation is just as much a calling as the "priests" or five-fold ministries. When work goes from an act to an attitude, your labor becomes the premier expression of worship, as Adam had in the garden. *"Whatever you do, you do your work heartily, as for the Lord"* (Colossians 3:23 NASB). One author wrote:

> All lay people have a special role to play in the economy of salvation, sharing in the task of furthering the faith by using their talents in complementary ways. Every person created in the image of God has been given certain natural abilities that God desires to be cultivated and treated as good gifts. If the gift happens to be an inclination for business, stock trading or investment banking, the religious community should not condemn the person merely on account of his or her profession.[4] [But help to keep them with a moral compass, and use their gifts within the context of faith.] (*Author's insert*)

Kings must also make sure they honor and respect the gift of the priest, *"...the eye cannot say unto the hand, I have no need of thee...."* If the revelation of the kings or priests is not valued and the message concerning the importance of this relationship not embraced, it can be extremely costly. God has placed pastors, ministers, teachers, and the other five-fold ministry gifts as spiritual coverings and resources for His people. Let there be mutual respect for both of the anointings, the kings and the priests.

PRIESTS: A MINISTRY GIFT TO KINGS

For leaders serving as kings and kingdom representatives in the marketplace, battles are necessary for success.

As leaders rise to the top of their sphere of influence, some conflicts should be even viewed as natural. As change agents sent to establish the kingdom of God, wherever we are sent, we should expect that satan is not going to relinquish his power without a fight.

> Finally, my brethren, be strong in the Lord, and in the power of his might. Put on the whole armour of God, that ye may be able to stand against the wiles of the devil. For we wrestle not against flesh and blood, but against principalities, against powers, against the rulers of the darkness of this world, against spiritual wickedness in high *places*. Ephesians 6:10–12

The good news here is that God already knows every battle a king will ever face, and has already provided a divine arsenal for his or her victory. The key is how to access it. The anointing of the priest is part of a king's arsenal to win in the marketplace. If marketplace leaders are to optimize their performance and have amazing results in their given assignment or profession, they need someone graced with spiritual acumen and discernment to teach and speak into their lives the words of the kingdom, and to give them the divine guidance and wisdom required.

THE ANOINTING OF THE PRIEST IS PART OF A KING'S ARSENAL TO WIN IN THE MARKETPLACE.

This "inside information" is given by God to assist leaders in making right decisions that would result in the highest and supreme good for their businesses, schools, industries, communities, and nations. Even non-Christians understand this principle. Again, many multi-national companies are hiring Vedic astrologers to "make predictions in the stock market, (predict) the success of business ventures, and offer astro-tips in financial management."[5] Why? They are seeking information and solutions on a supernatural level to give them a competitive advantage and to win in the marketplace.

My point is, even those who don't know Jesus Christ understand we do not live and conduct business in just a natural environment, but also a spiritual one. They even realize that the realm of the spirit is more powerful than our physical world, and actually controls the realm of the natural.

Just like divine wisdom, supernatural wealth, THE BLESSING, and God's favor, the anointing of the priest is a covenant gift to kingdom marketplace leaders. The priest is to help kings succeed in business or marketplace matters, mainly by taking them beyond the boundary of the natural or intellectual.

Examples of the priest's service to the king are shared throughout the Bible: Melchizedek, the *"priest of the Most High God,"* who reminded Abraham to tithe after Abraham had slaughtered the enemy and took the spoils; the prophet Nathan whom the Lord sent to King David to speak with him about his recent adulterous affair with Bathsheba and to call him to repentance, *"Thou art the man"*; or a Levite priest who spoke prophetically to King Jehoshaphat and all of Israel giving them inside information as to the outcome of an impossible-to-win battle and how they were to fight it, declaring, *"the battle is not yours, but God's."* In each case it involved a realm above this natural physical and intellectual world; the world of the spirit.

WHY EVERY KING NEEDS A PRIEST

> But when he saw the multitudes, he was moved with compassion on them, because they fainted, and were scattered abroad, as sheep having no shepherd. Matthew 9:36

If a person has confessed Christ and is born again, he or she falls into the category of a sheep; and every sheep needs a shepherd. If kings, no matter what their position or title, don't have a priest in their lives, something will be missing spiritually, and eventually, naturally. I heard someone say there are three main responsibilities of a pastor (shepherd):

1. To guard the sheep

2. To graze (feed) the sheep

3. To guide the sheep

Pastors should speak words of faith to inspire and empower kings for marketplace success and conquest, not words of fear and condemnation (see the story of R. G. LeTourneau and Pastor Devol, chapter 14, "Calling All Kings"). In an atmosphere of fear, the anointing does not flow, kings often don't see increase, and their marketplace ministry suffers.

In every nation there are "elites," or who some might call "plutocrats," who we call kings in the marketplace. They are not necessarily part of a monarchy, but some have a significant measure of rule. They are influencers and decision makers. They have authority that shapes opinions. However, many of these "kingly" elites are running without a priest.

With no spiritual insight, battles (e.g., economic, social, military) that should last 30 days could end up lasting 10 years and draining the revenues of a city or national treasury. The higher a person rises in influence, the more critically they need a priestly relationship.

For instance, where there should have been an end to this war on terror by now through divine intervention, we have seen a modern-day replay of the mythical fight between Hercules and the giant Hydra, a multi-headed monster. As I mentioned before, as soon as Hercules would cut off one head, two more heads would instantly take its place. Doesn't that sound similar to what is happening in today's terrorist's cells? We need the total solution from God's unbeatable team...kings and priests. This unbeatable team comes together to apply a total solution that deals with the full perception of reality—the spiritual and the physical. *"He maketh wars to cease unto the end of the earth"* (Psalm 46:9). Here are four important reasons why every king needs a priest.

Reason No. 1: Some Battles You Can't Win Without God

"A wise man is strong; yea, a man of knowledge increaseth strength...If thou faint in the day of adversity, thy strength is small" (Proverbs 24:5, 10). We need God in every area of our lives to be successful, and there are some battles you cannot win without His presence and power to defeat the unseen, massive forces of the enemy.

In 2 Kings 18–19, King Hezekiah knew his armies were not strong enough to defeat the King of Assyria. The nation of Judah was being attacked, and King Hezekiah needed strength. Sennacherib, the King of Assyria, had attacked all the fortified cities of Judah, and had set his sights to take all the people, property, and wealth of Judah. He even taunted King Hezekiah by boasting that his conquests must mean that God was with him, and not Hezekiah (2 Kings 18:19–25). But Hezekiah sought the counsel of the prophet Isaiah, his priest, who responded with these words,

> Thus says the LORD: "Do not be afraid of the words which you have heard...Surely I will send a spirit upon him, and he shall hear a rumor and return to his own land; and I will cause him to fall by the sword in his own land." 2 Kings 19:6–7 NKJV

Like Hezekiah, today's marketplace kings need a priest who can speak supernatural strength in the day of adversity.

General George S. Patton is a wonderful example of a modern-day military leader who knew the importance of relying on God's supernatural strength to win battles. The now famous "Patton Prayer," distributed to 250,000 soldiers and chaplains in the Third Army during World War II, documents forever in history General Patton's faith in God to achieve miracles on the battlefield. This great military leader said, "Those who pray do more for the world than those who fight; and if the world goes from bad to worse, it is because there are more battles than prayers."[6]

The backdrop for Patton's prayer was that rains were steadily falling and fog cover was threatening the Allied Forces advance against the German soldiers. General Patton requested Chaplain James H. O'Neill, Chief Chaplain of the Third Army, to find a prayer on weather.

Here are excerpts from Chaplain O'Neill's written account of what happened:

> "This is General Patton; do you have a good prayer for weather? We must do something about those rains if we are to win the war."
>
> My reply was that I know where to look for such a prayer, that I would locate, and report within the

hour. As I hung up the telephone receiver, about eleven in the morning, I looked out on the steadily falling rain...the same rain that had plagued Patton's Army throughout the Moselle and Saar Campaigns from September until now, December 8.

Keeping his (Patton's) immediate objective in mind, I typed an original and an improved copy on a 5" × 3" filing card: *Almighty and most merciful Father, we humbly beseech Thee, of Thy great goodness, to restrain these immoderate rains with which we have had to contend. Grant us fair weather for Battle. Graciously hearken to us as soldiers who call upon Thee that, armed with Thy power, we may advance from victory to victory, and crush the oppression and wickedness of our enemies and establish Thy justice among men and nations.*

This done, I donned my heavy trench coat...and reported to General Patton. (Patton speaking) "Chaplain, I am a strong believer in Prayer. There are three ways that men get what they want; by planning, by working, and by praying. Any great military operation takes careful planning, or thinking. Then you must have well-trained troops to carry it out: that's working. But between the plan and the operation there is always an unknown. That unknown spells defeat or victory, success or failure.

"It is the reaction of the actors to the ordeal when it actually comes. Some people call that getting the breaks; I call it God. God has His part, or margin in everything, That's where prayer comes in. Up to now, in the Third Army, God has been very good to us. We have never retreated; we have suffered no defeats, no famine, no epidemics. This is because a lot of people back home are praying for us.... Simply because people prayed."[7]

General Patton further instructed Chaplain O'Neill, "I wish you would put out a Training Letter on this subject of Prayer to all the chaplains; write about nothing else, just the importance of prayer...we've got to get not only the chaplains but every man in the Third Army to pray. We must ask God to stop these rains. These rains are that margin that hold defeat or victory."[8]

The letter was "Training Letter No. 5" and was distributed on December 11 and 12, 1944, to every man in the Third Army. The outcome was also described in Chaplain O'Neill's account:

> On the 19th of December, the Third Army turned from East to North to meet the attack. As General Patton rushed his divisions north from the Saar Valley to the relief of the beleaguered Bastogne, the prayer was answered. On December 20, to the consternation of the Germans and the delight of the American forecasters who were equally surprised at the turn-about, the rains and the fogs ceased. For the better part of a week came bright clear skies and perfect flying weather. Our planes came over by tens, hundreds, and thousands. They knocked out hundreds of tanks, killed thousands of enemy troops in the Bastogne salient, and harried the enemy as he valiantly tried to bring up reinforcements...General Patton prayed for fair weather for Battle. He got it.[9]

Another favorite modern-day example of a king and priest relationship in action is the story of President George H. W. Bush and Reverend Billy Graham, which I shared earlier in the book. President Bush had invited Reverend Graham to stay at the White House on the eve of the first Gulf War, which started after Iraq invaded Kuwait several months earlier. This is how the President described Reverend Graham's stay:

> Billy came to stay with Barbara and me at the White House...I told him what I was then having to do— our diplomacy and our quest for a peaceful solution having failed. I told him when the first cruise missiles would hit Baghdad, and we watched in wonder as the war to liberate Kuwait began. Just the three of us were there. Billy said a little prayer for our troops and for the innocents who might be killed....I cannot begin to tell what Billy's presence and his faith meant to me as President and as Commander in Chief. His own beliefs and abiding faith gave me great strength.[10]

The rest is history. American and Allied Forces began launching air attacks on Iraqi forces on January 17, 1991, "and on February 24 the ground campaign began. By February 27, the coalition had achieved their stated mission of ejecting the Iraqi army out of Kuwait. Exactly 100 hundred hours after the ground battle had begun, the allies suspended all offensive operations."[11] The war lasted a little over 40 days.

Reason No. 2: Kings Need a Priest to Help Them Stay On Course

David was perhaps the most powerful king in the Old Testament. But he still needed the priest—in this case Nathan the prophet—to keep him morally on course. Nathan gave King David direction, correction, and impartation when David had an adulterous affair with Bathsheba, whose husband, Uriah the Hittite, served in David's army. In an attempt to hide his sin when Bathsheba became pregnant, David eventually had Uriah killed in battle (see 2 Samuel 11).

David thought he had gotten away with his sin until Nathan, walking in revelation from God, revealed to David that God was aware of his secret sin and was going to correct him publicly, *"For you did it secretly, but I will do this thing before all Israel, before the sun"* (2 Samuel 12:12 NKJV). Nathan's revelation caused David to repent.

One of the deceptions that can easily trap people (referring to those in the Body of Christ) who attain great wealth and success is that they no longer feel the need for a spiritual covering or that they need to be accountable. That's not true! Actually, those leaders who have a significant measure of rule are in need the most of the priestly partnership and the godly influence, because of how many lives one of their decisions might affect. This level requires a priest who is not intimidated by money or power...one who is uncompromising in assisting kings to walk out their kingdom role or assignment, no matter how simple or how important. Again, I am first referring to those in the Body of Christ.

State governors, Supreme Court justices, congressmen and senators—even the President of the United States—and prime ministers need a covering. Every sheep needs a shepherd. Every king needs a priest. All kingdom citizens serving in the marketplace are sheep, and every sheep needs a shepherd. This is true in the natural world and the spiritual world. Top executives of our major corporations and global enterprises, well-paid athletes, famous actors and celebrities, and other cultural icons; if they claim salvation through Jesus Christ, all are sheep. God's divine order is for kings to have a priest in their lives. The prophet Elijah said to Ahab the king, *"get thee up, eat and drink; for* (I hear the) *sound of an abundance of rain,"* (1 Kings 18:41). This was in the midst of a drought, and wow, did it rain. Every king needs a priest.

Again, priests help kings through sermons, teachings, prayer, and advising them on the direction and timing of the move of God to stay right in line with the will of the Father. Even by speaking the Word from the pulpit, the pastor or minister can impart spiritual strength to help make tough decisions and to stay on the divine path God has set for them.

Reason No. 3: All Leadership Is Spiritual

> Billy Graham is one of the best ambassadors our country has but he told me, "I am an ambassador of heaven." Dwight D. Eisenhower

All leadership is spiritual. Again, Reverend Billy Graham has been referred to as the "Pastor to Presidents" because every U.S. president since World War II, including our present leader, President Barack Obama, has sought his counsel and prayers.[12] Two presidents, Lyndon B. Johnson and Richard M. Nixon, even offered him high positions in the government, which he refused.[13]

Here is what is written on the website of the Billy Graham Evangelistic Association:

> Billy Graham has often said, "Whether the story of Christ is told in a huge stadium, across the desk of a powerful leader, or shared with a golfing companion, it satisfies a common hunger. All over the world, whenever I meet people face-to-face, I am made aware of this personal need among the famous and successful, as well as the lonely and obscure.[14]

In almost every major nation, most heads of state and political leaders understand the importance of a man or woman of God praying and speaking a blessing over them, as demonstrated in the coronations of kings and queens and the inaugurations of U.S. presidents. This is because, throughout history, leaders of nations have understood that all leadership is ordained by God (or by some higher power in non-Christian nations) and must have His blessing. They understood that all leadership is spiritual.

Reason No. 4: Supernatural Help (Relief) from the Pressures of Life

A marketplace leader once confided in me that the pressures of life can be so overwhelming that he found it extremely valuable to have a relationship with a priest to confide his thoughts and feelings. He said the king-priest relationship was personally precious in helping him relieve stress.

Before I was born again, while serving in the military and later in the corporate world, I would seek ways to relieve the pressures that often came with certain assignments. Our Creator did not design us to live with stress. It is why many people party, overeat, drink, smoke, do drugs, or feel they need a long vacation on a secluded island somewhere. Deep down they are asking, "How do I get rid of this pressure?"

ALL LEADERSHIP IS SPIRITUAL.

When people don't have a relationship with the Lord and no one to talk to and no counsel, they seek to relieve stress the best way they know how—often through unhealthy choices. Why? Man was never designed to carry stress. Stress came as a result of Adam's fall in the garden. It leads to anxiety, which is fear-based, and connects a person with satan—the spirit of death. Once a person allows fear to enter his or her life, it provides an open door for the enemy to influence their thoughts, emotions, words, and behavior.

For example, read what Job said after he experienced major loss in his life: *"For the thing which I greatly feared is come upon me, and that which I was afraid of is come unto me"* (Job 3:25). Priests provide kings with supernatural help from stress by reconnecting them with faith in God. Faith comes only one way, *"by hearing, and hearing by the word of God"* (Romans 10:17). When the priest speaks the Word of righteousness to a king, it is designed to bring peace, quietness, and assurance in the midst of troubled times. The knowledge of God is a requirement if you are to enjoy the peace of God. The more knowledge you get, the more of His peace you enjoy.

In Psalm 23:1-2 David writes, *"The Lord is my shepherd I shall not want. He maketh me to lie down in green pastures: he leadeth me beside the still waters."* Being led by God will cause your peace to flow. The idea is for us to yield to His leading.

The Bible is filled with accounts of people who were stressed, but were delivered by a word from a priest. In Luke 5, Simon Peter, who was a fisherman when Jesus called him to be a disciple, was stressed. He had toiled all night and had caught nothing. No fish. No profit. No dinner to bring home to "Mrs. Simon Peter." Then Jesus (the Priest) spoke *"Launch out into the deep and let down your nets for a catch."* Peter did as instructed and caught so many fish his net began to break.

Then there was the widow woman in 2 Kings, chapter 4, who was in so much debt that her two sons were about to be taken by the creditor as slaves. The woman sought the help of Elisha, the prophet, who said to her, *"What shall I do for you? Tell me, what do you have in the house?"* And she said, *"Your maidservant has nothing in the house but a jar of oil"* (verse 2 NKJV).

Elisha instructed her to borrow vessels from all the neighbors, and that when she returned home, *"you shall shut the door behind you and your sons; then pour it into all those vessels, and set aside the full ones"* (verse 4 NKJV). When she did as told, a miracle happened. The oil supernaturally increased in every vessel she poured into. She then sold the oil, paid off her debt, and she and sons lived off what money remained. The woman was delivered from debt and stress with one miracle.

When Jesus announced *"the acceptable year of the Lord"* in Luke 4:19, He was announcing supernatural debt cancellation. By obeying the word of the prophet Elisha, the widow woman activated the anointing (THE BLESSING), the power of the kingdom of God, which supernaturally caused the oil to increase as she poured out into each vessel. She expected the prophet to give her the answer to her problem, and when she obeyed, she received her miracle. You must expect the supernatural. If you don't, it won't happen.

I refer again to Isaiah 48:17–18, the scripture God gave me in 1986 that opened up the revelation of kings and priests: *"Thus saith the LORD, thy Redeemer, the Holy One of Israel: I am the LORD thy God which teacheth thee to profit, which leadeth thee by the way that thou shouldest go. O that thou hadst harkened to my commandments! then had thy peace been as a river, and thy righteousness as the waves of the sea."*

God has ordered the divine partnership of kings and priests so that both roles need each other. Kings need priests, and priests need kings. For example, when Veronica and I came to Chicago to start our ministry, we only had $200. But two friends helped us: Sister Beverly, a television producer who opened her home to us, and Brother Steve (affectionately called Burt), a lawyer who kindly assisted and provided for us until we had planted the church and it began to grow. Today, we have a worldwide ministry that is touching millions of people and impacting many other ministries around the world. We cannot thank them enough for what they did for us. May God's blessing be upon them forever!

A WARNING ABOUT FALSE PROPHETS

As discussed in the previous chapter, the world has counterfeit kings and priests partnerships that mimic the biblical relationship created by God. Even within the Church, the enemy can send what are called "false prophets" who misrepresent themselves as being sent by God, but the truth is not in their mouths. Second Thessalonians, chapter 2, says,

> This man of sin will come as Satan's tool, full of satanic power, and will trick everyone with strange demonstrations, and will do great miracles. He will completely fool those who are on their way to hell because they have said no to the Truth; they have refused to believe it...so God will allow them to

> believe lies with all their hearts, and all of them will
> be justly judged for believing falsehood, refusing the
> Truth, and enjoying their sins. verses 9–12 TLB

Men and women who are called to the five-fold ministry, the priests, must be vigilant to submit themselves only to God and His Word. When they try to avoid speaking the truth, and become more interested in pleasing human authority or going after money, they open themselves to a lying spirit and false prophesy. Obedience to God is paramount, especially for a priest, and it can mean the difference between life and death, literally. The story in 1 Kings, chapter 13, gives a good illustration of this.

A young prophet of God from Judah spoke truth to Bethel's wicked king, Jeroboam, who was committing abominations before God. Jeroboam *"appointed priests for the high places from all sorts of people. Anyone who wanted to become a priest he consecrated for the high places"* (verse 33 NIV). His evil ways eventually led to his downfall and the destruction of his entire family. Unfortunately, a bigger tragedy in this story is what happened to the young prophet. He was tricked into disobeying God's command by an older prophet who lived in Bethel, and it cost him his life.

> (The old prophet) rode after the man of God. He
> found him sitting under an oak tree and asked, "Are
> you the man of God who came from Judah?" "I am,"
> he replied. So the prophet said to him, "Come home
> with me and eat." The man of God said, "I cannot
> turn back and go with you, nor can I eat bread or
> drink water with you in this place. I have been told
> by the word of the Lord: 'You must not eat bread or
> drink water there or return by the way you came.'"
>
> The old prophet answered, "I too am a prophet, as
> you are. And an angel said to me by the word of
> the Lord: 'Bring him back with you to your house
> so that he may eat bread and drink water.'" *(But he
> was lying to him.)* So the man of God returned with
> him and ate and drank in his house....
>
> When the man of God had finished eating and
> drinking, the prophet who had brought him back
> saddled his donkey for him. As he went on his way,

> a lion met him on the road and killed him, and his
> body was left lying on the road, with both the don-
> key and the lion standing beside it. verses 14–24
> NIV, emphasis mine

Serving the Lord may often put priests in opposition to what is socially popular or pleasing to those in authority. But they must speak *"what thus saith Lord"* regardless of others' reactions. It takes courage and the boldness that comes from knowing God and His Word...and who you are in Christ. The Bible calls it righteousness. This was the case of the prophet Micaiah in 1 Kings, chapter 22.

Ahab, the king of Israel, wanted king Jehoshaphat to join him in battle against Syria, and Jehoshaphat replied, *"First seek the counsel of the Lord"* (1 Kings 22:5). So the king of Israel gathered about 400 prophets who all said, *"Go, for the Lord will give it unto the king's hand"* (verse 6 NIV). But Jehoshaphat was not deceived and asked is there no longer a prophet of the Lord here of whom we can inquire? The king of Israel replied that there was one prophet, Micaiah, but he hated him because he never prophesied anything good about the king.

When the messenger went to summon Micaiah, he told him that all the other prophets without exception are predicting success in this war, and you better let your word agree with theirs. The prophet's response was, *"As surely as the Lord lives, I can tell him only what the Lord tells me"* (verse 14). After momentarily bowing to the pressure, Micaiah boldly declares,

> I saw all Israel scattered on the hills like sheep with-
> out a shepherd, and the Lord said, "These people
> have no master. Let each one go home in peace."
>
> ...Therefore hear the word of the Lord: I saw the
> Lord sitting on his throne with all the multitudes
> of heaven standing around him on his right and on
> his left. And the Lord said, "Who will entice Ahab
> into attacking Ramoth Gilead and going to his death
> there?"
>
> One suggested this, and another that. Finally, a
> spirit came forward, stood before the Lord and said,

"I will entice him."

"By what means?" the LORD asked.

"I will go out and be a deceiving spirit in the mouths of all his prophets," he said.

"You will succeed in enticing him," said the LORD. "Go and do it."

So now the LORD has put a deceiving spirit in the mouths of all these prophets of yours. The LORD has decreed disaster for you.

Only the prophet Micaiah, among 400 prophets, spoke the truth. It wasn't popular or the will of the king, but it was the will of God, and the Word of the King of kings. There are countless examples throughout history of God's people who had to stand alone against the majority because they heard and obeyed the voice of the Lord and all were proved right and vindicated.

THE LORD TEACHES YOU TO PROFIT.

So kings must beware of men and women who profess to be spiritual but actually have ulterior motives. They are often sent by the devil to control the money or the influence, and in most cases, both. Pray for discernment and that your spiritual eyes be open (2 Kings 6:15–17) to any deceptive attacks of the devil. David said, *"O my God, I trust in thee: let me not be ashamed, let not mine enemies triumph over me."*

WHO OVERSEES THE PRIESTS?

Some marketplace leaders may ask, "Who keeps the priest on course?" Given the tragic ministry scandals that have happened over the years, it's totally understandable why they would ask such a question. To answer this, one must first understand God's way of governing His Church— the government of God. To understand how leaders are held accountable in the United States of America, one should simply study the U.S. Constitution, the Bill of Rights, and the structure of our federal, state, and local governments. To understand how God's leaders are held accountable in the kingdom, one must study the constitution of the kingdom of heaven, the Bible, and the government of God.

God structured His Church as a theocracy, which simply means that God rules. God never intended His Church to be a democracy, no matter how precious and important the principles of liberty and democracy are in our national and state governments (Gordon 1990). His formula for success is one God, one man, no confusion.[15] God did not choose a senate to lead the children of Israel, but a man—Moses.[16]

As one pastor writes:

> When the government of God is understood, men will no longer cry, "what about accountability? To whom is our leader accountable?" Let me tell you to whom any pastor is most assuredly accountable: he is accountable to the One into whose hands it is a fearful thing to fall. A pastor would be the worst kind of fool to think that he could tamper with [the all-powerful and all-knowing] God (*Author's insert*).[17]

THE CONSTITUTION OF THE KINGDOM OF HEAVEN IS THE BIBLE.

God's true priests know the serious consequences "of being unfaithful to their calling that is holy before the Lord."[18] Priests are responsible to God to keep their relationship with the Creator and with those over which God has given them charge. This is kingdom, and the way the Lord set up His Church government (Gordon 1990).

Guaranteed, the democratic process would cry out at this arrangement. However, this formula does not produce a lack of accountability on the part of the priest; on the contrary, it increases it. The priest reports directly to God. This formula is supernatural and not only avoids confusion, but "produces a coalition that absolutely devastates the powers of darkness."[19]

When Moses, one man, died, God simply moved Joshua, another man, into the formula to lead three to six million Jews. Remember Gideon or Balaam's donkey that spoke? (See Judges 6; Numbers 22:27–28) God has no problem providing a mouthpiece for what He wants to do. "When God calls, God also equips."[20]

Ephesians 4:11–12 says, *"And he gave some, apostles; and some, prophets; and some, evangelists; and some, pastors and teachers; For the perfecting of the saints, for the work of the ministry, for the edifying of the body of Christ."* Pastors (priests or shepherds) are responsible before God to lead the Church, and *"perfecting of the saints,"* which consists of sheep or marketplace ministers. The shepherd (pastor) will lead them only as God directs, and must give account to God (Hebrews 13:17). The unfaithful could suffer the same outcome, whether king or priest, as the servant who buried his talent in Matthew 25. The eternal lesson in this story is that we are all judged based on how we use God's gifts of grace, and how well we manage our stewardship.

The conduct of a shepherd (pastor) is clearly spelled out in scripture:

> These pastors must be men of blameless lives because they are God's ministers. They must not be proud or impatient; they must not be drunkards or fighters or greedy for money. They must enjoy having guests in their homes and must love all that is good. They must be sensible men, and fair. They must be clean-minded and level-headed. Their belief in the truth that they have taught must be strong and steadfast so that they will be able to teach it to others and show those who disagree with them where they are wrong. Titus 1:7–9 *The Living Bible*

One last and very important point: God has not placed a shepherd or spiritual leader over the congregation of the local church for people to relinquish their spiritual responsibility to grow. There is an inheritance that cannot be delivered to you beyond your level of growth. You must grow to the place of being able to command more: more influence, more territory for the kingdom of God. Ultimately, the kings must place their faith in God Himself, while trusting that the Lord has given them spiritual leadership after His own heart. Whether a king or a priest, each of us is special to God, and He has mighty plans and purposes for every one of us.

PART 2
THE ECONOMY OF THE KINGDOM

CHAPTER 4

A MENTAL REVERSAL

In the Church we are all referred to as members of the Body of Christ. When the Bible speaks of members, it doesn't mean members in the sense of joining a club or fraternity or even a church. First Corinthians 12:12 teaches that every member of the Body has their own unique capability, gifting, design, and purpose to fulfill. We may not all look the same or have the same function, but we are all important and necessary for the proper functioning of the Body of Christ. For example, if your eye is itching, it can't scratch itself, it needs your hand; however, to see, you need your eyes not your hand.

When it comes to the local church 1 Corinthians 12:18 says God places you as it pleases Him—not as it pleases you (paraphrased). In reality, you don't go to the church of your choice; you go to the church of His choice. The reason is that God has placed gifts in you that you may not even know you have, so He places you in a certain church because the pastor (priest) there is going to give you the spiritual food you need to draw out those gifts and be perfected to fulfill your kingdom assignment.

Many kings are often pressured to be priests because their spiritual leaders mistake their passion for the things of God as a call into full-time (pulpit) ministry. Even though a king may lead a successful workplace Bible study, that does not mean he or she has been called to preach or teach as their profession. This mistake by spiritual leaders could result in a kingdom of priests without any kings, a kingdom with many unfulfilled kings, and a kingdom with unfinanced visions.

Kings and priests must come together for us to fully accomplish what God has planned. The vision of the priest comes from God and should resonate with the kings called to that ministry or local church. However, when the kings are not recognized as a vital, anointed part of the Body, they could become spectators, when God wants to use them to fight a battle, gather the spoils, and bring it back to help build the kingdom. Kings thrive off conquest. Profit to a king is like winning to an athlete.

GOD HAS PLACED GIFTS IN YOU THAT YOU MAY NOT EVEN KNOW YOU HAVE.

For example, when the Lord told me to buy a shopping mall, it was not my idea. God dropped the idea into my heart. He *gave me* the desire of my heart. This is why kings and priests must be open to the move of God, because it will take them to new levels of conquest and abundance. Due to some religious traditions, many kings (Christians) have been preconditioned to think that wealth, or even wanting to profit, is carnal or sinful. However, nothing could be further from the truth. That's why David (a king) asked, *"...What will a man get for killing this Philistine* (Goliath) *and ending his defiance of Israel?* (1 Samuel 17:26 NLT).

THE NEED FOR A COMPLETE MENTAL REVERSAL

Most traditional church leaders have not yet received a revelation of the kingdom and the idea of kings and priests working together for the advancement of the government of God. As a result, the world is stuck in inferior principles such as hatred, corruption, fear, and injustice, and getting the inferior results of poverty, sickness, and self-destruction. Church leaders must rethink how these two corporate anointings should flow together in the Body of Christ. In essence, there has been a problem with "the Church" paradigm and how the Church is seen by its average member. The Lord opened my eyes to the Church being about people and, as I've mentioned, when we limit our thinking or concept of the Church to only a building or the five-fold ministry, we make 95% of the Church irrelevant. He showed me that members of the Body of Christ working in the marketplace are also ministers.

After God gave me a greater understanding about the kingdom of God and the divine partnership of kings and priests, I had "to repent," which is a complete change of mind (a revolution in viewpoint usually expressed when a sinner turns to God). When "light" came, I changed my mind and belief system to embrace that in the kingdom, God "calls" entrepreneurs and other marketplace leaders, just as He "calls" pastors and church leaders to advance His kingdom.

One of the Greek words in the New Testament to describe genuine repentance is *metanoia*, which means "to have another mind or to change one's mind, attitude and purpose regarding sin."[1] When God gave me the revelation of kings and priests, I instantly had a shift in my thinking that changed the entire way I looked at ministry.

When your beliefs change, your behavior changes, which ultimately changes the results you are getting in life. Transform your thinking, transform your life. I had to reject my old, religious thinking and embrace the new thinking of a superior kingdom, the government of God, which is first established in us to finish the work of the Lord Jesus Christ. We must renew our minds to the way God sees things and, when we do, a radical transformation takes place. Romans 12:2 says, *"And be not conformed to this world: but be ye transformed by the renewing of your mind, that ye may prove what is that good, and acceptable, and perfect, will of God."* You can't transform a society you are conformed to.

The word *transformed* in *Thayer's Greek Lexicon* means "to change into another form."[2] It comes from the Greek word *metamorphoo*, which means "to change, transfigure or transform, literally or figuratively."[3] When you are transformed by the renewing of your mind to the Word of God, you "undergo a complete change."[4] The change is so radical that you are changed beyond recognition. Former friends and acquaintances won't even recognize you. Oh, you may physically look the same, but your speech and actions are so dramatically different that people see a new person. And you are!

When Jesus entered into full-time ministry, preaching and teaching the kingdom of God, He was so radically different that His own family thought He had lost His mind.

"For He healed many, so that as many as had afflictions pressed about Him to touch Him. And the unclean spirits, whenever they saw Him, fell down before Him...But when His own people heard about this, they went out to lay hold of Him, for they said, 'He is out of His mind'" (Mark 3:10, 11 and 21 NKJV).

You see, the kingdom of God teaching is the best thing that could happen to mankind and the worst thing that could happen to the devil because it reorients the mind. Manipulating the mind is how the devil keeps people in bondage. Your mind is never neutral; it's always thinking and everything is created from thought. This is how God functions. He creates everything from His thoughts. All that you have around you right now are products of your capacity to think. When God gives us a thought, we must be careful not to shrink it down or "reduce the request." Instead, enlarge your capacity to conceive.

Sad to say, most folks have "downsized" God's thoughts. In the book of Isaiah it says, *"For my thoughts are not your thoughts, neither are your ways my ways, saith the LORD"* (Isaiah 55:8). Someone once told me, "You don't manifest beyond your thinking boundary." You are designed to create whatever you think about continually. According to *Merriam-Webster Dictionary*, the word *paradigm*, in a broad sense, means a "pattern" or "a philosophical or theoretical framework of any kind."[5] A paradigm essentially is a mental map that shapes what you see and how you see it. The idea is often illustrated by the story of the one person who sees the glass half empty and the other person who sees the same glass half full. Notice, this view could affect a person's outlook about life, either positively or negatively. People could also perceive someone or something given to help them as someone or something sent to hurt them...depending on their paradigm.

THE GREEK AND HEBREW MINDSET

Two primary paradigms influence our Christian worldview: the Western Greek mindset and the Hebrew-Asian mindset. In the Greek mindset, which is heavily shaped by the teachings of Greek philosopher Plato, Christians view eternal life as detached from this world. In other words, when we finish life here on Earth, we go to heaven to receive all our rewards and blessings. While we are here on Earth, we basically experience hardships, trials, and struggle.

Philosophies, such as Plato's, lead to paradigms producing a behavior I call "Christian Dualism," where the Christian life is segmented into the sacred and the secular. Spiritual things are on the sacred side, and worldly things are on the secular side (Shepherd 2004). That's dualistic thinking, which also plays out in many social, civic, legal, and religious arenas. An example of dualistic thinking is the separation of church and state. Dualism says that God is with me in the church services, but not outside the church in the marketplace. He's with us on "Sunday" but not on "Monday."

In this view, a hierarchy is inevitably created, where the only meaningful things in life are on the sacred side. However, when people divide their lives like this, making distinctions between the sacred and the secular, one side—usually the secular side—dominates and then worldliness, a distorted view of human value and fulfilling the pleasures of the body, wins out (Shepherd 2004). In this paradigm, the person is programmed to act holy on Sunday and carnal on Monday; preach about the virtues of the Bible one day and buy slaves from the coast of Africa the next.

The Hebrew or Eastern mindset, however, is a view of the kingdom of God in which eternal life begins now, and there is no separation of God from any aspect of a person's life. The kingdom of God is inside of us (Luke 17:21), and should permeate wherever we go.

The Greek paradigm sees faith as an intellectual exercise with education being the highest attainment. The Hebrew mindset expresses life in terms of a relationship with God, where fellowship with God is the highest attainment. The ancient Greek mindset elevates reasoning, arguments, and philosophy. Unfortunately, with reasoning, however, there are no miracles. Miracles cannot be explained by the laws of the material universe. They are by God's Spirit and require the application of faith.

To operate the revelation of kings and priests, we must adopt this "kingdom mindset" or a "Hebrew mindset." We must shift our paradigm to see God and His kingdom influencing every aspect and sphere of society, in every nation, every day. With the right paradigm, Bibles never would have been legally removed from our public schools in the United States and corruption would never be at an all-time high in the global business environment.

BLESSED TO BE A BLESSING

Part of this kingdom or Hebrew mindset is that we are not our own. We are under the authority of the government of God. The apostle Paul calls us "Ambassadors," indicating that we are sent as representatives of a foreign government. He further writes, *"...all are yours; and ye are Christ's; and Christ is God's"* (1 Corinthians 3:22–23). When one understands the kingdom of God and that everyone functions under the authority of God, he or she can understand this

> **WE MUST SHIFT OUR PARADIGM TO SEE GOD AND HIS KINGDOM INFLUENCING EVERY ASPECT OF SOCIETY IN EVERY NATION EVERY DAY.**

kingdom authority arrangement. The apostle Paul goes on to say, *"...You are not your own, You were bought with a price [purchased with a preciousness and paid for, made His own]"* (1 Corinthians 6:19–20 AMP).

Let me give you an illustration how this kingdom mindset has operated in my life. Veronica and I have blessed people by giving them a car, making a mortgage or rent payment, and providing other assistance. In nearly every case, it was because we sensed a leading from the Lord. And because we are submitted to kingdom authority and understand that we belong to Him, we could give cheerfully, realizing that we are helping others and lifting the burden of the curse.

God once spoke to our hearts about giving someone some food around Christmas time. We went to the grocery store, purchased bags of groceries, and put them in the trunk of the car, not knowing who they were going to go to. We prayed and the Lord led us to drive a few miles to the home of a lady living in a government housing project. I knocked on her door and as she opened it, all I saw were young kids sitting on an old, torn-up sofa. I told her that I had a trunk full of groceries for her and she shouted.

After she brought me inside the small apartment, she began to tell me how her daughter was addicted to drugs, and she was keeping her kids; they had just run out of food and she didn't know what to do. She said she kept telling the young kids, "Don't worry, babies, the Lord's going to bring us something to eat..." and He did! Tears rolled down her face when I gave her the food. You see, I owned the food, but that's only half the picture. The full picture is that Christ owns me. As believers, kings or priests, you can see why we should be totally submitted to the King, Jesus, not because we are made to, but because we want to.

In the end, life in the kingdom is not defined by what you possess, but what you have done with what you possess; in other words, how much you have blessed others and served your generation. I like what it says in the book of Acts about David, who was a king and a man after God's own heart, *"For David, after he had served his own generation by the will of God, fell on sleep..."* (Acts 13:36). He was a servant-king and in many ways so are we.

> ESTABLISHING THE KINGDOM OF GOD MUST BE OUR NUMBER ONE PRIORITY.

God strategically and purposefully designed the Body of Christ with a great diversity of gifts, talents, and callings. We are many members, but there is still only one Body. We must learn to respect and value one another's unique role and gifting, as well as respect our contributions. We must shift our paradigm to understand that we are in a relationship with God, and this relationship should influence every area of our lives. Establishing the kingdom of God must be our number one priority regardless of our sphere of influence. As we do this, we will truly come together as one prophetic team. And His kingdom will come and His will be done on Earth, as it is in heaven.

CHAPTER 5

NO MORE TOIL

In Mark 2:27, Jesus makes a revolutionary declaration to the Pharisees, *"And he said unto them, The sabbath was made for man, and not man for the sabbath."* The Sabbath brings to mind how God created the world in six days. What came on the seventh day? Rest.

God made man at the end of the sixth day. The question is: Why did He wait until then? The main reason is that He wanted to provide everything that man would need so that he could step right into the seventh day with all his needs met, which was the foundation of what is now called the Sabbath, or rest. In the past, we have related only ceremoniously to the Sabbath. But the Sabbath instituted under the Old Covenant (Exodus 16) was a "type and shadow" of a much greater spiritual reality. The Old Testament, or Old Covenant, is the shadow, whereas the New Testament is reality.

"Let no man therefore judge you in meat, or in drink, or in respect of an holyday, or of the new moon, or of the sabbath days: which are a shadow of things to come; but the body is of Christ" (Colossians 2:16–17). This is saying that the Sabbath is a reminder of God's promise to bring His man back to completeness so that he could rest in God's provision. It is a picture of restoring the provision that Jesus was going to make possible.

You see, God has not called us to endure hard labor and heavy toil, but to enter into His rest. Because of being conditioned under the curse, surprisingly, many of God's children have the idea that if it's not hard, it's not God. No. God planned for us to live exactly like He lives, believing, speaking, and walking by faith. I like what one man of God said: "We should live like we're on vacation 365 days out of a year." He wasn't saying we shouldn't work. He was saying, "What we do should be enjoyable and without any toil."

A good example of life without toil is found in Luke 5:4–9, where Jesus used Peter's fishing boat while teaching. After He finished teaching, Jesus commanded Peter to launch out into the deep and *"let down your nets and you will catch a lot of fish"* (verse 4 TLB). Peter said, *"We have toiled all the night, and have taken nothing: nevertheless at thy word I will let down the net."* *Toil* is defined as "labor with pain and fatigue, labor that oppresses the body or mind"[1]—now you can see why people are looking forward to retirement; they are "tired."

Peter obeyed the Lord and pulled in a boat-sinking, net-breaking "draught" of fish (verse 9). He even called his partners and they filled both boats. The whole experience brought Peter to his knees. Why? Because he did it with no toil. Toiling and running after provision is under the curse and came because of Adam's transgression in the garden of Eden. By the way, Jesus was not telling Peter to "launch out into the deep" so that he could find a good "fishing spot." Jesus was going to make the fish come to Peter.

In Proverbs 10:22 it says, *"The blessing of the LORD, it maketh rich, and he addeth no sorrow with it."* The *NIV* translation says, *"The blessing of the LORD brings wealth, without painful toil for it."* Again, you and I were not designed to run after fish. They are supposed to come to us, under the command of THE BLESSING or Blessed One (God). We serve an all-powerful God. As we put our faith in God and make Him our only Source, only then will our expectations not end in frustrations. David writes, *"for my expectation is from Him"* (Psalm 62:5). **I decree your days of frustrations are over and all His blessings are now upon you and overtaking you!**

OUR ORIGINAL MODE OF OPERATION

When Adam sinned in the garden of Eden, he not only lost fellowship with God, but he lost his spiritual sight, and his ability to function like God, to think or believe like God, and talk like God. Man was never to be driven by his environment, but to be led by his spirit; to live by his spiritual discernment, not by his five physical senses or wit. God never made our bodies to relate to the spiritual or the supernatural world. He said, *"The flesh* (without the spirit) *profiteth nothing."*

Jesus came to restore us back to where Adam left off and to destroy everything that would mock our redemptive testimony. His mission was to bring mankind back to his original mode of operation, God's ability at man's disposal, taking the kingdom of heaven everywhere he went. Adam's "spiritual eyes" worked perfectly before the Fall. He didn't have to learn...he discerned. He didn't just have information, he operated by revelation. Adam could see things in the spirit— he had full perception of reality. A clear picture of this is found in 2 Kings 6:17 when the prophet prayed for his servant *"...LORD, I pray thee, open his eyes, that he may see."* Anyone reading this knows that the young man's eyes were opened already; that's how he saw the Syrian army on the mountain surrounding them. But those were not the eyes the prophet prayed for to be open.

It goes on to say, *"And the LORD opened the eyes of the young man; and he saw...the mountain was full of horses and chariots of fire round about Elisha."* These chariots were angels of God, which were invisible to the natural eye. God has always intended for mankind to rule this earthly physical realm from the invisible realm. Through one command given by Elisha—*"Smite this people, I pray thee, with blindness,"* (verse 18)—it put an immediate end to this war or conflict. The lesson here is this: You'll never fully function in God's kingdom until you discover you already have provision. Everything God is going to do for you, He's already done. As you read this book, I pray that your eyes will be open to everything God has for you.

Today, the world is experiencing problems that are almost impossible to be solved with only natural sight or human solutions. These problems become, as I've said before, like Hercules fighting with the giant Hydra; every time he cut off one head two grew back in its place. This war on

> **EVERYTHING GOD IS GOING TO DO FOR YOU, HE HAS ALREADY DONE.**

terrorism needs a godly solution only administered through the unbeatable partnership of kings and priests.

Just imagine how short our wars would be today if this unbeatable team of kings and priests, accessing the entire spectrum of reality, would partner together when engaging in conflict. Proverbs 20:18 tells us *"Every purpose is established by counsel: and with good advice make war."* Another translation says, *"...so if you wage war, obtain guidance"* (NIV). I think you will agree there is no better guidance than God's. Through a priest (Levite), God told Israel's army the exact strategy for winning the battle in one day. After the prophetic instructions were given by the priests, the king said, *"...believe his prophets, so shall ye prosper"* (2 Chronicles 20:20). They didn't even need to fight the battle...the Lord fought for them as they praised Him. The result, the enemy was crushed, all dead in one day. Remember, the Babylonian system is characterized by a people trying to meet their needs without God.

THE KINGDOM PROCESS

In the kingdom of God, our goal and covenant obligation is to change the world into a "kingdom culture." God created a man, put him in the garden of Eden, and gave him both an assignment and a prohibition. He instructed the man to tend the garden and cultivate it. He also commanded him not to eat of a certain tree or he would "surely die." Adam was to produce the culture (garden) of the kingdom everywhere he went. Adam fell and sin created a culture outside of God, one coming from man's own imagination and producing without God, based on inferior principles.

A few thousand years later, Christ came and reintroduced the kingdom of God and a "new order" of living by faith with God as our Provider. Jesus taught His followers how the kingdom works saying, *"The sower soweth the word."* So, for every assignment or project God gives us, we must start with the Word of God or a promise from God. Why? Because the promise or "seed" has the potential to bring forth what it says.

God stimulates our imagination through a thought or idea, or a dream or vision as He did with Jacob to deliver him from years of unfair servitude under his uncle Laban (see Genesis 30). Or, He may tell us to do something that, at the time, may seem impossible. For example, Jesus told the disciples in the middle of a desert place as He ended a three-day meeting, *"Feed them."* *"Philip answered, 'For everyone to have even a little, it would take more than two hundred silver coins to buy enough bread'"* (John 6:7 GNT). What Philip didn't realize was that it was not money they needed, it was faith. The scriptures tell us, *"the just shall live by faith."* With two fish and five loaves of bread, they ended up feeding 5,000 men plus women and children.

LET YOUR SPIRIT PRODUCE WHAT YOU NEED

The Lord called me to do the impossible one Sunday morning. "Buy that mall," He said, as I was leaving our worship service. I looked across the street at this huge, almost vacant retail shopping mall. He gives you the "What to do," or "What to think." He then gives you the "How to do it" in the form of a revelation that comes through meditating the seed or promise (a scripture) from His Word.

In my case, when God told me to "Buy that mall," He gave me the scripture, Joshua 1:3, *"Every place that the sole of your foot shall tread upon, that have I given unto you...."* I planted (or sowed) that seed into the soil of my heart (spirit man), which is designed to produce or bring forth what the Word says. In other words, the soil (spirit) is the production center, and like the soil of the earth, it is designed to grow or produce the things sown into it.

The way we sow spiritual seed into our heart is to speak it, or in the case of Abraham, *"Call things that be not* (physically seen) *as though they were."* It is not lying when you confess the promises of God when it has not yet happened. Confession, or agreeing with God, is the way you make it happen.

God knew the situations we would encounter as we fulfilled our kingdom assignments and He laid up the answers on how to solve them before the situation ever showed up, even before the foundation of the world. This one "word seed" in Joshua 1:3 contained it all, from wisdom, guidance, and strategy, to timing and miracle-working power to buy the mall. The seed has everything built in; it's like a "one stop shop." It is a miracle seed.

After God gave me Joshua 1:3, I then had to commit to meditate (ponder) it until my thinking was transformed, until I could see it the way God saw it or receive a revelation. In God's kingdom, only what you see becomes yours. Another way of saying this is, "What we see is what God delivers."[2] God said to Abraham, *"For all the land which thou seest, to thee will I give it."* One man said it like this, "Whatever is revealed to you will be restored to you."

So, as I meditated the "word seed" that the Lord gave me (He gives seed to the sower), it became so alive in me that I no longer saw the obstacles but now I saw the opportunities. Revelation had come, and now manifestation was not far behind. All I had to do from this point was follow the guidance of the Holy Spirit. No one on planet Earth can stop you from having what you are seeing and saying—we are made that way, invincible and unshakeable.

Understand that all the things of God are first spiritual and then they become physical. In fact, material things are dependent on spiritual things for their existence. Things exist first in the invisible, eternal world where God is, and faith brings spiritual things into the natural, physical world. How do we know there is a spiritual, eternal world and things are there? Our heavenly Father told us about it in the Bible. That's why the Bible is so important. There is an abundant supply of everything you could ever need or want awaiting your appropriation through faith.

Jesus taught this process. He said, *"The sower soweth the word...and the seed should spring and grow up, he knoweth not how...but when it is sown, it groweth up, and becometh..."* (Mark 4:14, 27, 32). In the book of John, chapter 1, it says the same thing, but in a little different way, *"In the beginning was the Word, the Word was with God, and the Word was God...And the Word was made flesh, and dwelt among us"* (verses 1, 14).

So, when the seed is planted and grows up *"it becometh"* (Mark 4:30–32). Matthew 13:32 says it's the *"...least of all seeds: but when it is grown, it is the greatest among herbs, and becometh a tree, so that the birds of the air come and lodge in the branches thereof."* This is how I manifested our possession of the Forest Park shopping mall. It all started with a seed.

Where God is taking the Body of Christ we must transform our thinking, and biblical meditation is the way to do this. Faith comes as biblical meditation brings revelation, and where God is taking us, faith will no longer be an option, but a requirement.

To accomplish anything for God, we must first believe God's Word. This believing is with the heart (spirit man), not with the intellect or our natural mind, and believing God takes a decision. You must first decide or choose to believe God's Word. When the angel of the Lord appeared to Mary, the mother of Jesus, and told her that she was going to have a child without being with a man, her response was *"Be it unto me."* She chose to believe the Word spoken to her by the angel. The Bible tells us that *"all things are possible,"* if we know how to believe.

Once you begin to meditate or confess the promise, you are sowing the seed. Then the soil, which is your spirit or heart, conceives the seed and begins the process of searching the wisdom of God for the answer, or how to bring it forth into manifestation. It's like searching through the library for certain books that contain information relative to your situation. In this case, it's for the wisdom to bring your desire to pass. James 1:5 says, *"If any of you lack wisdom, let him ask of God, that giveth to all men liberally, and upbraideth not; and it shall be given him."*

God does not want us to take responsibility for what He does. Our job is to first believe. I warn you, don't look at your bank account. Our job is only to believe. I decided to believe that our church could "buy that mall" and that God would do His part. Belief is committing to the Word. After we make a decision to believe God and meditate His promise, then we take action. Faith is acting on what we believe.

God has no backup plan. Why? Because the first one always works. This is why possessing things according to "His Righteousness," the kingdom way of doing things, is no toil. The plan that the Lord gives is so custom-made it takes even your background and experiences into consideration. It has been calibrated for accuracy. It will work perfectly. Just follow His instructions and guidance and do what He tells you. In Proverbs it says, *"The Spirit of the man is the candle of the Lord, searching all the inwards parts of the belly"* (Proverbs 20:27). This simply means that God will use your spirit to guide you.

This kingdom process will give you solutions, strategies, and thoughts you never had before. Why? Because you never planted that seed before. Your spirit had not called on God's Spirit for this revelation. You are not forcing God to do something, but calling for the harvest He promised. Again, this is not man's method, this is God's method. Proverbs 2:7 says, *"He layeth up sound wisdom for the righteous...."*

The scriptures tell us *"wisdom is the principle thing"* ... not the problem. God told Joshua after he meditated, *"See, I have given into thy hand Jericho"* (Joshua 6:2). Then He proceeded to give Joshua specific instructions as to how to take delivery.

The kingdom process first starts with a promise from God. Then you must believe that promise. Believing starts with a decision.

Third, you must meditate the promise to start believing the unbelievable. Meditation brings revelation and faith to take delivery of your inheritance. As one man of God said, "Revelation is your greatest asset in the school of faith." Meditation also brings you to a place where you begin to see your victory, not some time in the future, but NOW! Finally, when faith comes, you act on the promise and you are certain to experience your miracle.

THE IMPORTANCE OF PRAYER

Prayer is vital in the life of every believer, whether a king or priest, because it connects you to the supernatural by getting God's thoughts and insights on every situation and problem you face. Therefore, kingdom process must include prayer. In the kingdom, you listen to God for your goals, objectives, and plans, because only God knows who you really are and what your true purpose is on Earth. You must beware of satan's attempt to cap your potential by shrinking your thoughts. You

FAITH & THE MARKETPLACE

are much bigger on the inside than you are on the outside, and God is the one who knows all about you.

First Corinthians 2:11–12 says, *"For what man knoweth the things of a man, save the spirit of man which is in him? even so the things of God knoweth no man, but the Spirit of God. Now we have received, not the spirit of the world, but the spirit which is of God; that we might know the things that are freely given to us of God."*

> **"REVELATION IS YOUR GREATEST ASSET IN THE SCHOOL OF FAITH."**

The word *body* in Greek is *soma*, which means "slave."[3] It was never meant for your body to tell you what you can and cannot do. An example of this is Peter walking on water. When he came back to his reason or natural mind and the dictates of the five physical senses, he sunk. So, I've developed a habit of always checking the source of my thoughts (see 2 Corinthians 10:3–5).

Before I begin a new project or venture, I pray for God's wisdom and direction. According to Mark 11:24, I receive His wisdom by faith when I pray, and then God begins to reveal it to me. Realize, the ideas, visions, and plans that God gives you are a form of currency. You can sell them, trade them, and monetize them in various ways, and they are given to advance you in every area of your life.

Prayer and following the leading of the Holy Spirit are vital in every phase of a new business or project. Kingdom entrepreneurs and marketplace leaders must set aside some time for prayer or devotion for their companies, organizations, and all marketplace responsibilities. I recently read a powerful story of how prayer saved one businessman's company from the brink of disaster. Customer orders had seemingly dried up and closing his factory seemed like the only solution. Here is the excerpt from his book:

> Frequently the Lord used our (business) circumstances to teach us to pray, and then His glory was manifest on the factory floor in the most remarkable ways!

The first example came through the pots and pans business, which I later sold. Our sales figures were automatically logged as we were linked with major department stores and received their orders as the computers logged the sales. Our daily output was approximately 3,000 casserole pans, and this was very satisfactory. However, by May there were no new orders, and so I contacted the customers asking them what was wrong. They simply reassured me that everything was fine and orders would be coming in. But towards the end of the month we had only received $700 USD worth of sales. Virtually nothing. I was deeply troubled.

Again we phoned the customers to check, but meanwhile, the warehouse was filling up with casseroles. As I surveyed the crowded warehouse I knew there was nothing else I could do. Production had to be stopped. Our customers had confirmed that nothing was wrong, and yet orders were drying up. I prayed, spoke to Asther (my wife), and told her that there was nothing more we could do. The factory would have to be closed if we were to survive the crisis.

As it was a Friday night, we went along to the prayer group with heavy hearts and that evening one of the women shared a passage of scripture: "Five of you will chase a hundred, and a hundred of you will chase ten thousand, and your enemies will fall by the sword before you" (Leviticus 26:8). As she read these words, my spirit leapt and I knew what I had to do. Inspired by the Scriptures, I immediately shared my problem with the rest of the group. "We have 90,000 unsold casseroles sitting in the warehouse," I said as I finished describing our dilemma.

A brief discussion followed and we knew we had to use our unity as a group to pray and command those casseroles to move out of the warehouse. So we took authority in the name of Jesus Christ and commanded those casseroles to move out and give glory to God!

During that weekend we didn't discuss the matter, and on Monday morning the office manager met me on the stairs. "Good news! I guess we should praise the Lord! Some of our major customers called and they've bought everything we have except the one litre and three litre casseroles. They want us to ship the order today."

Quickly, we began packing and loading and the warehouse gradually emptied. However, it soon dawned on me that this was not a total answer to prayer because we had commanded all the casseroles to move and give glory to the Lord. I called the office manager into my room and shared the situation with him. We had taken authority over the situation in the name of Jesus and commanded all the stock to go. Surely we needed to agree that the remainder went as well? So in unity, now with the office manager, we prayed once more. This time we specifically spoke to the one litre and three litre casseroles to obey the command!

Half an hour later the phone rang. It was one of our customers. They had an emergency and they desperately needed one and three litre casseroles. Did we have any ready to dispatch immediately? And so our entire stock left the warehouse in one day.

Since the company had been given over to God, I realized there were other forces resisting us apart from the normal market fluctuations. We had to pray as well as work, and unity was a key factor in our prayers. This was a principle I never forgot and used many times when faced with impossible situations.[4]

This powerful testimony illustrates that kingdom citizens (God's people) in the marketplace must have prayer and that more can be accomplished when a group of believers pray. This is why our ministry has launched a prayer hotline for our partners, business entrepreneurs and leaders alike, or anyone facing problems and obstacles preventing them from moving forward. As this businessman points out, there are spiritual forces resisting kingdom citizens that can only be stopped through prayer and the Word of God. These spiritual forces are designed to offer resistance to the Church and those committed to advancing God's kingdom that the secular world does not have to contend with or fight. If we don't resist the enemy he is allowed to remain. "Normal market fluctuations" are not normal in the kingdom of God.

SUPERNATURAL RESULTS

Doing business the kingdom way will lead you to results that will be far superior to what reason and human effort alone could achieve—and with no toil. Again, look at the story in Luke 5 where Peter had "toiled all night." That is, Peter was fishing during the expected time of day to fish, which was at night, but had caught nothing. Then Jesus told him to launch out into the deep for a draught. He basically told Peter to go back out and fish according to faith instead of according to time, natural laws, or economic climate. Peter obeyed and caught a boat-sinking load of fish—supernatural results.

FAITH TAKES US ABOVE THE RESTRICTIVE DICTATES OF TIME

Many times toil and struggle come when we allow ourselves to be controlled by human reason and our five physical senses, instead of doing things God's way. We then become servants to our external environment and time, instead of time and our environment serving us, as was originally intended.

A good example of how faith can override time is the supernatural start of our ministry's business school, the Joseph Business School. Human intellect and research said it would take one to two years to start the school, but God spoke to my heart, "It will take two months." To the natural mind this seemed impossible. But when we started planning and executing by faith according to what God spoke, the project began following heaven's timeline and attracting heaven's "mysterious supply." Remember, real faith says (declares) when a thing will happen, and time must bow to that decree. Faith is the dominant force given to man to rule over time. The business school opened in the time frame God spoke to me and is now fully accredited—and planted in five continents.

If we believe with our minds, we will believe only what our body or five senses tell us; that's human reason and we will ultimately doubt God's power. However, if we believe with the heart (spirit), then the revelation knowledge that comes directly from God into our spirits will illuminate our mind with information that supersedes our natural senses. Our minds then dispatch this information to the body for appropriate action. Now the mind is no longer governed by what makes sense, but by what makes faith.

REST AND WORK

At the start of this chapter, I shared that God introduced the Sabbath to the children of Israel (mankind) in the wilderness. He told Moses to tell the people that for five days they were to gather enough food (provision) for each day and save none of it until the morning. If they did, they would find the food spoiled; the scriptures say the food *"bred worms, and stank."*

On the sixth day, however, God told Moses to tell the people to gather enough food for two days, because on the seventh day they were to rest rather than go out and gather provision. Exodus 16:21–23 NIV says,

> Each morning everyone gathered as much as they needed, and when the sun grew hot, it melted away. On the sixth day, they gathered twice as much—two omers for each person—and the leaders of the community came and reported this to Moses. He said to them, "This is what the LORD commanded: 'Tomorrow is to be a day of sabbath rest, a holy sabbath to the LORD....'"

When God provided manna from heaven daily for the children of Israel—between 2 and 3 million people—what did they have to do to get it? Gather it! And that was it. God made daily provision. Their job was only to gather it. On the sixth day, God provided twice as much to carry them through the Sabbath. It was His way of reminding them of the reality of Sabbath rest.

The Sabbath is a picture of the divine provision of rest. And "keeping the Sabbath" was a reminder of God's promise to someday restore back to man provision through Christ. In the wilderness, Israel fell into unbelief, and the Lord swore that He would not let them "enter" into His rest (Psalm 95:8–11). The rest that Israel was to enter into was the "Promised Land," a place of abundant provision. It was the *"land of milk and honey,"* where Israel would cease from their labor (toil) and possess all the blessings that God had prepared for them. They would live in houses they didn't build, and enjoy the fruit of vineyards they didn't plant.

Hebrews, chapter 4, verses 3 and 9, say, *"For we which have believed do enter into rest...There remaineth therefore a rest to the people of God."* Notice, however, there can be no real rest without provision. The concept of Sabbath rest is also a mandate for kingdom provision.

Understand, I am not saying that we are not supposed to work. In fact, God requires us to work. One of the best things a parent can do for a child is demand that they learn about the responsibility of work. However, the work we do is not going to be the "toil" that we were used to before we came into the kingdom. We no longer have to "earn" a living by the sweat of our brow, as mankind did after the sin of Adam.

God is saying, "Those days for you are over. No more toil! No longer a survival mentality and struggling trying to 'make ends meet'! You are going to be a representation of the kingdom of God." He is saying, "I am going to provide everything that you need just as it was for Adam and Eve in the garden of Eden in the beginning. Even in a time or place of economic famine you will gather plenty" (see Psalm 37:19). Where we live, in the kingdom of God, does not have a bad economy.

Think of it this way, in the garden of Eden how much did Adam and Eve have to worry about provision for their lives? Here's the answer. The thought about provision had not existed yet. In Jesus' teaching He said, *"...therefore, take no thought for your life, what you shall eat...."* He was showing them how they could access a supernatural supply through the spiritual law of sowing and reaping. He demonstrated how to put an immediate end to any need.

As a covenant child of God, when you plant good seed in good soil, you will get a harvest, and no man can abrogate (nullify) it (Oyedepo 2005). You can actually function in this world's economy according to heaven's economy, no matter where you are on this planet or what the circumstances.

Under the curse, sorrow and toil became tied to obtaining provision. However, when Jesus restored THE BLESSING to mankind, He restored us back to God as our original Source and Sustainer of every need or desire we (mankind) would ever have. Instead of toiling for provision through hard labor, like I did in borrowing and getting a second job, we are to trust God, and by faith and obedience, work His system, manifesting His goodness. Remember, *"the just shall live by faith."*

As I said earlier, living by faith does not mean that we are not supposed to work, for there is dignity in work. Sometimes your work or employment could be the channel God might use to bless you. In Deuteronomy 28, God said, *"The LORD shall open unto thee his good treasure, the heaven to give the rain unto thy land in his season, and to bless all the work of thine hand"* (verse 12), as He did Simon when he went fishing with Jesus, or me when I was in sales working for IBM. What happened in both cases is that we didn't toil, we gathered.

Dr. George Washington Carver, an African American scientist on the faculty in the early days of Tuskegee University, or Tuskegee Institute as it was called then, said, "I never have to grope for methods. The method is revealed to me the moment I am inspired to create something new. Without God to draw aside the curtain I would be helpless."[5] The word *grope* means "to search by feeling in the dark."[6] Carver said that once he is inside his laboratory alone with the Creator the answers just come to him. Notice, he doesn't struggle and toil for answers...he just "gathers," and that's called "work" in the kingdom of God.

Also, we are made to bless others through our labor. See Figure 1: Eight Reasons Why You Work in the Kingdom (Adelaja 2008). The bottom line is: If a person does not work, he or she gives nothing of value to the world. When we engage in the labor that God has assigned to us, we serve the greater good of humanity and bring glory to God. Maybe you can now better understand the scripture that says, *"Let your light so shine before men, that they may see your good works, and glorify your Father which is in heaven"* (Matthew 5:16).

Figure 1: Eight Reasons Why You Work in the Kingdom

1. Work is the way you can give something of value to the world.
2. Work releases and develops your gifts and talents.
3. Work keeps you mentally healthy by focusing your mind on something productive.
4. Work is a means by which dreams, ideas, and goals become a reality.
5. Work makes you a blessing to other people.
6. Work allows you to become a co-creator with God.
7. You will not fulfill your potential and purpose in God's kingdom without work.
8. Work provides avenues by which revenues can be directed into your hands supernaturally...avenues through which God can give you seed to sow.

WORK PLACES A DEMAND ON YOUR POTENTIAL

The Greek word for *work* is *ergon*,[7] which is where the word *energy* derives from. Work is activating stored energy. Through work, your potential is expressed in tangible form. If you refuse to work, your ability or potential to express God's image and to bear fruit remains sealed up inside of you. One man said, "Potential without work is poverty."[8] *Potential* means "hidden abilities." The dictionary definition is "existing in possibility: capable of development into actuality...expressing possibility."[9] You have seeds of greatness placed inside of you by God; the potential is given in seed form. Without work, your potential and abilities remain hidden.

Proverbs 18:16 AMP says, *"A man's gift makes room for him and brings him before great men."* You and I were designed to work out the genius God placed in us when we were created.

Think of it this way: By your work, you are becoming what you already are. It brings your potential to the surface, into manifestation. No one comes into this world without a gift or calling, and everybody has potential. But without work, those gifts and talents remain underdeveloped. God uses work to place a demand on our potential because potential needs a demand to draw it out.

Abraham was given potential but it had to be worked out. God told him to walk through the land, *"for I will give it unto thee"* (Genesis 13:17). As you know, he and his "seed" had to fight those who lived in the land. They could not just go in and possess the land with no effort. He also commands us to put forth effort to receive what He has promised. *"Let us labor therefore to enter into that rest."* Our primary labor, however, is in the Word of God.

Situations and circumstances can place a demand on your potential, but you don't have to wait to be challenged. You can intentionally place a demand on your own potential, as Peter did in Matthew 14:28 when he saw Jesus walking on the water. He said to Jesus, *"Lord, if it be thou, bid me come unto thee on the water."* And, *"he walked on the water, to go to Jesus"* (verse 29).

WHO WANTS TO BE A BILLIONAIRE?

Problems can place a demand on your potential, ultimately for the benefit of mankind. Many billionaires know that problems are what make life so great. Like David ran toward the giant Goliath, they run toward problems, and once they conquer them, emerge with a marketable solution or product. Thus, the rich get richer. The average person tries to run away from problems.

I believe that your work should be so fulfilling that someone has to remind you to take a day of rest. Also, in the kingdom, you're not working for money (that puts money in control). You're working to work out the potential God placed in you. There can be no greatness without work—no effort, no increase. Again, "Potential without work is poverty." The Scriptures tell us that a lazy person will come to poverty

(Proverbs 24:30–34). So, work is not something to be avoided but toiling is. Work (not toil) is a gift from God. It's a way to make all your dreams come true.

I am convinced that once a person comes into the kingdom, the next thing they should focus on after being filled with the Holy Spirit is the release of the potential and energy God gave them for the good of the world. God also uses our work to establish His kingdom wherever He sends us, so we must make sure we develop the right attitude about work.

GOD USES WORK TO PLACE A DEMAND ON YOUR POTENTIAL.

> Therefore, take no thought, saying, What shall we eat? or, What shall we drink? or, Wherewithal shall we be clothed? (For after all these things do the Gentiles seek) for your heavenly Father knoweth that ye have need of all these things. But seek ye first the kingdom of God, and his righteousness; and all these things shall be added unto you. Matthew 6:31–33

This scripture reminds us that the job is not our source; it is a resource. God is our Source. A "job" provides a paycheck, while work releases potential. Where God sends you, you are not being employed but deployed. You are on a heavenly assignment. God may direct you to take a lower-paying job or position just because He has an assignment or plan for you there. There may be someone to reach or something to change for the kingdom. He may tell you to start a business selling lemonade only because He's got BIG plans for you in the juice or beverage manufacturing business. Wherever God sends you, He fully takes care of you while you are serving in your assignment. This is how my wife and I were able to come to Chicago with only $200 to start a ministry that now reaches most of the known world.

CEASE FROM YOUR OWN WORKS

Hebrews 4:9–11 says:

> There remaineth therefore a rest to the people of God. For he that is entered into his rest, he also hath ceased from his own works, as God *did* from

his. Let us labour therefore to enter into that rest, lest any man fall after the same example of unbelief.

This passage is important because it demonstrates again that our days of toil are over. Of course we work, but without toil. God has provided a better way for us to bring something to pass (work is bringing something to pass). Dr. George Washington Carver revolutionized the agricultural industry by discovering more than 300 uses for the peanut. His discoveries also included over 118 uses for the sweet potato, as well as for the soybean, including cosmetics, shaving cream, salad oil, instant coffee, and nontoxic color dyes from which crayons were eventually created.[10]

Henry Ford, founder of Ford Motor Company, became personal friends with Dr. Carver after being fascinated with his method of deriving rubber from milkweed. He tried many times to convince Dr. Carver to join him in business, but Dr. Carver was committed to Tuskegee, Alabama, and helping his people in the South. Thomas Edison offered him a position with a six-figure income, but Carver turned it down.[11] Did Dr. Carver toil for any of those discoveries? No! Only God can show a man 300 uses for a little old peanut.

All that he sought was already there. He said: "No books ever go into my laboratory. The thing I am to do and the way of doing it are revealed to me."[12] Many of us have been trained in the Babylonian world system to run after money or things, but that isn't what Deuteronomy 28:2 says. It says that *"all these blessings shall come on thee, and overtake thee, if thou shalt hearken to the voice of the LORD thy God."*

> **WORK (NOT TOIL) IS A GIFT FROM GOD.**

I read a book about a man who had made a trip to heaven.[13] An angel escorted him around and showed him a place that looked like a trade show warehouse with different rooms or sections throughout. He said that one section was a storage area for body parts...limbs, eyeballs, teeth, gums, hair, everything. Some of the items were specifically designated. One even had a tag on the toe for someone who needed a foot. He said that all God's people had to do was believe for what they needed, because it was all their inheritance—it was already there in the heavenly realm (1 Peter 1:3–4).

In 2 Kings, chapter 7, the king of Syria had besieged Samaria and cut off all Israel's provision. This assault caused a dreadful famine, which turned some people to cannibalism even eating other people's babies. In the midst of this, the prophet Elisha, a priest, came in. He basically said, "Tomorrow about this time, there is going to be plenty, and it's going to be cheap" (Winston interpretation). That was a welcomed word, because that famine had caused outrageous inflation and soaring food prices.

The prophet spoke deliverance and hope to the people. What happened? Four lepers right outside the king's gates heard the prophetic word. Something happened on the inside of one of them and, in so many words, this is what he said: "Why are we going to sit here until we die? Let's see; if we go in there to Israel, they are starving to death. If we sit here, we are going to die. So, why don't we just go into the enemy's camp? If we live, we live. If we die, we die." I once heard it said: "Faith answers to crazy people." "Crazy people" are those people whose minds are no longer governed by what makes sense. In other words, the lepers were no longer fearful of what might happen to them. So the Bible says they rose up at twilight and began to go forth.

The lepers in this passage of scripture probably could do no fighting, but the battle was not theirs anyway, because they had come into their rest. That battle was the Lord's. When they reached the enemy's camp, the enemy had scattered. Why? Because God had made the enemy hear the sound of horses and chariots so numerous that it frightened them, and they left everything behind. When the lepers arrived at the camp, the Syrians had left their tents, their food, the gold, the silver, their clothing, everything. The lepers went into each tent and carried away silver, gold, and clothing and went and hid it. As they continued going from one tent to the next tent, eventually they said, "Why are we keeping all this to ourselves? Let's go back and tell Israel the good news." The best news is that they didn't have to sweat for it; all they did was gather the spoils.

There are several things we can learn from this story. First, the priest, the prophet Elisha, gave a prophetic word of hope and deliverance. Second, that word cast out fear and caused faith to come into the lepers, who could represent marketplace leaders. Third, the lepers acted on their faith and went into the enemy's camp not knowing what they would find. This illustrates that faith doesn't always show you the total outcome up front. And what did they find? They found all the spoils—food, clothing, gold, and silver—that the enemy left behind. This leads to my final points: All the lepers had to do was to gather, and the spoils weren't just for them but to share with others. We are blessed to be a blessing.

COME INTO YOUR REST

I personally think that the world is entering into a time of creative revolutionary advancement, and most all of it will come through the Church (Ephesians 3:10). These "flashes of light" (revelation and creative ideas) in our minds and imaginations will bring new inventions to all spheres of the marketplace, from the arts to economics, from education to politics, and from media to the family. All industries will enjoy these discoveries.

We, in the Body of Christ, are now going to experience an "innovation download," or what one man calls a "mental revolution," that will help bring us to the top of every mountain of influence without sweat. This time of "ingenious waves of creativity" will greatly affect the quality of life for all people and nations. This is partly what is meant by the verse, *"For the LORD taketh pleasure in his people: He will beautify the meek with salvation"* (Psalm 149:4).

I'm speaking into your life now: **I decree that your days of struggling for money and provision are over.** God is empowering His people to get wealth, even to become millionaires and some billionaires, in the Body of Christ, out of every nation. There will be more than enough provision for any and every kingdom project. Some of you reading this may not even have much education right now, but God is getting ready to raise you up, like He did Gideon, empowering you academically, intellectually, and practically to take your place of leadership in the world.

Our faith is the conduit or the vessel that transports the abundant harvest from where everything is stored (spiritually) up in heaven, to us here in the earth—anytime, anywhere. As the apostle Paul says in Philippians 4:19, *"But my God shall supply all your need according to his riches in glory by Christ Jesus."* In heaven, there is an unlimited, inexhaustible supply of everything you'll ever need. You can live now, just like you were already there!

CHAPTER 6

LIVING IN THE KINGDOM

The kingdom of God was the Father's original plan for mankind. In fact, to this day, it continues to be what every person longs for here on Earth, whether they know it or not. Most people desire to live under a government that provides peace, purpose, prosperity, security, and everything necessary for a productive life. Well, this describes the kingdom or government of God that existed in Eden. When mankind fell because of Adam's treason, they were put out of the garden of Eden and the kingdom was lost. Jesus, the Son of God whom the apostle Paul calls the last Adam, came to reestablish this heavenly government on Earth and to reconnect mankind to the original power and provision he had before the Fall. This reconnection first happens in the heart of mankind, and eventually flows outward to touch the world. He said *"I am come that you might have life* (not religion) *and that you might have it more abundantly."*

In the kingdom all authority flows from the King, whose Word is supreme. The King is obligated to care for and protect its citizens. Their well-being and welfare is a reflection on the King himself. As kingdom citizens and ambassadors for Christ, if we are ever being told or forced to do something that is in direct conflict or violation of the "Word of the kingdom," we are commanded to keep God's Word, regardless of the threat or circumstances. Just as Daniel kept the Word of his God and the Lord shut the lion's mouth; or the three Hebrew men who refused to bow, honoring the laws of the one true God, and the fire could not burn them. They were heard saying, *"The God that we serve, He will deliver us."* And He will also deliver you. When we are divinely positioned, we are divinely protected. The Scriptures even tell us that Jesus, our King, is at the right hand of God making intercession for us (Romans 8:34).

The Bible, or God's covenant, is the constitution of the kingdom and expresses the Word, the will and the laws of the King. It also contains the benefits and privileges of its citizens. The laws of the kingdom cannot be changed by its citizens nor are they subject to opinion or debate.

Jesus said that the number one goal of all men is to seek first the kingdom of God (Matthew 6:33), meaning seek its priority and its operation. He even declares in Luke 4:43, *"I must preach the kingdom of God...for therefore am I sent."* The *Amplified Bible* says, *"I must preach the good news (the Gospel) of the kingdom of God...for I was sent for this [purpose]."*

Although the gospel of the kingdom of God was a new message to Jesus' followers, the kingdom itself, as I mentioned, was not something new. God created the kingdom for His children from the foundation of the world, *"Come, you blessed of My Father...inherit (receive as your own) the kingdom prepared for you from the foundation of the world"* (Matthew 25:34 AMP).

HOW THE KINGDOM WORKS

Every kingdom or government has laws, and the government of God is no different. God's government has spiritual laws and these laws are His Word. Living in obedience to God's Word keeps us from self-destruction and is the only guarantee of freedom. As you willingly follow its instructions, by faith, the Bible says, *"You shall eat the good of the land"* (Isaiah 1:19).

There are several (what I call) master laws that govern how the kingdom of God works here on Earth. Among them are the laws of sowing and reaping, tithing, the law of confession, the law of faith, the law of love, and so on. These last two work very closely together. In fact, the Bible tells us **"Faith worketh by love."** If we stop loving with "the

God kind of love," which is unconditional love, the faith of God eventually stops working. The Scriptures tell us *"God is love."* This means that you and I, who are made in His image and likeness, are designed to love, the same as our Creator.

Jesus teaches on the law of love saying, *"A new commandment I give unto you, That ye love one another; as I have loved you, that ye also love one another"* (John 13:34). Keeping this love commandment is important for the continuous flow of God's benefits into our lives (Mark 11:24–25). Unforgiveness, jealousy, envy, hate, and anger are all principles of the kingdom of darkness and have no place in the kingdom of God's dear Son. So, love is vital to our continuous promotion and kingdom expansion.

> **LOVE IS VITAL TO THE KINGDOM'S CONTINUOUS PROMOTION AND EXPANSION.**

THE LAW OF SOWING AND REAPING

In the kingdom of God, all increase comes from seed sown. Once you come into the kingdom, if there is a need, you can sow a seed. Sowing and reaping is a powerful spiritual law that no man can nullify. No amount of crying, fasting, or praying can make it work. It requires your participation and your practice (Oyedepo 2005). If you, by faith, plant good seed into good ground, you will get a harvest. Sowing and reaping is the method God has chosen for this planet and it will be that way as long as this Earth is in existence (Genesis 8:22).

Jesus teaches that sowing and reaping is the "granddaddy" law that controls everything in the kingdom:

> So is the kingdom of God, as if a man should cast seed into the ground; and should sleep, and rise night and day, and the seed should spring and grow up, he knoweth not how. For the earth bringeth forth fruit of herself; first the blade, then the ear, after that the full corn in the ear. But when the fruit is brought forth, immediately he putteth in the sickle, because the harvest is come. Mark 4:26–29

Anywhere you see God talk about prosperity, notice that the Word of God is the foundation (Oyedepo 2005). For example, I used to suffer from hay fever every year at a certain season. When I received Christ and became aware that I had been legally redeemed from the sickness of hay fever, I began to confess God's Word concerning the promise. The Word of God brought forth revelation that gave me the faith to access my God-given inheritance of health. I haven't suffered from hay fever since. Again, all increase answers to the quality of seed sown into your heart. "Prosperity in the kingdom is Word-seed-determined...the Word of God controls all increase in every area of the believer's life."[1]

Jesus even told His disciples in Mark 4:13 that understanding the parable of the sower was foundational for understanding all His other teachings. *"Don't you understand this parable? How, then, will you ever understand any parable?"* (*Good News Translation*).

> **"PROSPERITY IN THE KINGDOM IS WORD-SEED DETERMINED AND CONTROLS ALL INCREASE IN A BELIEVER'S LIFE."**

This revelation of sowing and reaping is seen again in the story of Jesus feeding the multitude in Matthew 14:15–20. It was evening in a desert place and the disciples wanted Jesus to send away the crowd so they could buy food to eat in the nearby villages. But Jesus told them, *"You give them something to eat."* The disciples responded that they only had *"five loaves, and two fishes."*

Now look what happens in verses 18–19.

> He said, Bring them hither to me. And he commanded the multitude to sit down on the grass, and took the five loaves, and the two fishes, and looking up to heaven, he blessed, and brake, and gave the loaves to *his* disciples, and the disciples to the multitude.

Jesus first told His disciples to bring the five loaves and two fishes to Him. For God to supernaturally multiply our seed, He has to have legal jurisdiction or authority over it (Keesee 2011). This same principle is seen when He handles our problems and cares..."*Casting all your care upon him (God); for he careth for you"* (1 Peter 5:7). If we don't cast our cares, He can't legally handle them and you'll walk away with exactly what you brought to Him. The same applies to sowing and reaping. A seed, whether fish, or money, or Peter's boat, has to be placed in the hands of Jesus before the anointing of multiplication can take over. One man of God said it has to be considered dead or useless to you.

Jesus then looked up to heaven and blessed the bread and the fish. He invoked the power of the covenant, or THE BLESSING, breaking the limits off of what one naturally has to submit to in the earth. The loaves and fishes began to multiply as He gave it to His disciples to distribute to the people. *"And they did all eat, and were filled...and they took up of the fragments that remained twelve baskets full."* Overflow...abundance... more than enough are what God has planned for us. Jesus spoke or invoked THE BLESSING over the seed. Many people don't understand that our words carry spiritual power. To bring God's goodness in any area of your life you must speak "life." Speak life over your family, finances, business, community, and even your nation. Confessing words in agreement with God's Word is a vital part of manifesting His abundance. I will discuss this in more detail shortly.

In the kingdom, a seed will meet any need. There was a widow woman whose sons were about to be taken and put in bondage because her husband had died and left them deep in debt. She cried to the man of God, Elisha, and he asked her in 2 Kings, chapter 4, "What do you have in your house?" She said that she only had a pot of oil, which we can describe as her "seed," and God supernaturally multiplied it as she poured oil into all the vessels that she borrowed from her neighbors at the instruction of the prophet. She then sold the oil, paid off her debt, and she and her sons lived off the rest. Remember, in sowing and reaping you are not forcing God to do something, but planting the seed that calls for the harvest God has already promised.

THE LAW OF THE TITHE

Some Christians have been taught that tithing was under the Law given to Moses and that since we now are under grace, tithing has passed away. The Bible shows, however, that

Abraham, Isaac, and Jacob all tithed hundreds of years before God gave the "Law" to Moses. Genesis 14:19–20 says, *"And he (Melchizedek) blessed him, and said, Blessed be Abram of the most high God, possessor of heaven and earth: and blessed be the most high God, which hath delivered thine enemies into thy hand. And he* (Abraham) *gave him tithes of all."*

> **IN SOWING AND REAPING, YOU'RE NOT FORCING GOD TO ACT BUT CALLING THE HARVEST HE'S ALREADY PROMISED.**

What is the tithe? The tithe is 10 percent of your income and all legal increase, and it does not belong to you. I submit to you that tithing is a spiritual law that when acted on, in faith, releases certain benefits into the life of a believer. The Bible tells us it belongs to the Lord (Leviticus 27:30). As citizens of the kingdom, God expects us to faithfully return to Him the tithe. Just as paying taxes is your civic responsibility in the country you live in, paying your tithe is "your covenant responsibility as a citizen of the kingdom of God. It is an inescapable covenant obligation."[2]

Tithing is actually covered under the law of sowing and reaping. Here is what the late Oral Roberts said about tithing after the Lord gave him revelation of seed-faith. "From that one experience, I changed the way I looked at my tithing to God—not as a debt I owed, but as a seed I sowed." Roberts went on to share this:

> Many years ago the Lord showed me what He meant when He said in Malachi 3:10, "Bring your tithe, your tenth, into My work and prove Me now and see if I will not open the windows of heaven and pour out a blessing on you more than you can contain."
>
> I said to the Lord, "I've always been able to contain any blessing You gave me. But you said You would pour out a blessing on me that I wouldn't be able to receive or contain it all. How can that be?" God said, "You haven't proven Me. If you bring in the tithe as a seed of your faith, I will open you the windows of heaven and POUR you out blessing after blessing. You need to expect 'exceedingly abundantly above ALL you can ask or think'" (see Ephesians 3:20).

Then He gave me a revelation about ICI: Ideas, Concepts, and Insights.[3]

Roberts said that God told him, "Tell the people I don't pour money out of heaven. Money doesn't fall out of heaven. Houses don't fall out of heaven. Cars don't fall out of heaven. And jobs don't fall out of heaven. Stop looking to heaven for those things. The blessings of God come through ideas, concepts, and insights (ICI)...."[4] Think about it: God is the creator of ideas, concepts, and insights, and gives strategies and guidance to those who honor Him through the tithe.

In Malachi 3:10 God instructs us, *"Bring ye all the tithes into the storehouse, that there may be meat in mine house, and prove me now herewith, saith the* LORD *of hosts...."* The storehouse is the place where you are being "fed" spiritually; that is, where you are taught the Word of God, and it should be the local church. When we bring all the tithes into the storehouse by faith, and not legalistically, God promises to open the windows of heaven and pour out a blessing that we don't have room enough to contain.

R. G. LETOURNEAU AND THE TITHE

Robert Gilmour ("R. G.") LeTourneau was a successful businessman during World War II and the decades after the war, but he didn't start out successful. His story, which I share in more detail later in the book, is a modern-day testimony of the power and importance of the tithe.

Mr. LeTourneau was a deeply committed Christian who was very poor when he first gave his heart to the Lord Jesus Christ. But he had a big dream and a great desire, and when he read Malachi 3:10 he decided to take God at His Word, literally. LeTourneau gave God 10 percent of all he earned for the work of the kingdom. He then decided to "prove" God regarding his dream of building great earth-moving machines that had never been made before, and he asked God how to make them. The more faithful he was in tithing, the more the ideas came. "As he continued to tithe, God caused his dream to manufacture earth-moving equipment to become a reality. He prospered so much that instead of giving God 10 percent of his income, he eventually gave the Lord 90 percent for the work of His kingdom and lived off the 10 percent!"[5] I can only imagine how big that 10% was.

When a manager at one of LeTourneau's manufacturing plants was asked how LeTourneau knew his ideas were because of his tithing, he responded, "Oh, he could easily tell that. If he stopped tithing, the ideas became blurred or stopped coming altogether. As he began to tithe again, the ideas would begin to come again."[6] LeTourneau tithed because God's Word said to do it and he was obedient to God's Word. LeTourneau's trust was completely in God, no matter what anyone said or thought.

What is LeTourneau's legacy today? His earth-moving equipment is still manufactured today and used all over the world. The university he and his wife founded in 1946, LeTourneau Technical Institute (now LeTourneau University) to help train returning World War II veterans, is still educating thousands of Christian professionals who view the marketplace as a mission field. The current president remarked, "The University has a legacy of uniquely equipping its graduates to be involved in the workplace, hearkening back to when R. G. LeTourneau was told that God needed businessmen as well as preachers."[7]

ALL INCREASE COMES FROM THE WORD OF GOD

Each time I've talked to God about a need, He's talked to me about a seed. It is the way God does things and it is a present tense covenant for every generation. Harvest under this covenant only answers to seed sown (Oyedepo 2005). No seed...no harvest! This is God's foundational plan to provide for His people and He will not change it, *"As long as the earth remains..."* (Genesis 8:22). No economic dearth or crisis can break the power of this covenant to produce in our lives (Oyedepo 2005; Genesis 26:1–3, 12).

Again, sowing and reaping only operates by practice; you can't cry or fast long enough for it to work. A covenant takes practice (Oyedepo 2005). You must act on what it says and it has guaranteed results. In fact, you can stake your life on it! Jesus did with His own life. He was the Seed planted by the Father, and in three days He was raised from the dead. He had to trust that the Father would raise Him up the same as we do, *"...Except a corn of wheat fall to the ground and die, it abideth alone: but if it die, it bringeth forth much fruit"* (John 12:24).

Kingdom prosperity starts from the inside first, with our thoughts, understanding, and our faith. By speaking words or confessions, Word seed is first planted into the soil of our heart or spirit. And just like a garden, the soil produces an inner image or faith for whatever is to be. Now you can see why we were never made to speak what we don't want in our lives, because you will eventually have what you believe and speak. In my early days of ministry one of my Bible teachers said that the Lord spoke to him one day saying..."Instead of my people having what they say, they are saying what they have." God's way is to first prosper your soul (3 John 2), which is nothing more than receiving revelation of the Word of God. To do this, you must say exactly what God says. Someone might say, "Well, what if it's not true?" The answer is, "How can you lie saying what God said?"

ANSWERING MY CALL TO FULL-TIME MINISTRY

Prosperity of the soul is what happened to me before I was able to leave my employment at IBM to answer my call to full-time ministry. I meditated Mark 10:29–30:

> Verily I say unto you, There is no man that hath left house, or brethren, or sisters, or father, or mother, or wife, or children, or lands, for my sake, and the gospel's, but he shall receive an hundredfold now in this time, houses, and brethren, and sisters, and mothers, and children, and lands, with persecutions; and in the world to come eternal life.

Understand my image of preachers at this time was not a good one. I saw many as broke and begging for money as well as some other ungodly images. Until these negative images that dominated my thinking were replaced with godly images I didn't have the strength to leave. Oh, I wanted to leave, but each time I delayed and set another date. I'm sure this was the same with this rich young ruler in Mark, chapter 10, who came to Jesus asking what he must do to inherit eternal life.

Jesus told him to *"...sell whatsoever thou hast, and give to the poor, and thou shalt have treasure in heaven: and come, take up the cross, and follow me"* (verse 21). The scripture records his response as he *"went away grieved: for he had great possessions."* I know the feeling. This man thought he was going to go broke and so did I.

Without revelation or faith in God's promises, you'll never sow your last or your best. The Lord was not asking this young ruler or me to leave something. No. He was asking us to sow it. I believe the Lord was going to make this man one of the richest men of his day, but he couldn't see it. And at first, neither could I. The scriptures tell us, *"If thou faint in the day of adversity, thy strength is small"* (Proverbs 24:10). In Proverbs 24:5 it says, *"A wise man is strong; yea, a man of knowledge increaseth strength."* So, if you lack strength, you need more knowledge not more time.

One day, without warning...breakthrough! Without warning, light came in while I was driving down the street. Revelation! Revealed knowledge! I called my wife on the telephone and said to her, "Honey, I'm leaving this company." I think IBM was, and still is, one of the best companies in the world, but it was time for me to move to my "higher calling."

MEDITATING GOD'S WORD

For some people to experience and enjoy the abundance that God has for them, they will first have to uproot or destroy the old images that lack and poverty have produced. Perhaps it was planted from years of living in constant insufficiency and financial struggle, or from seeing generations of family members in debt and never having enough. Destroying these images and prospering the soul is mainly done by meditating and confessing God's Word. Meditation is thinking or pondering the Word of God. It is continually confessing or muttering the Word of God until the Word carries more authority than satan's lies or your circumstances—until one begins to think like God. When this new way of thinking or revelation comes, you will not be disappointed in your expectation.

If you have a need or desire, or cannot seem to get ahead in a certain area in your life, go to the Bible and find scriptures that provide a promise from God about your situation. Meditate and confess those scriptures until revelation or light comes. Once the light comes, it will bring the strength and the strategy to take full possession of your desire. As one evangelist said, "One word from God can change your life forever."

Jesus teaches *"the sower soweth the word"* (Mark 4:14), so you cannot leave God and His Word out of the process; however, in manifesting material abundance, it also takes a material seed. This seed does not have to be money. In Luke 5, Peter sowed his fishing boat for Jesus to teach the people gathered along the shoreline. The widow in 1 Kings, chapter 17, had only one meal left and she gave (sowed) it into the life of the prophet. And, in 1 Samuel, chapter 1, Hannah, longing for a child, sowed a vow to God and received back a miracle of her womb being opened and she miraculously conceived. She later gave birth to a son, the prophet Samuel.

I even heard a story about people sowing painted rocks and getting a harvest. An evangelist friend shared that he had ministered at a new church on an Indian reservation where the people were so poor they had no money to give in the offering. So to give something to God, they decorated beautiful rocks and sowed them as their offering. The man of God said that when he spoke at that same church the following year, several of the people who had been in lack the previous year were now driving brand new sport utility vehicles (SUVs)!

Your harvest does not always come back in the same form of the thing that you sowed. It may come in the form of new contracts for your business, opportunities for work, a bonus at the job, or half off the price of something you are purchasing. Whatever the form, your harvest is guaranteed! Expect it.

A MIRACLE OF 27 ACRES

Pastors Greg and Celeste lead a church in Alexandria, Louisiana, and desired to build a ministry center that would be a blessing to the entire region of Central Louisiana. They had learned the principles of seed-sowing, and knew that if they wanted God to bless them and their church, they needed to bless others. So for years they sowed into the lives and ministries of others.

Pastor Greg began believing God for 25 acres for the ministry center—a vision he shared with a close friend and prayer partner. One day, as the two prayed about the land, the friend told Pastor Greg, "I keep praying and I see 27 acres, not 25." When Greg responded that he would be grateful to have 25 acres, his friend smiled and said, "Well, there's two more acres out there for you."

In January 2009 Pastor Greg and his wife traveled to Fort Worth, Texas, for a three-day ministers' conference where I was a guest speaker. During one of my sessions I was led by the Holy Spirit to receive a "spontaneous" offering. Pastor Greg, remembering everything he had learned about seed-sowing, later said that he wanted very much to be part of it.

Reaching into his pocket, he pulled out a $10 bill—all the money he had on him. He reasoned that this wasn't enough seed for him to sow. He started to put the money back into his pocket, when he had a nudging from the Holy Spirit to give what he had. The Lord told him, "Give it. You've already sown a lot of seed."

In obedience, Pastor Greg stepped out into the aisle and moved toward the front of the auditorium to give his offering. As he approached the platform, he heard me say, "Stop thinking small. God is a big God, and He's ready to do big things for you…. You're sowing because you have a need or there's something you desire and you're sowing a seed to get it."

Pastor Greg said he was going to put the offering on the platform, but then heard that same Voice say…"No, go and put it in his hand." As he handed me the money, he said "25 acres of land" and walked away.

I stopped and pointed to him and said: "Twenty-five acres of land. Praise God. You'll have that land in seven days. You go out there on that land and you point at that land. You'll have that land in seven days."

Within days of returning home, Pastor Greg called a real estate agent to search for the land. They were convinced there was nothing available inside the city, and focused their search outside the city. But when the agent spoke with an associate, he was told about a piece of land inside the city that used to be a drive-in movie theater that had been closed for about 30 years. A tree line had grown up around the property, making it barely visible from the road. It was 27 acres of land!

There is more to Pastor Greg's story, but I will summarize what happened next. The owners wanted $990,000 for the property, but after Pastor Greg prayed he sensed that the Lord wanted him to offer no more than $500,000. So, he offered $400,000. The owners countered, and he made one final offer of $486,000, this time giving the owners three days to respond. The next day, the agent called him and said "I don't know what happened, but they accepted your offer."[8]

Just like the widow with the oil in 2 Kings, chapter 4, Pastor Greg would not have received his ministry's financial miracle if he had not sowed in obedience (giving the $10 to God, not to a man), and then taken immediate action on what the prophet had spoken under the direction of the Holy Spirit. Some harvests are hidden for you (not from you) to protect them from being stolen or delayed by the enemy (Keesee 2011). In this story it was hidden for 30 years. But God will divinely direct you to these hidden harvests when you look to Him as your Source, sow a seed in faith, and take action quickly on what the Holy Spirit tells you. You then tap into the supernatural and God gets involved in your situation.

SOWING A SEED FOR A NEW HOUSE

My wife and I got our home by sowing a seed at a Believers meeting in London, England. At the time, we were in the midst of believing God for a new house, and God spoke to us during the meeting. We had confessed the promise of God (our scripture was Deuteronomy 6:11), and had prospered our soul (our mind, will, and imagination) to line up with God's will for our prosperity in owning a house. We had some money saved for the purchase of a house, but not nearly enough. God told us to sow out of our need from some of that money. We were obedient and sowed a seed of a sizeable amount where He directed us.

When we returned home from the meeting, the Lord led my wife to a new house that was under construction. The people building the house had a death in the family, and they were searching for someone to take over the contract to buy the house. My wife saw it and said, "That's the same house the Holy Ghost had me write down on this list" (she had written on paper what she wanted in our new house).

We claimed the house in prayer and within six weeks, money started coming in from everywhere—unexpected sources. We took over the contract and, because we understood and worked kingdom principles, we were able to pay cash for our new home, debt-free.

Supernatural prosperity is your heritage. Through the practice of sowing and reaping the King and His kingdom become the source to prosper you. No more second jobs or working overtime trying to make ends meet. For business owners, no more employee layoffs or securing bank loans to offset weak company profits. For those holding political office, no more raising taxes or borrowing from other nations to fund the government.

Joseph in the Old Testament is a wonderful example of a covenant person who rescued and prospered not only his family who was feeling the effects of the famine, but also Pharaoh who, through Joseph, was able to provide more than enough for the whole world (Genesis 39–47).

THE LAW OF CONFESSION

Declaring God's Word or confession is vital in the kingdom process to manifest provision and God's promises for your life, but it is a step that many Christians have missed. To confess in this context comes from a Greek word *homologeo*, which literally means "to say the same thing"[9] or to say what God said. Abraham said what God said, and he called things that *"be not as though they were."* Declaring God's Word is especially critical during the "waiting period," the time between sowing your seed and reaping your harvest.

You can cancel your harvest by speaking negative words that are contrary to the harvest you desire. As was discussed, sowing money or material seed is not all that is required.

Your confession rules you, and you can negate the harvest God has already prepared for you by saying the wrong thing. That is, saying words of doubt, worry, and unbelief instead of saying what God has already said and done (read Numbers, chapters 13 and 14).

BREAKTHROUGH IN MARRIAGE

For example, I remember about six months after marrying Veronica, I began to be critical of everything she did. Nothing she did was right and I became completely antagonistic toward our future together. Realize, we were both born again, but my inner image of marriage had not been changed. It had been distorted years ago by my parents' divorce.

Then I went to a meeting where the minister was teaching on the power of confession and that we could have what we say according to Mark 11:23. I purchased a small book on prayer, which included a prayer confession on marriage, and began to pray and speak that confession every day. As the seed of the Word of God went into my heart, things immediately began to happen. The Word began to root out the old image of divorce and replace it with the image of a healthy, stable, loving marriage. I now saw that God designed marriage to be an asset rather than a liability, and that Veronica was sent to help both of us win in life. Now we have a marriage made in heaven!

The story about my marriage illustrates that your mind takes you to what you believe, not necessarily to where you want to go. It doesn't matter if what you believe is not true; if it is true to you it becomes your reality. Your thoughts and beliefs about financial abundance work the same way. You may desire financial freedom and abundance, but if you subconsciously believe you will never have enough that is what you'll produce in your life. And, without being born again into the kingdom of God, one is trapped in a limited perception of reality.

HOLDING FAST HER CONFESSION FOR NEW EMPLOYMENT

A second example of the law of confession is when I was in full-time Bible School in Tulsa, Oklahoma, and Veronica was seeking employment. She had gone to several employment agencies and the report was the same. "There are no jobs...people are being laid off by the hundreds because the economy is in bad shape." We labored in the Word of God, and found scriptures that said that every need and want of ours had already been met before the foundation of the world.

We agreed and took a piece of paper and fashioned the exact kind of employment she would get, how much she would make, and how far she would have to drive in the car they would give her as a perk to get to her place of employment.

Interestingly, during Veronica's waiting time before she was hired by her new employer, one of my classmates came over to visit me and happened to ask her about the job she had believed God for.

> "Sister Veronica, have you got your job yet?"
> She quickly answered, "I sure do."
> He then replied, "Where is it?"
> She said, "I don't know where it is, but I believe I have it."

How she answered my classmate was critical. Her words could have cancelled her harvest and so can your words. Someone might ask, "If I say that, wouldn't I be lying?" No. Again, how can you lie saying what God said?

One day I came home from seminary class and there was some homemade soup cooking. Its aroma filled the house so much so that I asked her to prepare me a bowl, "I'm ready to eat." She quickly told me that this soup was not for us, but for one of my classmates, because he and his family had fallen on hard times. She was sowing a seed. We received a call days later with exactly the kind of job we had described on the paper...with the car! She didn't toil and struggle to find this job. The job found her.

I wrote a book called the *Law of Confession* based on a teaching I had done about the power of our words. Here's a passage from this book, "Much of what happens in your life starts with the words you speak—if you want your life to change—then you must change the words you speak. When your words are right in line with God's Word, your life will be transformed in a supernatural way."

Remember, our combat has been fought and won. The devil has been defeated (Colossians 2:14–15). There isn't any battle for us to fight except the battle of faith. We are to fight the good fight of faith. This means that most of our battles are won with words. Most people have not made the connection between what they say and what they have in life. They have no idea that the two are connected. Words have spiritual power and many Christians have not understood this. Jesus said, *"For by thy words thou shalt be justified, and by thy words thou shalt be condemned"* (Matthew 12:37).

> **YOUR MIND TAKES YOU TO WHAT YOU BELIEVE, NOT TO WHERE YOU WANT TO GO.**

When you sow your seed into the kingdom of God, you must speak over it and declare the harvest you desire, just as Veronica and I did for her job in Tulsa. We meditated the Scriptures related to our need, wrote down her desired job, and declared by faith that she had received her job, and eventually it manifested.

The other part of this testimony is that not only did God give Veronica the desire of her heart during an economic downturn when no one was hiring, but we also later learned that her company, which was based in Denmark, had only recently opened an office ten minutes from where we lived in Tulsa. This demonstrates that faith and the laws of the kingdom are so powerful that if God has to move a company from across the globe to answer your prayer, He will. So, when shortage of provision arises, there's only one thing to do...sow a seed.

BLESSED ARE THE POOR

God's Word is written for both the rich and poor. As the scriptures tell us, *"God is no respecter of persons."* His laws and principles apply to everyone. So when Jesus taught, *"give, and it shall be given unto you; good measure, pressed down, and shaken together and running over, shall men give into your bosom..."* (Luke 6:38), He was speaking to rich people and poor people alike. Only the devil came up with the idea that a poor man shouldn't be expected to give, because it's a way that he can keep the poor...poor.

You see, giving, or the spiritual law of sowing and reaping, is God's idea, not man's... *"While the earth remains, seedtime and harvest, and cold and heat, summer and winter, and day and night shall not cease"* (Genesis 8:22 ESV).

There are millions of poor people right now on this planet, some are even starving. Why doesn't God just provide for them? The answer is, "He can't," because God cannot violate His covenant. It's the way He set up the system in the beginning, giving mankind the authority over this planet and giving him faith to operate the spiritual law of sowing and reaping to bring forth provision. Someone has to sow a seed to release provision and someone else is responsible for its distribution.

"Blessed be ye poor, for yours is the kingdom of God" (Luke 6:20). This does not mean that God loves the poor more than the rich, nor does it mean that the poor are blessed because they will get their rewards in heaven. No. Jesus was saying that the poor are blessed because they now have a new kingdom and a new economic system. They now can live in this economy according to heaven's economy. Once born again into the kingdom, those who were poor have access to unlimited provision, a supply that is not based on their background or pedigree or their minimum wage job. In fact, their job can become a source for their seed. By sowing and reaping they can tap into that supernatural supply of the "New Economy." Remember, everyone who makes God their Source becomes as rich as God, no less. How is that? It's the way the covenant works. The world and all the wealth belongs to Him. He gave it to Jesus and we are joint heirs with Him.

> **YOU WILL EVENTUALLY HAVE WHAT YOU BELIEVE AND SPEAK.**

Again, sowing and reaping is not forcing God to do something, but planting the seed that calls for the harvest He has already promised. Also, whenever God makes a kingdom demand on you, He's about to affect your destiny. So, the statement that they are "too poor to give" is a myth. One of the favorite tricks of the devil is to keep the people of God operating by human reason, which is, in most cases, completely opposite of the way God thinks and does things.

So, God would have everyone, whether rich or poor, on welfare or faring well, to sow seed and to pay tithes. Why? So He can measure back to them His pre-planned provision. Remember, this is not man's method but God's method. This was proven by Jesus when a poor widow threw in two mites (copper coins worth about a penny) for her offering in Mark, chapter 12, verses 41–44. Jesus, who always did the will of the Father, did not object when this widow, although poor, threw her last into the bucket. She heard the Word and caught a revelation of this timeless principle. He didn't say, "Hold on there now! You don't need to give your last. There are plenty of rich people at this meeting. Save your pennies and wait until you're able to give."

No! He didn't say that. Instead He blessed her offering and said it's the biggest offering that anyone had given at this meeting, *"This poor widow has cast more in, than all they which have cast into the treasury...."* Again, Jesus always did the will of the Father. If God didn't want the poor to give, Jesus would have objected to her giving. One man of God said that he believes this woman eventually became extremely rich and ended up being one of the biggest givers.

THE KINGDOM DISMANTLES POVERTY AT ITS ROOTS

> Save when there shall be no poor among you; for the LORD shall greatly bless thee in the land which the LORD thy God giveth thee *for* an inheritance to possess it. Deuteronomy 15:4

God has custom-made ideas and solutions for every nation. He has ingenious ways to confront the demon of poverty, destroy its work, and replace it with kingdom prosperity and productivity in the most hopeless environment. Dr. Booker T. Washington, the famous black educator who founded Tuskegee University, proved this. In his mission to educate and train emancipated but disenfranchised ex-slaves, Dr. Washington set out to lift an entire race from poverty, despair, and hopelessness, often speaking about the kingdom of God in his talks. In doing so, Dr. Washington was fulfilling the plan of God to raise and lift up *"the poor out of the dust"* and *"the needy out of the dung hill. That he may set him with princes, even with the princes of His people"* (Psalm 113:7–8).

True, God calls us to *"give to the poor,"* but what happens in most cases is that we end up financing poverty, instead of eradicating it. This is another reason why many of the poor remain in poverty. I believe God's plan for the Church from the beginning was to destroy poverty at its roots and to work continually until there is no more poor among us.

One of Dr. Washington's favorite verses of scripture was *"As he thinketh in his heart, so is he"* (Proverbs 23:7). I believe Washington had a revelation that we are made to function like our Creator, and that whatever we think on continually we will end up creating. So, people are poor not so much because they have no money or a job that pays them well, but because of what they choose to think on continually, which is what they will eventually create. If a person doesn't know this, they will blame someone else, the government, or their ethnic background for not being rich. If you can think abundance, you will end up there. *"The rich man's wealth is his strong city: the destruction of the poor is their poverty"* (Proverbs 10:15).

PART 3
ACCESSING PROVISION FOR KINGDOM BUILDING

CHAPTER 7

MANIFESTING KINGDOM ABUNDANCE

Having wealth serves a very important role in spreading the gospel, eradicating poverty, and rebuilding the nations and the waste places wherever they may exist. One of my favorite passages of scripture says,

> Thus saith the Lord God; In the day that I shall have cleansed you from all your iniquities I will also cause *you* to dwell in the cities, and the wastes shall be builded. And the desolate land shall be tilled, whereas it lay desolate in the sight of all that passed by. And they shall say, This land that was desolate is become like the garden of Eden; and the waste and desolate and ruined cities *are become* fenced, *and* are inhabited. Then the heathen that are left round about you shall know that I the Lord build the ruined *places, and* plant that that was desolate: I the Lord have spoken *it,* and I will do *it.* Ezekiel 36:33–36

I believe that this passage in Ezekiel 36 is part of the Church's "greater works" that Jesus speaks about in John 14:12 AMP, *"I assure you...anyone who believes in Me [as Savior] will also do the things that I do; and he will do even greater things than these [in extent and outreach], because I am going to the Father"* (emphasis mine). I am convinced that the rebuilding of ruined and desolate cities and nations around the world is part of our kingdom assignment, and it's going to take the wealth of the kingdom of God to accomplish it. Therefore, this chapter is not just about money, but about having THE BLESSING of the Lord on our lives to produce kingdom abundance primarily for kingdom expansion. More specifically, it is about wealth creation and divine provision, without the wrong attitudes of covetousness, greed, and the love of money, to accomplish the greater works to which God has called us, as the Church.

I firmly believe no one wants to be poor, not even in the most remote places on Earth. Just as God placed in the nature of man a desire to live and be at peace, I also believe that it is human nature to desire to have abundance and live with more than enough. Unfortunately, because of the curse, constant failures, generational and systemic poverty, and spiritual oppression, the desire for abundance has been lost or perverted.

GOD PLACED IN US A DESIRE TO LIVE, BE AT PEACE, AND HAVE ABUNDANCE.

Nevertheless, deep down inside this desire is still there, hidden away until stimulated by some environmental influence, or by the power of the Word of God. Jesus said pray this way, *"Thy kingdom come. Thy will be done in earth, as it is in heaven."* This is proof that God never changed His mind about planet Earth being like heaven, having the same atmosphere and the same abundance. That is what *Eden*, which comes from the Hebrew word that means "live voluptuously, a place of pleasure, or place of delight,"[1] was all about. Many believers are going to be shocked when they see how much this planet is like heaven itself.

God made man in His image, with His same nature and method of operation. There is nothing around the throne of God that even remotely resembles poverty or lack. I like what one man said, "If God likes poverty so much, why isn't He poor?" The answer is: He isn't. He has wealth beyond anything anyone on Earth can comprehend, and He has stocked the earth with riches making it available to us. Just as the father said to the elder brother in the parable of the Prodigal Son, *"...all that I have is thine."*

In the Old Testament, God led His people, the children of Israel, into the Promised Land describing it as *"a land flowing with milk and honey."* "Milk and honey" symbolizes abundance. Realize they had been enslaved for over 400 years.

They were poor, miserable, and conditioned to having "not enough." The Bible says that God heard their cry and sent a deliverer, named Moses, to bring them out. Poverty and lack were not their portion. God's plan for them, and for us as the seed of Abraham, is abundance and nothing short of it!

Prosperity or abundance is the covenant birthright of every child of God, and God takes pleasure in our prosperity (Psalm 35:27). It is part of our inheritance in Christ. The book of Revelation even speaks about our inheritance (benefits) package left to every believer through the price paid by our Lord, the "Lamb of God." The Bible says that Jesus was slain for us, raised from the dead, and then seated at the right hand of God so that we could *"...receive power, and riches, and wisdom, and strength, and honour, and glory, and blessing"* (Revelation 5:12).

Today, unfortunately, this is not the case for many of God's children. They are in the kingdom and have inherited a life of walking on streets of gold, if you will, but still operating with a scarcity or slave mentality, struggling trying to do better under a failing, cursed system called Babylon. They switched kingdoms but failed to switch systems for getting their needs met, which I believe is mainly because of unbelief, fed primarily by their observations, associations, and bad teachings. They have declared that "Jesus is Lord," but are still trying to produce

PROSPERITY IS THE COVENANT BIRTHRIGHT OF EVERY CHILD OF GOD.

provision through the old method of toil and struggle, living from paycheck to paycheck, instead of by grace through faith...God's way of doing things.

Here's an example of what I mean: In the gospel of Luke, Peter had fished all night and caught nothing. Jesus entered into his boat and sat down and taught. He wasn't teaching the law, because that would not have produced the faith needed to produce a miracle. No. What He taught was THE BLESSING. Proverbs 10:22 says, *"The blessing of the LORD brings wealth, without painful toil for it"* (NIV). After He had finished teaching, He turned to Peter and said, *"Launch out into the deep and let down your nets for a draught."* Reluctantly, Peter launched out but he pulled in so many fish until the net broke and he had to call for his partners, who also filled up their boats. *"When Simon Peter saw it, he fell down at Jesus' knees, saying, Depart from me; for I am a sinful man, O Lord. For he was astonished, and all that were with him, at the draught of the fishes which they had taken"* (Luke 5:8–9).

Notice the operation of THE BLESSING and the grace of God, which caused Peter to experience an enormous catch without toil or struggle. Again, this is God's way of doing things. Oh yes, he had to work, but not through struggling, "trying to make ends meet," so to speak, as he was doing before. This is a picture of how God plans for things to work for any New Testament believer.

Whatever you gain in the kingdom must be received— not achieved. You don't "earn" anything in the kingdom— from God's love to your daily living, from your salvation and through the rest of your Christian walk—it's all by grace… all about receiving. *"For by grace are ye saved through faith; and that not of yourselves: it is the gift of God: not of works, lest any man should boast"* (Ephesians 2:8–9). Today, on the average, almost every member in the family daily goes out to work if they are old enough, and in some countries even if they are not old enough. There's nothing wrong with work except that many of those same households still barely make enough, or have enough savings to take a rest or vacation, not to mention if someone in the house gets sick and they have medical bills. Toiling and struggling were never God's plan for humanity. In fact, we should be living like we are on vacation 365 days a year.

THE BABYLONIAN SYSTEM

Let's go back to the beginning and see how this "toiling" happened. When Adam and Eve sinned in the garden of Eden, they fell to a life of toil, struggle, insufficiency, and hard labor (Genesis 3:17). Satan became the "god of this world," and he enslaved mankind to build Babylon, the kingdom of darkness. In this kingdom, the adversary uses mainly deception, unbelief, and the fear of not having enough to control not only people, but whole cities and entire nations.

Instead of making decisions based on truth (God's Word on abundance), their decisions are filtered through the limited supply of this earthly provision: "Do I have enough?" "How much does it cost?" "When do I get paid?" "Can we afford to send our child to that school?" When there is not enough, the thought comes..."Maybe a second job will help to remove this pressure I am under." Now, the person is on this Babylonian treadmill and it's speeding up while they're running faster trying to make more money. That is exactly what happened in my situation while working at IBM...anything to relieve the pressure.

The Babylonian system, or what I call a socialistic system of government, is one in which people try to meet their needs without God. People are taught to bear the weight of their own provision by running faster and faster, chasing mainly after money or things. Maybe you've heard the expression, "Robbing Peter to pay Paul." Notice, they are two Bible figures...satan's attempt to remove the Judeo-Christian influence from society, to remove all traces of the Word of God, and to jettison God from all the nations.

In the beginning it was not so. Adam didn't serve things; everything was created on Earth to serve him. And when people become too provision-minded, or develop what I call "a paycheck mentality," the enemy, with a little financial pressure, can cause them to let go of their true purpose for being on this planet, or what is their God-given assignment, and run after whatever job or vocation pays the most. Money becomes their master. Under this cursed Babylonian system, almost everyone sees their job as their security, instead of God. Soon they become content and comfortable with surviving or having just enough until they reach the age of retirement, but never feeling fulfilled or having any distinguishing accomplishments in life.

Some years ago, I was in this same place, on a treadmill, running faster but getting nowhere; working hard but with little money to show for it. I could hardly enjoy the necessities of life without borrowing money. I took a second job and ended up working six days a week, again, with little to show for it. Once I was born again and learned about the kingdom, my breakthrough came. I discovered a whole new way of living by faith, and how I could meet my needs without the pain and fatigue of two jobs. I discovered, through biblical teaching, that I have "THE BLESSING" on my life. And this blessing of the Lord is something that supernaturally empowers me for success...which entails financial breakthroughs, supernatural favor, protection and longevity, along with business strategies and insights. Furthermore, I found out that God has a supernatural supply of wisdom and healing, already laid up for me and everyone in His family, all that we could ever need or want.

Now it became clear that no job or company could pay me enough to live like God has planned for me to live. True, your employer should provide a decent wage for the work performed, but that job was never meant to replace God, nor can it. According to the economy of heaven, what I call the new economy, and the wealth that is already in the earth, there is enough provision available for the Church to totally eradicate poverty anywhere on the earth. God has provided a higher lifestyle for His *covenant* people...an independent lifestyle full of abundance that is transferred only by faith. God's unfailing, unstoppable distribution system, called the kingdom of God, which operates far above the earth-cursed system of lack, toil, and financial uncertainty, is what we should be trusting in.

NEW ECONOMY

Again, I call this the new economy of the kingdom of God. One main reason Jesus came to Earth was to redeem mankind from the curse and the old system of lack, to reintroduce the kingdom of God, and to provide access again to heaven's inexhaustible supply. Understand, this is the same kingdom that existed in the garden of Eden before the Fall of Adam and Eve.

As I mentioned in one of the earlier chapters, the kingdom of heaven is not another religion, but it is a government—the government of God—with its own wisdom, protection, health, and wealth to care for all its citizens, much like a commonwealth. As I mentioned in chapter 2, a *commonwealth* is "an economic system of a kingdom, which guarantees each citizen equal access to financial security." Remember, there was a woman in 1 Kings that was on her last meal during a famine. She said that she and her son were going to eat it and die. The man of God said, "Fear not...feed me first." And when she did, everything she had left, both the oil and jar of meal began to multiply. That was from heaven's inexhaustible supply.

How about in the New Testament when they ran out of wine at the wedding in Cana? Jesus turned water into wine, about 180 gallons of the best in the world! That was heaven's supply. That same heavenly supply is available for every child of God no matter what type of job you have or how much you make. The government of God functions independently of the system of the world.

Matthew 6:25–33 says,

> Therefore I say unto you, Take no thought for your life, what ye shall eat, or what ye shall drink; nor yet for your body, what ye shall put on. Is not the life more than meat, and the body than raiment? Behold the fowls of the air: for they sow not, neither do they reap, nor gather into barns; yet your heavenly Father feedeth them. Are ye not much better than they? Which of you by taking thought can add one cubit unto his stature?...Therefore take no thought, saying, What shall we eat? or, What shall we drink? or, Wherewithal shall we be clothed? (For after all these things do the Gentiles seek) for your heavenly Father knoweth that ye have need of all these things. But seek ye first the kingdom of God, and his righteousness; and all these things shall be added unto you.

God never intended for His children to depend upon the world's economic system to provide for them. The same way God "planted" the garden of Eden to provide for all the needs of Adam and Eve is the same way the kingdom has been given to us to produce and provide everything we would ever need or want in staggering and enormous portions. And everything God's going to do for us...He's already done. Scriptures tell us that *"the works were finished from the foundation of the world."* I believe we will never fully function in God's kingdom until we discover that we already have provision.

GOD HAS PLANNED A CLEAR DIFFERENCE BETWEEN YOU AND THE REST OF THE WORLD.

As I said, this does not mean that we don't work, but that our work is now mainly for the fulfillment of our purpose and not for "earning a living." We accomplish this through first laboring in the Word of God and spending time in prayer. As kings and priests, God intends for our focus and priority to be on His assignment, and not on struggling to earn enough to pay the mortgage.

One man said it like this: "It doesn't matter whether you are pastoring a church or running a lemonade stand, whatever you are called to do is kingdom business. Since kingdom business is supernatural, the key to succeeding is doing whatever Jesus says to do. If He calls you to open up a lemonade stand, He has a reason for it and a way He wants it to be done. He may want you to corner the lemonade market and pour millions of dollars into spreading the gospel. He may be planning to send the next president of the United States to buy a glass of lemonade from you so that you can pray for him, bless him and change the future course of the nation."[2]

The point is, in the kingdom, you just can't "be anything you want to be" or "go anyplace you want to go" or "join the church of your choice." No, not so in the kingdom. He already has a plan for you, and where your job or business or church is. It's where your protection is and where your prosperity is.

God's abundant provision, His supply set aside for us in what I refer to as "heaven's warehouse," goes beyond just finances. It includes wisdom, inventions, new songs, businesses, custom-made body parts, names for your kids, material things, peace, success, good marriages and relationships—nothing is left out. The secret or mystery, as Jesus calls it, is that it is in heaven's invisible inventory waiting for us to take delivery, to access it by FAITH.

God saw what we would need or want during our time on Earth and He has already laid it up for us in an invisible warehouse before the foundation of the world. He is Jehovah-Jireh, the God who sees and provides. There is an abundant supply waiting for you. People in the world (without God) don't have this storehouse of unlimited provision.

So, they work with, or in some cases literally fight over, a limited supply from what already exists in the physical, visible realm. But when you become a citizen of the kingdom of God, and begin to operate according to the new economy, the enormous supplies that have been set aside for you in the heavenly warehouse of God become available to you. This is a supply that will last until Jesus comes, waiting for all those who would partner with God and call it forth by faith. As I said before, no company or job can pay you enough to live like God has planned for you to live. The decision is yours.

Jesus taught how to live in the earth according to heaven's economy, and demonstrated how to use the principles and laws of the kingdom to manifest this abundance for any need anywhere, anytime, independent of geographical location or the world's economic system. These same principles work today for any kingdom citizen who will believe and act on them by faith...whether it's a government facing an economic dearth similar to the time of Joseph (Genesis 41), or a CEO facing a severe downturn in company sales and profits, to the head of a household desiring no longer to live paycheck to paycheck in caring for the family. Jesus said:

> Come unto me, **all** *ye* that labour and are heavy laden, and I will give you rest. Take my yoke upon you, and learn of me; for I am meek and lowly in heart: and ye shall find rest unto your souls. For my yoke *is* easy, and my burden is light. Matthew 11:28–30 (emphasis mine)

Jesus' teaching on how to operate in this world's economy according to heaven's economy is the primary focus of this chapter. Again, the Father never intended for His children to depend on the world and its system to provide for them. My desire is that you will know and begin operating in these biblical economic principles to supernaturally produce provision, know how to fix any financial or material need or problem that comes your way, and be able to accomplish any dream or vision God places in your heart...because money or provision will no longer be an obstacle.

God has BIG plans for us. And one reason we are saved (born again) is to display God's wealth on Earth. We are supposed to feed the hungry and clothe the naked. Again, that's one reason abundance is our birthright and wealth is our heritage. Deuteronomy 8:18 says, *"But thou shalt remember the LORD thy God: for it is he that giveth thee power to get wealth, that he may establish his covenant which he sware unto thy fathers, as it is this day."*

I was told about a sign that Oral Roberts had in his office at Oral Roberts University. It said, "No Small Plans Made Here." That's why He gives us, what I call, "Blank Check" scriptures such as *"...What things soever ye desire, when ye pray, believe that ye receive them, and ye shall have them."* Or, *"...ye shall say unto this mountain, Remove hence to yonder place; and it shall remove; and nothing shall be impossible unto you"* (Mark 11:24; Matthew 17:20). It is obvious God wants us to think BIG. Why? There is a big job ahead and He is a "more than enough" God. With Him, the more you can desire the more you have. His way, however, is for you to depend on Him and not on your performance. Think "No More Limits." His plan is for there to be a clear difference between you and the rest of the world.

SUPPLY AND DEMAND

> For I will pour water upon him that is thirsty, and
> floods upon the dry ground.... Isaiah 44:3

During a recent trip overseas, I spoke at a breakfast meeting for business leaders. Part of my teaching was on "Supply and Demand." Some time ago I heard a well-known man of God speak on this topic to a church group. However, when I heard it, I immediately applied it to business: "The Big Business of the Kingdom of God."

Most of the world's business principles come from the Bible. A lot of people don't know this. They think that they came from an Ivy League business school, or some famous economist such as Keynes, Friedman, or Malthus. No. They came from God and are used by a society void of the superior principles of the kingdom of God. These basic biblical principles are used by the kingdom of darkness to rule over mankind and shape a world economy. Why would satan, the architect of the world system, who Paul refers to as *"the god of this world* (system),*"* use God's system? Because he knows that whatever God creates works best.

However, satan removed some of the essential ingredients, such as the motive of love (compassion); the necessity of faith, justice, and integrity; and the importance of being led by the Holy Spirit. Furthermore, he substituted the master spiritual law of sowing and reaping (seedtime and harvest) for the fear-based inferior principles of the Babylonian system whose economy is based on buying and selling. One system is characterized by giving (abundant supply), good, selflessness, and following the leading of God, while the other system is characterized by hoarding, shortage (limited supply), selfishness, and man's own (vain) imagination.

Like those who were building the tower of Babel, the Lord said concerning these men who knew not God, *"And now nothing will be restrained from them which they have imagined to do."* These were not "full gospel" businessmen. No. These were devil worshippers, constructing a city without God.

Well, after I finished my teaching at that breakfast, I opened the meeting up for questions and answers. One man stood up and asked, "I hear you say supply and demand. I was taught it was demand and supply. Why do you say, 'supply and demand' in that order?" I quickly responded, "Because in God's economy, the supply

EVERY CHILD OF GOD HAS A SUPERNATURAL SUPPLY FOR EVERY NEED OR WANT.

was here long before the demand was ever made."

I went on to explain how the world system has a limited view of reality and is prospering in the world in a very limited economy. Psalm 73, verse 12, says, *"Behold, these are the ungodly, who prosper in the world; they increase in riches."* But for every child of God there is a supernatural supply of all that we would ever need or want, provided for us before the foundation of the world. Think of it this way: Everything that Adam needed was already placed in the garden before God created him.

MIRACLES ON DEMAND

In the book of 2 Kings, there was a story of a woman whose husband had died and left her in debt. The creditors were coming to take her two sons to put them in slavery until the debt was paid. The Bible says, *"She cried to the man of God."* Or a more accurate way of saying it is, "She cried *out* to the man of God." In the kingdom of God, we must place a demand on God's (invisible) supernatural supply.

She was provoking a release of the blessing or anointing that was on his life as a prophet. In this case, it was the anointing of wisdom and revelation as to what to do about her situation. He began to give her specific instructions, identifying first what was of value in her house. He told her, *"Borrow as many vessels as you can from your neighbors, come into the house, shut the door, and pour out into these vessels..."* which she followed to the letter. As she was pouring her jar of oil, it began to multiply and filled up many vessels. She said to her son, *"Bring me yet a vessel. And he said to her, There is not a vessel more. And the oil stayed"* (2 Kings 4:6).

The *Living Bible* says it this way, *"...And then the oil stopped flowing."* She went and told the man of God, who told her to go and sell the oil, pay the debt then live on the rest with her family. Notice, as long as a demand was there, the oil flowed. As long as the demand was placed on the anointed man of God, he kept speaking prophetically. But once the demand was not there, the supply stopped and he ceased to give her any more instructions. It stopped even though there was plenty more where that came from. This was supernatural provision and produced supernatural debt cancellation.

Again, notice the dynamic duo of "kings and priests." Her first step was to locate the "sent" one, the prophet sent by God. Then she placed a demand on his life and began to follow his words. The scriptures tell us, *"...believe his prophets, so shall ye prosper"* (2 Chronicles 20:20); also, *"how shall they hear without a preacher?"* (Romans 10:14). She believed in her man of God, followed his instruction, and got her miracle. Her debt was cancelled! This principle works the same for a family, a company, or a country. It works for "whosoever" will work it. The team of "kings and priests" (and

God) is virtually unbeatable. You have a supernatural way out of your financial situation, no matter how bad it looks. No generation in God's creation ever has been left without "sent" men and women with profitable solutions to the calamities of humanity.

We can see another example of this supernatural "supply and demand" when Jesus and His disciples fed 5,000 people in a desert place in John, chapter 6. Jesus instructed His disciples to feed the people but Philip answered Him saying, *"It would take more than half a year's wages to buy enough bread for each one to have a bite!"* (verse 7 NIV). Philip was being controlled by shortage thinking or a shortage mindset, which causes a person to be only mindful of "things" instead of being mindful of the greater good or purpose. Jesus then demonstrated the "kingdom way" to fix their need for provision without leaving their assignment. With two fish and five loaves, He used as seed, Jesus, the Anointed One, placed a demand on God's great invisible warehouse to manifest enough provision to feed 5,000 men plus women and children, as much as they could eat with twelve baskets left over all. The need was met without the disciples ever leaving their assignment to serve the Lord Jesus—which was their assignment and for the greater good!

A COVENANT OF PROSPERITY

> Now the LORD had said unto Abram, Get thee out of thy country, and from thy kindred, and from thy father's house, unto a land that I will shew thee: and I will make of thee a great nation, and I will bless thee, and make thy name great; and thou shalt be a blessing. Genesis 12:1–2

Abram was 75 years old when he departed out of Haran. Just by acting on the Word of God, applying himself to it, he prospered. *"And Abram was very rich in cattle, in silver, and gold"* (Genesis 13:2). This same covenant principle is spoken about in Deuteronomy 28:1–2 *Amplified Bible, "If you will listen diligently to the voice of the Lord your God...all these blessings shall come on you and overtake you,"* further saying in verse 11, *"And the Lord shall make you have a surplus of prosperity...."*

This Bible covenant is like a contract that cannot be broken. It involves two or more people, each having to do their part for it to work. Originally if one failed to honor the contract, their lives could be taken, even by their own relatives. In the New Testament, if you are born again, you have a covenant with God through the blood of Jesus Christ. God is the "Covenantor" and you are the "covenantee," which means you are the beneficiary of the covenant. God is a covenant keeper and His side of every covenant is forever secured.[3] He even declares in Psalm 89:34, *"My covenant will I not break, nor alter the things which have gone out of my lips."*

It's on our side of the covenant where there is the variable. When we understand and lay hold of its terms, and apply ourselves to them, God is committed (Oyedepo 2005). As long as Israel kept the covenant, there weren't enough enemies in the whole world to conquer one little village. If we do not lay hold, then He does not commit Himself to us and our situation. The covenant is all about the fulfillment of our part of any scripture in order to commit God to deliver His promise. Put another way, when your part is fulfilled, God is then committed (obligated) to fulfilling His part.

God's covenant of prosperity will always prevail, even in the midst of a famine. Again, look at 1 Kings, chapter 17, the prophet Elijah, in a time of famine, was instructed by God to go to a widow's house and ask for a meal. She said, *"I have not a cake, but a handful of meal in a barrel and a little oil in a cruse and I'm making a cake for me and my son that we may eat it and die."* The prophet gave her instruction to sow what she had and the barrel of meal and cruse of oil would supernaturally multiply. She acted on the Word (covenant), tapping into the economy of heaven. The famine could not stop the covenant, or THE BLESSING, from working.

> WHEN WE UNDERSTAND AND APPLY OUR COVENANT RIGHTS, GOD IS COMMITTED TO FULFILL HIS PART.

What I am about to say is ever so vital for receiving your inheritance or manifesting God's abundance. Living a covenant lifestyle demands that God must not only be your Source, but He must be your *only* Source. One man said it like this, "When God is not the only Source of your expectation you will end up in frustration."[4] As the Psalmist said, *"My soul, wait silently for God alone, For my expectation is from Him"* (Psalm 62:5 NKJV). The *Amplified Bible* says it this way, *"My soul, wait only upon God and silently submit to Him; for my hope and expectation are from Him."*

Realize that when the Holy Spirit gives you instructions to follow in manifesting His plan, He has no backup plan. Why? Because the first one always works. Jesus sat in Simon Peter's boat and taught the people out of the ship, He then said unto Simon, *"Launch out into the deep and let down your nets for a draught."*

He wasn't trying to get Simon over into "a good fishing spot" where the fish were biting. No. He was repositioning his faith, taking Simon from sense-knowledge faith to the same faith as Abraham, which was real Bible faith where you don't have to see it before you believe. Faith was now about to cause every fish in the lake of Gennesaret to try to get in that net. Remember, nothing and no one can say "No" to God, whether it is birds feeding Elisha, Boaz being attracted to Ruth, or every fish jumping into the nets that Simon and his partners threw out into the water. The scriptures tell us that *"The LORD shall command the blessing upon thee in thy storehouses, and in all that thou settest thine hand unto; and he shall bless thee in the land which the LORD thy God giveth thee"* (Deuteronomy 28:8).

The word *command* in Hebrew is *tsawah* or *tsavah*, which means "to charge, to appoint, to order."[5] God ordered those fish to get into that net the same as He can order contracts to come to your business or givers to bless your offering bucket. He can command the blessing. So, when Simon Peter obeyed God and acted on the spiritual law of sowing and reaping, God literally ran his boat over.

God's covenant is tied to His throne and will work for you wherever you are every time without exception. Every environment is conducive to the covenant, which is why God can send you to any place or nation on Earth to advance His kingdom. He is Lord over all. The secret is to embrace His covenant and its infallibility. God cannot break it. I repeat, God cannot break His covenant and it is an "everlasting covenant." Again, the only variable in the covenant is our obedience to act on it.

CHAPTER 8

STEPS TO MANIFESTING KINGDOM ABUNDANCE

Manifesting kingdom abundance and how it is done is vital to the Church for the end-time, rapid evangelization of the world. It doesn't matter whether this abundance is through the supernatural transfer of enormous wealth being held by the wicked; or through the discovery of amazing amounts of material wealth deposited here when our God created this opulent planet; or simply by using our faith and sowing seed to manifest God's invisible store of supernatural supply, as Jesus did when he turned water into wine or fed five thousand people. Whatever the case, we must have an "abundance mentality." Not so we can hoard, but so we can be the distributors of the wealth as God intended us to be. God said to Abraham and to his seed, *"... and I will bless you [with abundant increase of favors] and make your name famous and distinguished, and you will be a blessing [dispensing good to others]"* (Genesis 12:2 AMP).

So, the mindset of having "just enough" for yourself is *not* having enough. And those who teach a doctrine that reinforces that mindset have made a significant and unfortunate contribution to the harvest still being left in the field and not being reaped and brought into the kingdom. In Jeremiah 8:20 AMP it says, *"The harvest is past, the summer is ended, and...we are not saved!"* I believe there is a penalty for blocking the door to the kingdom. For example, in the Old Testament, the ten spies who brought back an evil report about the Promised Land, causing the children of Israel to murmur against the Lord, died early (see Numbers 14:36–37). The converting of souls from serving idols to serving the living God is of the highest priority. In fact, ask any farmer. Harvest time can sometimes be quite expensive.

When your heart is with God, His hand will be upon you for blessings. Why does God bless? One reason is so we can bless His kingdom and build His house. Hear what the Lord said to His people in the book of Haggai... *"Consider your ways...ye looked for much, and, lo, it came to little; and when ye brought it home, I did blow upon it. Why? saith the Lord of hosts. Because of my house that is waste, and ye run every man unto his own house. Therefore the heaven over you is stayed from dew, and the earth is stayed from her fruit. And I called for a drought..."* (Haggai 1:7–11).

The statement I'm about to make may come as a shock to some Christians but, "One of the reasons you are saved is to display God's wealth on Earth." You and I are not here on Earth to beg. No one representing the kingdom and its King should be poor. The Bible even says, *"...the poor man's wisdom is despised, and his words are not heard"* (Ecclesiastes 9:16). Prosperity is part of your identity and abundance is your birthright.

Surprisingly, some of God's children get squeamish even petrified when the man of God talks this way. They are more concerned about the perception others might have of them than they are about financing the gospel and building the kingdom. Granted, there have been some in the Body of Christ that have abused the message of prosperity. Some spiritual leaders have exploited God's desire to bless His people abundantly for selfish ambition and greed. But we cannot "throw the baby out with the bath water." We cannot reject certain aspects of the gospel just because some preachers have perverted it for personal gain. Hear this beloved: We are moving into the most exciting time in the history of the Church, a time of worldwide revival financed by the unselfish giving of the rich and righteous.

The scriptures clearly state that those who *"hearken diligently unto the voice of the Lord thy God, to observe and to do all his commandments...that the Lord thy God will set thee on high above all nations of the earth: and all these blessings shall come on thee, and overtake thee...The Lord shall command the blessing upon thee in thy storehouses, and in all that thou settest thine hand unto...And all people of the earth shall see that thou art called by the name of the* LORD... *And the* LORD *shall make thee plenteous in goods* (surplus of prosperity)...*and thou shalt lend unto many nations, and thou shalt not borrow"* (Deuteronomy 28:1–12).

Understand, I'm not saying that all rich people are righteous, not by any means. What I am saying, however, is that all the righteous should be rich. In the Bible, *rich* simply means "having more than enough; abundant." Father Abraham is a very good example. *"Abram was very rich in cattle, in silver, and in gold"* (Genesis 13:2). And, get this, God made him that way. God even called Abraham "His friend." Abram (Abraham) said to the king of Sodom, a heathen, *"...I will not take so much as a single thread from you, lest you say, 'Abram is rich because of what I gave him'"* (Genesis 14:23 TLB). The *Webster's 1828 Dictionary* defines the word *rich* as "wealthy, opulent, possessing a large portion."[1]

The Babylonian world system has programmed most people to think shortage or just enough. How many people today are living from paycheck to paycheck, or work for 40 years and have little or nothing to show for it? You have heard people say..."There are no jobs," not knowing that they have been given gifts and the capacity to build their skills or talents by Almighty God and, with training, they can build the skills that can produce goods and services that people are willing to pay for. The truth is: There is no shortage on planet Earth. The only shortage is in the individual's mind. If you dare to believe, God will make water come out of a rock...get your buckets ready.

A personal story that illustrates this "shortage mentality" happened some years back in the early days of my ministry. It was a Monday, the day that I usually take off to rest after Sunday services. I went to a gas station to fill up my car. When I was done, as customary, I went inside the station to pay. The attendant asked, "What pump do you have, sir?" I said, "Pump nine." He said, "That'll be $36." As I reached into my pocket for the cash, a gentleman beside me shouted, "$36!" It kind of startled me, and he quickly shouted it again, "$36!" I looked at him and tried to calm him down, telling him "I've got this."

After this incident, I went back out to my car and immediately began to reflect on what had just happened. The Spirit of God spoke to my heart saying, "This man has a shortage mentality." From this incident I taught an entire series called *Renewing Your Mind*. Through fear, this man envisioned himself paying that much and it forced him to cry out emotionally and he just lost it. He was saying, "No way, I can't pay that!" And this is one way the enemy keeps the poor...poor. He keeps them seeing obstacles versus opportunities, a fear of running out versus faith in running over. So, whenever my gas tank is about half full, I usually "top it off," filling it up to the brim. This is one way I have of doing personal "mental maintenance."

Please observe that there is nothing in the Word of God that supports poverty, shortage, or even "just enough." The following scriptures reveal God's plan for your life. It is "abundance."

> The abundance of the sea shall be converted unto thee.... Isaiah 60:5 (God's design is to produce a conversion of the world's wealth to the Body of Christ)

> And God is able to make all grace (every favor and earthly blessing) come to you in abundance, so that you may always *and* under all circumstances and whatever the need be self-sufficient [possessing enough to require no aid or support and furnished in abundance for every good work and charitable donation]. 2 Corinthians 9:8 AMP

> I am come that they might have life, and that they might have *it* more abundantly. John 10:10 The *Amplified Bible* says, ...have it in abundance [to the full, till it overflows].

> The blessing of the LORD brings wealth, without painful toil for it. Proverbs 10:22 NIV

> For ye know the grace of our Lord Jesus Christ, that, though he was rich, yet for your sakes he became poor, that ye through his poverty might be rich. 2 Corinthians 8:9

The *Amplified Bible* says, ...might become enriched (abundantly supplied).

So then they which be of faith are blessed with faithful Abraham. Galatians 3:9

The heaven, *even* the heavens *are* the Lᴏʀᴅ's: but the earth hath he given to the children of men. Psalm 115:16 (God created this world for us, His children, and He gives it to us all the way, from the justice to the curse.)

We, as the seed of Abraham by faith, are to be blessed the same as Abraham, *"And the Lᴏʀᴅ hath blessed my master greatly...and he hath given him flocks, and herds, and silver, and gold, and menservants, and maidservants, and camels, and asses"* (Genesis 24:35). This blessing will cause us to be financially and materially independent, which I guarantee will put us at odds with the world. This independence is a large part of why the material aspects of the gospel are so often criticized. The purpose of the criticism is to frighten and intimidate you from ever moving into abundance and from ever becoming financially and materially independent.

> **THERE IS NOTHING IN THE WORD OF GOD THAT SUPPORTS SHORTAGE OR EVEN "JUST ENOUGH."**

Interestingly, no one criticized me in the beginning of starting our ministry in Chicago. We were struggling and had barely enough to pay the rent and keep food on the table. It is only when we began to grow and prosper in people, property, and influence that we began to receive criticism. No matter how many cars our ministry gave to families in need or how many Joseph Business Schools we started that produced entrepreneurs to help communities overcome their unemployment, we still were the object of envy and ridicule. Jesus Himself said that we would *"receive an hundredfold now in this time, houses, and brethren, and sisters, and mothers, and children, and lands, with persecutions; and in the world to come, eternal life"* (Mark 10:30). One man said it like this, "Can you stand to be blessed?"

Proverbs says, *"A good man leaveth an inheritance to his children's children: and the wealth of the sinner is laid up for the just"* (Proverbs 13:22). God plans for us to be so blessed that long after we leave this Earth, our wealth will be at least two generations strong. And He expects us to be compliant saying, *"So shall my word be that goeth forth out of my mouth: it shall not return unto me void..."* (Isaiah 55:11).

Manifesting kingdom abundance is not hard; it simply has not been taught. In the book of Romans the Apostle Paul teaches, *"How then shall they call on him in whom they have not believed? and how shall they believe in him of whom they have not heard? and how shall they hear without a preacher"* (Romans 10:14). And, if it has not been taught, then how can people have the faith to receive what legally and rightfully belongs to them? Remember, everything God is going to do for us He's already done. You're not trying to get Him to heal you.

According to His Word, that's already done. You're not trying to get Him to give you abundance; abundance is the basis of God's kingdom, *"...I am come that they might have life, and that they might have it more abundantly"* (John 10:10).

In teaching about manifesting kingdom abundance, it's important to note that people don't become rich by just giving money. They become rich by first thinking rich thoughts. God prospers us first by prospering our soul (3 John 2). The scriptures also teach us, "As he thinketh in his heart, so is he." It did not say, "As he giveth, so is he." The first real step to creating abundance is to align your thoughts with the thoughts of God. What you think about continuously, guaranteed, you will end up creating.

People also become rich by creating value, as I alluded to earlier. Let me explain further. We all are born into this world with gifts and talents. I call it "treasures in an earthen vessel" (2 Corinthians 4:7). It's what each person was born with and given as a gift to serve humanity. As they develop and expand that gift, they will, over time, produce a product or service that people will be willing to buy. Soon their income will be greater than the expense used to create that product or service. Now we understand, *"A man's gift maketh room for him, and bringeth him before great men"* (Proverbs 18:16).

Dr. George Washington Carver, a black scientist who invented some 300 products from the peanut, was invited to speak before the Ways and Means Committee in Washington, D.C., in 1921 about his discoveries and creations. Initially, he was given only ten minutes to speak, but the Committee became so instantly enthralled that the Committee's chairman said, "Go ahead Brother. Your time is unlimited!" Carver spoke for one hour and forty-five minutes.[2] At the end of his address, the chairman asked, "Dr. Carver, how did you learn all of these things?" Carver answered, "From an old book." "What book?" asked the Chairman. Carver replied, "The Bible." The Chairman inquired, "Does the Bible tell (us) about peanuts?" "No Sir," Carver replied, "But it tells (us) about the God who made the peanut. I asked Him to show me what to do with the peanut, and He did."[3] Dr. Carver's uses for the peanut and other new crops drastically improved the economy of the southern United States.[4] God said through the prophet Isaiah, *"I am the LORD thy God which teacheth thee to profit, which leadeth thee by the way that thou shouldest go."*

Here are three simple steps to supernaturally manifest covenant abundance from God. Study them and meditate the Scriptures until the Word of God carries more authority than any of the devil's lies or your present circumstances.

Step 1: Make God Your Only Source

He is the Source of your total supply. The apostle Paul writes: *"But my God shall supply all your need according to his riches in glory by Christ Jesus"* (Philippians 4:19). God wants a relationship with us and wants us to totally depend on and trust in Him. *"This is what the LORD says; Cursed is the one who trusts in man, who draws strength from mere flesh and whose heart turns away from the LORD...they will not see prosperity when it comes, But blessed is the one who trusts in the LORD..."* (Jeremiah 17:5–7 NIV). Allow me to put this verse in my own words, "Either we trust totally in Him or He takes His hands off our affairs." Again, *"If God is not the only Source of your expectations, you will end up in frustration"* (Psalm 62:5). Remember, everyone who makes God their Source has just stepped into unlimited prosperity. That's the way the covenant works.

The Lord introduced Himself to Abraham in Genesis 17:1 as *"I am the Almighty God."* God was saying to Abraham, "I have all you need." God never planned for His children to have to go "begging" the world to take care of them. He refuses to allow an economic slump to affect His Church's ability to build, grow, and flourish and evangelize the world. No! We are to live in this economy according to heaven's economy. Just suppose this Babylonian system one day, without warning, switched off all credit cards. Ask yourself, what would you do? Jesus came to show us how to get our needs met independently of this world system.

Step 2: Sow a Seed for Your Need

The spiritual law of sowing and reaping is God's way of meeting the needs of His people and no man, system, or drought can abrogate it or stop its function. Jesus taught "Give, that it may be given unto you" (Luke 6:38 paraphrased). No one ever sees increase in the kingdom without sowing seed, whether they are poor or rich (Mark 12:41–44). The scriptures tell us *"where there is no seed...there is no prosperity"* (Zechariah 8:12). As believers, we are under a covenant with God, a covenant of increase, where only what you give can be multiplied. When your seed is sown (given to the Lord) it comes under God's legal jurisdiction (of the kingdom) and God multiplies it back to you (Keesee 2011). This is what the woman did who had only one meal left, and what the little boy did who sowed his lunch box. As long as they held onto it, God could do nothing with it. It would have remained as it was. In each case, their "seed" was blessed and multiplied.

Remember, "God gives seed to the sower," meaning that you'll never be without a seed. You always have something to give (sow). You always have something in your house, hand, or your heart. One woman, Hannah, even made a vow and got her need met (1 Samuel 1). A vow allows God to accept your promise to Him as your seed. There is a warning, though, that comes with a vow, *"Better is it that*

GOD WANTS US TO TOTALLY DEPEND ON AND TRUST IN HIM.

thou shouldest not vow, than that thou shouldest vow and not pay" (Ecclesiastes 5:5).

Also, the Word of God, not money, is the platform upon which we prosper in the kingdom. Every time the Scriptures talk about blessings and prosperity, it talks about the Word of God to produce it. It's only after Abraham heard the Word of God and acted on it did God's blessings manifest in his life. So, sowing and reaping is here to stay. From the beginning, the scriptures tell us, *"While the earth remaineth, seedtime and harvest, and cold and heat, and summer and winter, and day and night shall not cease"* (Genesis 8:22).

Step 3: Expect a Miracle

A dear friend and prophet of God once told me, "Expect the supernatural. If you don't, it won't happen." Why did he tell me this? Because our expectation is vitally important in receiving anything from God. Too many Christians give, for the good of the kingdom, with no expectation of receiving anything in return. Religion had taught us that it is selfish to expect a return on our giving. Child of God, this is wrong thinking. It's wrong if your motives are wrong. If you are not looking for or expecting it, it could pass you by or go right over your head. Again, see it this way, you are not forcing God to do something, but planting seed that calls for the harvest or promise He has already provided.

If you were hired by a farmer and after sowing seed you left his harvest in the field, you would be fired. Quick! Why? That would be poor stewardship. The Lord has provided an inexhaustible supply for all the things we would need in this life. Sowing seed and expecting a miracle harvest is God's way of our taping into it. This is how we can live in this world's economy, according to heaven's economy. "This is not greed, it is growth."[5]

Here are some examples:

In 2 Kings, chapter 4, there was the widow who cried to the prophet Elisha when the creditors were about to take her two sons to work off the debt her dead husband owed. Elisha asked her, what can I do for you? What do you have in your house? She only had a pot of oil, but it was enough to produce a financial miracle. As she obeyed the prophet's instructions, the oil supernaturally multiplied into all the vessels that her sons had borrowed from the neighbors. *"Then she came and told the man of God. And he said, Go, sell the oil, and pay thy debt, and live thou and thy children of the rest"* (verse 7). The widow expected a miracle and she received one.

There is the account of the miracle of feeding 5,000 men plus women and children in John, chapter 6, all from five barley loaves and two small fishes given by a young lad. *"And Jesus took the loaves; and when he had given thanks, he distributed to the disciples, and the disciples to them that were set down...When they were filled, he said unto his disciples, Gather up the fragments that remain, that nothing be lost"* (verses 11–12).

God operated this same principle when He sent His precious Seed...His Son. *"For God so loved the world, that he gave his only begotten Son."* When God gave, He planted His best seed in all of creation, His only begotten Son, for a desired result—that His family that was lost would return to Him and have everlasting life. Jesus said, speaking about His own death and resurrection, *"Verily, verily I say unto you, Except a corn of wheat fall into the ground and die, it abideth alone: but if it die, it bringeth forth much fruit"* (John 12:24).

God fully expected a return or harvest on His precious seed (His Son) that was sown, and you and I are part of that harvest. Once you sow, and release your seed in faith, start thanking and praising God for your miracle before your return is manifested. **To be thankless is to be fruitless.** And keep your speech and confession in line with what you believe you've received. Here are three scriptures you might meditate on and commit to memory.

> My soul, wait thou only upon God; for my expectation *is* from him. Psalm 62:5

> Be not deceived, God is not mocked; for whatsoever a man soweth, that shall he also reap. Galatians 6:7

> But my God shall supply all your need, according to His riches in glory by Christ Jesus. Philippians 4:19

LET THEM HAVE DOMINION

God designed us to be limitless. He also wired us to operate like He does. He empowers us to return to our original mode of operation, which is by faith. Real faith says or declares when something will happen, and time must bow to that decree. You might ask, "Well, how can that be?" Here's the answer: Time, along with space and matter, falls in the category of creation. Time, as we know it, was created on the fourth day and is included in *"the works of His hands"* along with the moon and stars (Psalm 8:3). Because God made mankind to have dominion over the works of His hands (Psalm 8:6), time is therefore subject to our dominion. Time, like money, was meant to be our servant, not our master. Faith is the dominant force given to us to rule over time.

King David worked this faith principle when he told Goliath, *"This day the LORD will deliver you into my hands"* (1 Samuel 17:46 NIV). He was putting an end to what the army of Israel had tolerated for going on forty days. The prophet Elisha also declared when something would be. *"Elisha answered, 'Listen to what the LORD says! By this time tomorrow you will be able to buy in Samaria ten pounds of the best wheat or twenty pounds of barley for one piece of silver'"* (2 Kings 7:1 *Good News Translation*). They went from being poor to having an abundant supply within 24 hours.

I recall when my family and I had first come to Chicago to start our ministry and a dear sister (Beverly) took us in until we could get established. Every time we would make plans to move out and get our own place to live, something would happen to take the little money we had saved. We experienced delay after delay. Time was ruling mercilessly as an undisputed king. Something inside me knew that this was not God, that it was not the will of God for us to be delayed this way, so I fasted for three days. Then God spoke to me very clearly saying, "Declare what you want." I knew exactly what He was saying. He wanted me to set a date or time by faith of when it would happen and believe it was done when I spoke it.

So I declared, "WE'LL BE MOVING IN SEVEN DAYS!" Understand, I didn't have a clue of how or where or with what money, but when you operate by faith you break the laws of time, space, and matter. So, as the days began to click off one by one, I would tell my wife, "We'll be out of here in six more days...We'll be out of here in five more days...." All of a sudden...miracles! A series of them! And we moved in seven days into a nice luxury apartment building. I had to decree a thing, releasing my faith for the miracle, and it happened right on time. When I said it would be is when God did it. He said Himself, *"Thou shalt also decree a thing, and it shall be established..."* (Job 22:28). Again, faith is a dominant force given to us to rule over time.

RECEIVING OUR HOUSE—DEBT FREE!

As I shared in chapter 6, "Living in the Kingdom", when Veronica and I believed God for our first home in the Chicago area, we started with the promise of God found in Deuteronomy 6:11, *"...houses full of all good things, which thou filledst not...."* Confessing and meditating this scripture led us to describe how we wanted the house to look, in detail. We then were prompted by the Holy Spirit to sow out of the money we had started saving up for a house. Once we sowed the sacrifice seed, supernaturally our brand new home came into our hands—debt free! As I said earlier, "We are not waiting for God, He is waiting for us." There is plenty in Daddy's House! And it's in God we trust. You may not have developed this level of faith yet, so just start where you are. That's what I did and in time moved to greater levels of faith.

In the kingdom, expecting and producing a harvest from a seed sown in faith is operating biblically. Expecting to receive something in return is a godly way to give. As I said, God demonstrated this Himself in *"for God so loved the world that He gave,"* and He expected His family back in return.

Once your seed is sown, remember to listen for the voice of God for His instruction. Again, He may speak to you through a sermon, a prophet (priest), or directly to you in prayer or even in a dream. Whichever way, He will lead you to, bring to you, or create for you, your supernatural harvest or provision.

RECEIVING HER BUSINESS SUPERNATURALLY

A graduate of our Joseph Business School shared this awesome testimony of how she received her business—supernaturally—by working the laws of the kingdom. Here is her story in her own words.

My school is called the Illinois Welding School and on October 28, 2013, I celebrated 5 years in business. I have 7 employees and we offer welding techniques to students from ages 16 to 60. Our employment rate is around 91% so we have been very successful in placing people in jobs. This is my third business but for this particular business, I didn't pay a dime for it. It came out of nowhere but I was in expectancy. I had been looking for a business to pursue and knew the Lord had something for me but I didn't know what field it was in. One day while I was reading Isaiah 45 that scripture gave me confirmation that this business was mine. Illinois Welding School (IWS) was one of my clients at the time and someone there told me the owner was thinking about selling the business. So I called the owner, a millionaire, and just asked him to transfer the business to me during our conversation. He said no, he wouldn't transfer it because, of course, he could make money on it by selling it. I told him okay have a good day. But I hung up the phone and said, "Oh no, it's a done deal. I own IWS."

As I said before, I was just expecting. I happened to get an introduction to the owner through a high-level associate and set up a meeting. Now I knew nothing about welding, but as Dr. Winston says, sometimes you just have to have "crazy faith" and get on out there. I have crazy faith and will jump out there as long as I know God is in it. So I went for it. When I met with the owner, I took a book with me I had written, *Job Search Made Simple,* just so he could get a feel for who I was personally since I didn't have the experience in welding or a degree in that field. I was confident it would all work out because I had said prayer confessions over this meeting and when

> I was in his office, I literally saw Jesus sitting next to me and angels in the room with me.
>
> One thing that I make sure I do, even today, is to confess over my business what I desire to see because I know that my words have power. Something I also found very important is that I had to sow seed. In this case, I also knew God wanted me to sow upward to others who are already prosperous because the blessing is there. When you give more to someone who has more, God loves that. He'll give you more seed. All of this I've described about communicating with the owner happened in March and by October 28th the owner had signed the papers drawn up by his lawyers to transfer the business to me with no money. Praise God![6]

The apostle Paul writes, "No soldier goes to war at his own expense" (1 Corinthians 9:7 paraphrased). Here is an example: When I was in the military I would receive orders to go from one station to another. When I got to my new station, my house, the school for my children, my airplane, and uniforms were all provided for me. I didn't have to pay a dime. The government took care of all my military needs. So it is, in the kingdom of God, *"My God shall supply all your need according to His riches in glory by Christ Jesus."* All your stuff is paid for and laid up for you. Jesus paid it all. Now, believe it and receive it!

WE ARE JOINT HEIRS WITH CHRIST

I said earlier that financial prosperity is part of our redemptive inheritance package (Revelation 5:12) that Jesus died and left to us. Hebrews 1:2 says, *"Jesus is the lawful owner of everything"* (*Charles B. Williams Translation*). The Bible also says that you are a joint heir with Him (Romans 8:17). Whatever He owns, all that He has, He shares with us; and all that we have belongs to Him, if He needs it. That's the way the covenant works. This is a powerful revelation that was key for me in manifesting kingdom abundance. We must see ourselves as owners with stewardship responsibility.

Let me share a story that will illustrate this point in a humorous way. I was a speaker at a conference jointly hosted by two ministries, one was led by a dear friend who is a military chaplain and pastor, and the other led by another dear friend and mentor who has a large worldwide ministry. The audience included many of our men and women serving in the military. While this chaplain was on stage, the co-host and main speaker ministering at the conference joined him on stage unexpectedly and said, "God has just spoken to my heart saying that whatever size offering is collected in this three-day conference meeting, I was to match it from my ministry." Of course, the audience started clapping as they witnessed an astounding display of faith and giving. Then he went on to say: "The Lord also said for me to give you (the chaplain) my Cadillac Escalade as a gift."

Well, then the audience went wild. But what especially caught my attention was the pastor's wife who was sitting in the front row. And before the speaker could hardly finish his sentence, she jumped out of her seat, twirled around and started shouting and dancing. "Thank you Jesus! Praise the Lord!" I thought to myself, he wasn't talking to her; he was talking to the chaplain. Why is she so excited? Plus, she hasn't even seen the car yet; she only has this man's word that it even exists.

Then the Lord showed me the revelation of biblical ownership. She got excited because she **saw** herself as a **joint heir** with her husband. As his wife, whatever he gets, she gets. Whatever he owns, she owns. She believed the speaker's words and by **faith**, with no physical proof that the car even existed, she had taken possession of it.

Her reaction is how every child of God should be when they read in the Bible about the promises of God. We are the "bride of Christ" and joint heirs with Him. The only reason many have not been excited when they hear the preacher preach or read in the Word of God concerning their inheritance is because they don't believe it or they have yet to receive the revelation of being a joint heir. I believe that through this book you will get a breakthrough in this area and see your inheritance clearly, and when you do, you will be like the pastor's wife...nothing will be able to keep you in your seat!

The apostle Paul has a powerful revelation in 1 Corinthians 3:21–23, *"Therefore let no man glory in men. For all things are yours...and ye are Christ's; and Christ is God's."* Paul goes on to say, *"Wherefore thou are no more a servant* (slave)*, but a son; and if a son, then an heir of God through Christ"* (Galatians 4:7).

Notice, He did not say "All spiritual things." He said "All things." Houses, businesses, lands or real estate, cars, and so on; each qualifies as a "thing," everything without exception, nothing left out. Paul is writing this revelation to every person in the family of God. He did not receive this revelation from man or for his own personal benefit, but he received it from God to communicate it to you and me, the Body of Christ. Then He goes on to say, *"Ye are Christ's."*

Thus, manifesting abundance starts with being born again into the kingdom of God. Once born again, through faith and right thinking, you can tap into an inexhaustible supply, provisions that God has prepared from *"before the foundation of the world."* And guaranteed, once you experience kingdom prosperity you will never covet earthly prosperity again. You will rest in the finished work of Jesus, and be fully persuaded that there is more than enough in "Daddy's House" to meet the need of every God-given vision or assignment and have plenty left over.

CHAPTER 9

VENGEANCE & RECOMPENSE
THE JUSTICE SYSTEM OF GOD

This is our season of kingdom manifestation, a set time when the government of God will be established throughout the earth. Every spiritual force that has been assisting the ungodly against God's people is now being put down. This is a part of what the Bible calls, *"the vengeance of the LORD."* It's that "day" when the believer's "mourning is turned to dancing." A time when we, the Church, will be distinguished as prophetically packaged to lead the world, which must take place before Jesus comes. God says, *"...I will render vengeance to mine enemies, and will reward them that hate me"* (Deuteronomy 32:41).

This *"vengeance of the LORD,"* or the justice and judgment of God, is a vital part of kingdom manifestation, and the lack of its teaching is one of the main reasons why society has not reflected the Church's influence. In times when we should have been victorious in holding back iniquity, we have been victims and evil has been expanding at an alarming rate. In the book of Isaiah it says, *"Therefore my people are gone into captivity, because they have no knowledge..."* (Isaiah 5:13). Our kingdom authority and anointing gives us the power to regulate, legislate, enforce, and establish God's rule and reign wherever we are sent. We are called to dominate this planet. In the book of Revelation, God gives us a picture of the eventual outcome between good and evil *"...The kingdoms of this* (evil) *world are become the kingdoms of our Lord, and of his Christ; and he shall reign for ever and ever"* (Revelation 11:15).

We, the Church, cannot for a moment shrink back from confronting evil and unjust laws of the land through fear or intimidation. Sir Winston Churchill once said (as quoted in Kachaje 2014), "The power of the wicked is always enhanced by the timidity and indecision of the righteous."

THE VENGEANCE OF THE LORD IS A VITAL PART OF KINGDOM MANIFESTATION.

In Daniel, chapter 6, Daniel defied King Darius' decree (a law) *"...that every man that shall ask a petition of any God or man within thirty days, save of thee, O king, shall be cast into the den of lions...."* (verse 12). *"Now when Daniel knew that the writing was signed, he went into his house; and his windows being opened in his chamber toward Jerusalem, he kneeled upon his knees...and prayed..."* (verse 10). Daniel continued to honor his God by praying three times a day publicly as he had always done before. He placed his faith and trust in his God for everything he needed, including divine protection.

The result was that Daniel was cast into the den of lions. Today we call that "capital punishment." I think you remember the outcome. Daniel lived, being untouched, declaring, *"God sent his angel to shut the mouths of the lions so that they would not hurt me. He did this because he knew that I was innocent and because I have not wronged you, Your Majesty"* (Daniel 6:22 GNT). God had commanded vengeance (justice and judgment) on behalf of His servant Daniel *"because he believed in his God."* Then at the king's command, *"...they brought those men which had accused Daniel, and they cast them into the den of lions, them, their children, and their wives; and the lions had the mastery of them, and brake all their bones..."* (verse 24).

This all happened without Daniel trying to fight his own battle or seek revenge. We are in the time that the prophet Joel speaks about saying, *"...and my people shall never be ashamed."* It is a time when systems, institutions, codes, cultures, laws, and legislations will adjust to accommodate our divine purpose, and the *"hand of the Lord"* will be upon anyone who touches us.

For centuries the justice system of the world has been one of the main targets of demonic abuse, and without heaven's justice system, everything in society will eventually collapse. Why the justice system? I believe it's because it's the most efficient and effective way to shift a culture. When ungodly laws are passed and go unchallenged, they affect the thinking and behavior of the masses. People think that wrong is right, causing nations to continue in ungodliness and a moral decline.

American slavery, which allowed people to sell and own another human being based on the color of their skin, was once justified by law. The economy of almost the entire South was built upon it, affecting the thinking of millions of Americans for generations, even after slavery ended. Even though the Emancipation Proclamation was signed, African Americans still could not buy land, attend schools with whites, nor have competitive businesses, and so on. This was unjust. Dr. Martin Luther King, Jr., in his famous "I Have a Dream" speech, referenced Amos 5:24. In speaking to the nation about the terrible injustice of segregation and the denial of civil and legal rights to African Americans, he said "we will not be satisfied until justice rolls down like waters and righteousness like a mighty stream."[1]

There was a time when movies and television programs were not allowed to show certain things that were considered inappropriate to watch, but a shift in the culture changed all that and laws have been passed to make it legal and seem right. The scripture tells us, *"There is a way which seemeth right unto a man, but the end thereof are the ways of death"* (Proverbs 14:12).

In the beginning Adam was to *"...Be fruitful, and multiply, and replenish the earth..."* spreading the culture or quality of the garden of Eden throughout the whole Earth. Adam and Eve fell into sin, lost their relationship with God their Father, and began to create another culture outside of God. Jesus came to reintroduce the kingdom and put us back on track with Adam's original assignment.

When Jesus, at the age of thirty, stood to read the Scriptures in the synagogue as written in Luke, chapter 4, He intentionally left out *"the day of vengeance."* He said, *"The*

Spirit of the Lord is upon me, because he hath anointed me to preach the gospel to the poor; he hath sent me to heal the brokenhearted, to preach deliverance to the captives, and recovering of sight to the blind, to set at liberty them that are bruised, to preach the acceptable year of the Lord. And he closed the book..." (verses 18–20).

But now, through the ministry of the Holy Spirit, we have stepped into the part that was left out, *"...the day of vengeance of our God; to comfort all that mourn...ye shall eat* (consume or devour) *the riches* (wealth or substance) *of the Gentiles, and in their glory shall ye boast yourselves"* (Isaiah 61:2, 6). Through vengeance, or God's justice, we will see the complete plan of God manifested. The Church, as an institution, will be recognized as the most gifted and revered in the world. God is beautifying the Church in this hour and every work of the wicked one is being destroyed and dismantled.

> **THE CHURCH, AS AN INSTITUTION, WILL BE RECOGNIZED AS THE MOST GIFTED AND REVERED IN THE WORLD.**

As comfort comes to the Church, judgment will come to the world system bringing the greatest transfer of wealth ever seen on Earth into the hands of the righteous where it legally belongs. This will be such enormous prosperity that it will stagger the imagination of the world. Isaiah 60 says, *"...the LORD shall arise upon thee* (His people)*"* and the *"wealth of the nations shall be converted* (overturned) *unto thee"* (verses 2, 5 KJV and GNT).

A LOVE OF JUSTICE

The vengeance of the Lord has nothing to do with hate, emotional resentment, or retaliation, but involves the necessity of punishing offenders, which proceeds from a love of justice. This vengeance is the judgment of God for a specific people: mainly those standing in the way of establishing God's kingdom; those stopping the spread of the gospel; and those interfering with the rights of God's kingdom citizens. Again, this vengeance is not about revenge that springs from enmity, bitterness, or ill will, but from a love of justice, *"For I the L*ORD *love judgment* (justice)..." (Isaiah 61:8).

God loves people. The Bible also says that *"God is love"* (1 John 4:8). The Lord declares in Ezekiel 33:11, *"Say unto them, As I live, saith the Lord G*OD*, I have no pleasure in the death of the wicked; but that the wicked turn from his way and live...."* God demonstrates His love for us in His plan of salvation through Jesus Christ, *"God so loved the world, that he gave his only begotten Son..."* (John 3:16). Jesus Christ redeemed us from the curse that came through Adam's fall declaring that "I came to save men's lives, not to destroy them" (Luke 9:46 paraphrased). But if people do not accept the grace that Jesus died to give us and the love God has for us, they remain subject to the law of sin and death that still operates in the children of disobedience.

I am firmly convinced that in these last days, it will be impossible to fulfill your destiny without the vengeance of the Lord, or apart from the justice system of God clearing the way. We are moving into a place and time unlike any before, a time of extreme darkness and gloominess; yet, right from the midst will emerge a great army of light, the Church, men and women of unquestionable dominion who nations will respect as they will decide the destinies of nations (see Joel 2:2). Armed with the *"garments of vengeance,"* this army to advance the kingdom will not be running away from trouble but causing trouble for the enemy (1 Kings 18:17 NIV), putting down every demonic work troubling humanity.

ABRAHAM, SARAH, AND KING ABIMELECH

God said to Abraham, who was chosen by God as the father of the faithful, *"...In thee shall all nations be blessed."* And Abraham believed God. Anyone now standing in the way of God's "high calling" for Abraham was going to encounter His vengeance. King Abimelech found this out when he took Sarah for himself into his palace, *"But God came to Abimelech in a dream by night, and said to him, Behold, thou art but a dead man, for the woman which thou hast taken; for she is a man's wife. Now therefore restore the man his wife; for he is a prophet, and he shall pray for thee, and thou shalt live: and if thou restore her not, know thou that thou shalt surely die, thou, and all that are thine* (all your people)*"* (Genesis 20:3, 7).

By this time satan knows that Abraham and Sarah are chosen to bring forth this godly seed, and I'm convinced he was attempting to contaminate the gene pool of the Messiah. They had a divine mission the same way you and I are on a divine mission for God to establish His kingdom and prepare for His coming. We are here to make what God has already planned and prepared come to fruition in this hour, and are protected by God's anointing, which executes vengeance upon all our adversaries.

Not only did King Abimelech restore Abraham's wife, but the scriptures tell us that he told Abraham, *"'Look my kingdom over, and choose the place where you want to live'...Then he turned to Sarah. 'Look,' he said, 'I am giving your "brother"* (Abraham) *a thousand silver pieces as damages for what I did, to compensate for any embarrassment and to settle any claim against me regarding this matter. Now justice has been done'"* (Genesis 20:15–16 TLB).

> YOU AND I ARE ON A DIVINE MISSION FOR GOD TO ESTABLISH HIS KINGDOM.

God will bring judgment upon your adversaries, and in doing so will punish and penalize them for what they have put you through and force them to compensate you for damages that they have caused.

Again, *"...Vengeance belongeth unto me, I will recompense, saith the Lord..."* (Hebrews 10:30). *Recompense* means to "compensate, pay damages, return an equivalent for anything done or suffered to make amends."[2] So whatever is afflicting or humiliating you, whatsoever is against your peace, progress, career, business, or family, God is going to command vengeance.

GOD IS THE JUDGE

It took the vengeance of the Lord for Moses to enforce Israel's release from Egypt. Notice, whatever or whoever was resisting Moses did not go unpunished. When it was time for the children of Israel to be delivered from Egypt, the Lord told Moses, *"And I am sure that the king of Egypt will not let you go, no, not by a mighty hand. And I will stretch out my hand, and smite Egypt with all my wonders which I will do in the midst thereof: and after that he will let you go"* (Exodus 3:19–20). To fulfill God's mandate, Moses didn't go to Pharaoh or Egypt's court for permission, but invoked the justice system of God, the Supreme Court of the universe. Psalm 75:7 states, *"But God is the judge: he putteth down one, and setteth up another."* Isaiah 33:22 says, *"For the LORD is our judge, the LORD is our lawgiver, the LORD is our king; he will save us."*

It took vengeance for Joseph and Mary to stay in the plan of God regarding baby Jesus after King Herod *"...slew all the children that were in Bethlehem, and in all the coasts thereof, from two years old and under..."* (Matthew 2:16). The scriptures go on to say, *"But when Herod was dead, behold, an angel of the Lord appeareth in a dream to Joseph in Egypt, saying, Arise, and take the young child and his mother, and go into the land of Israel: for they are dead which sought the young child's life"* (verses 19–20).

Notice, this scripture still refers to Jesus as a young child, so within a relatively short period of time, perhaps three or four years, Herod and all his company who were re-sisting the plan of God to redeem mankind and establish His kingdom were terminated. Whatever is resisting God's plan for your life, whatever is tampering with your destiny, Isaiah 61:2 promises that your day is here *"...the day of vengeance of our God; to comfort all that mourn."*

Another example of God's vengeance is found in Acts, chapter 13, when a false prophet and sorcerer named Bar-jesus (or Elymas) was opposing Barnabas and Saul from preaching the Word of God to Sergius Paulus, the governor of Paphos. The governor, who had great influence, had asked to hear the gospel, but the sorcerer was blocking this from happening.

> Then Saul—also known as Paul—was filled with the Holy Spirit; he looked straight at the magician (sor-cerer) and said, "You son of the Devil! You are the enemy of everything that is good...The Lord's hand

will come down on you now; you will be blind and will not see the light of day for a time." At once Elymas felt a dark mist cover his eyes.... Acts 13:9–11 *Good News Translation*

Again, the false prophet was trying to stop the advancement of the gospel, but God's vengeance removed the disciples' adversary. God knows that satan is our true adversary, and that he uses people, especially those outside of God's covenant, to frustrate and fight God's servants from carrying out His instructions.

> **WHATEVER IS RESISTING GOD'S PLAN FOR YOUR LIFE, WHATEVER IS TAMPERING WITH YOUR DESTINY...YOUR DAY IS HERE.**

We must remember that our enemy is never flesh and blood. Our true warfare is never with what we can see or feel. This is why vengeance only operates supernaturally by faith. General George Patton understood this when he was fighting the Nazis in 1944 during WWII. Patton knew that he needed God's intervention to help win a crucial battle or countless lives and peace for the world would be lost. As I shared previously, Patton prayed a prayer for good weather written by the chaplain of his Third Army to invoke the *"hand of the Lord"* to move on his behalf. The next day the weather was clear and perfect. His men went forward and won the battle.[3]

The vengeance of the Lord is one of our covenant rights, but because vengeance has not been taught in the Body of Christ, many Christians end up fighting their own battles instead of resting in the assurance of God's deliverance and vindication. The Bible says that *"My people are destroyed for lack of knowledge."* This does not say that God's people have "no knowledge"; it says, a "lack of knowledge." Christians have some knowledge but not enough. Today's priests must begin to preach and teach the whole counsel of God, including the vengeance of the Lord, so that people can have the faith for putting it into operation. In so many cases, because we have not known vengeance, we have been victims. *"How then shall*

> **OUR TRUE WARFARE IS NEVER WITH WHAT WE CAN SEE OR FEEL.**

they call on him in whom they have not believed? and how shall they believe in him of whom they have not heard? and how shall they hear without a preacher?...So then faith cometh by hearing, and hearing by the word of God" (Romans 10:14, 17).

Vengeance is designed to protect you, your family, your business, your church, and everything that you own or are involved in. Our God sits in a place to judge anyone, any system, or any army who touches you (see 2 Kings 19). You are God's property, which means you can no longer be molested, tormented, assaulted, or harassed. Zechariah 2:8 says, *"...for he that toucheth you toucheth the apple of his eye."* You are the "apple of God's eye."

This word *apple* in the Hebrew translates as "pupil."[4] Have you noticed that you cannot touch the pupil of your eye? Your eyelid immediately closes to protect it. It's the same with our relationship with God, especially when we are actively advancing His kingdom. Anyone who tries to harm or hurt you, God's presence comes to cover and protect you. But you have to believe this. Everything received in the kingdom is according to your faith.

A TRUE DAVID AND GOLIATH BUSINESS STORY

A speaker at one of our business conferences, a born again, real estate entrepreneur, shared a powerful personal encounter of the Lord's vengeance in the early days of his business.[5] He said he had partnered with a wealthy businessman on a successful commercial real estate deal, but when it came time for the man to pay our speaker his portion of the profits, the man refused to pay him. The money owed was more than a half million dollars, and it meant the survival of our speaker's new company. The business partner, who our speaker called George (not his real name), decided he was simply not going to pay what was rightfully owed.

Although the law was on our speaker's side, he knew that suing George was not an option. George had much deeper financial pockets and could keep them tied up in litigation for years—draining his finances and eventually destroying his new business. He saw no way of winning except that he knew God was a God of justice.[6]

He prayed to God about the situation and surrendered the battle to Him. Once he did, he received the confidence that God would fight the battle against George. He also knew that he had to fight the battle against the spirit of fear, which he did by praising and worshiping God.

Our speaker followed the Lord's instructions to call George every week, which he did for ten weeks, to calmly ask him about his payment. Each time George refused. During their tenth telephone call, George became very angry and said that he was going to fly to our speaker's hometown and tell him to his face that he was never going to pay him the money. A meeting was arranged, and the two met a week later at the local airport.

As they entered an airport conference room, our speaker said he didn't know what to say so he decided to keep quiet and hold his peace. As they sat down opposite one another, he said something strange began to happen. Instead of looking at him, George kept staring at something over our speaker's head. All of a sudden, the color drained from George's face as if he were going to have a heart attack. Our speaker said he was about to ask George if he was okay, but the Lord spoke to his heart not to speak. God was handling this. In obedience, our speaker said he held his peace and kept quiet. *"The LORD will fight for you, and ye shall hold your peace"* (Exodus 14:14).

As they sat at the table, George's shoulders suddenly began to slump, as though the Lord had drained every bit of resistance and arrogance out of his body. George then started trembling and weakly mumbled, "We will pay you." Two days later, our speaker checked his bank account online and found there had been a wire transfer for the half million dollars he was owed.

What happened to George in that meeting? As our speaker said: "My best guess is that He [God] opened George's eyes into the spirit realm and let him see, either the angel that stood guard over me, or a glimpse of the Lord Himself."[7] Again, God said in Ezekiel 33:11 that he has no pleasure in the death of the wicked, but that they turn from their evil ways. I believe God gave George the opportunity "to repent" or change his wicked decision, and if he had not, he might have died in that airport conference room.

Whatever will not let God's plan come to pass in your life is now being removed. Everything prepared for your destiny must be released. Now is your set time and season, the time of the former and latter rain. No more delays, denials, or substitutes, and wherever the enemy has been holding you back, you are breaking forth! Your responsibility is to believe this.

The apostle Paul addresses this in Romans, which clearly indicates that this is an end-time Church reality. The apostle says: *"Dearly beloved, avenge not yourselves, but rather give place unto wrath: for it is written, Vengeance is mine; I will repay, saith the Lord"* (Romans 12:19). The Lord will execute vengeance on behalf of His people as we advance His kingdom. He will torment your tormentors. Whatever tampers with your destiny, peace, progress, children, or business, He will deal with! *"No weapon that is formed against thee shall prosper; and every tongue that shall rise against thee in judgment thou shalt condemn. This is the heritage of the servants of the Lord, and their righteousness is of me, saith the Lord"* (Isaiah 54:17).

Nothing resisting us in these last days shall go unpunished, for there shall be comfort and vengeance. Get ready for this: Your days of struggling are over! *"For we know Him Who said, Vengeance is Mine [retribution and the meting out of full justice rest with Me]; I will repay [I will exact the compensation], says the Lord. And again, The Lord will judge and determine and solve and settle the cause and the cases of His people"* (Hebrews 10:30 AMP).

A TIME OF FRESH OIL

Psalm 92:10–11 says, *"But my horn shalt thou exalt like the horn of an unicorn: I shall be anointed with fresh oil. Mine eye also shall see my desire on mine enemies, and mine ears shall hear my desire of the wicked that rise up against me."* Psalm 94:1 also says, *"O Lord God, to whom vengeance belongeth; O God, to whom vengeance belongeth, shew thyself."*

There is coming a new anointing, which the Bible calls "fresh oil," to empower the end-time Church to fulfill its destiny as kings and priests. This is the anointing of the Holy Spirit to execute vengeance on all your adversaries. Ministries that are trying to get by on the old oil and yesteryears' anointing (that old wine) had better come into the knowledge of the truth. God has fresh oil, a new anointing, that will raise up a nation of kings and priests so that the kingdom of God will fill the whole Earth. Get ready for the "fresh oil"!

Some clergymen and laymen say that this revelation for God's vengeance is not true or applicable for today. But by the authority of God's Word, it is true and it is for today. Once Jesus was raised from the dead and was seated at the right hand of the Father, His ministry was completely handed over to the person of the Holy Spirit.

And, as mentioned earlier, one of the jobs of the Holy Spirit is to execute vengeance on behalf of the Church. *"The* LORD *works righteousness and justice for all the oppressed"* (Psalm 103:6 NIV).

MY PERSONAL ENCOUNTER WITH VENGEANCE

I personally experienced the vengeance of the Lord in the acquisition of our shopping mall and worship center. My pursuit of purchasing the mall as the new location of our church home was based on a direct word from the Lord. The church had just signed the deal, with money paid, when without warning we were told by the local village officials that we would not be able to hold our worship services in the complex. I reached out to some professionals about what we should do and one said, "Find another place quickly." Another said, "Sue the village." But it was New Year's Eve, and the church had nowhere else to hold services. It was an impossible situation.

GET READY FOR THIS: YOUR DAYS OF STRUGGLING ARE OVER.

Early that morning, I began praying in the Spirit to get a breakthrough and to receive direction from the Lord on how to handle this situation. Understand, we were expecting thousands of people to attend that night.

In answer to my prayer, the Lord gave me some very specific instructions. He said, "Call a meeting with the mayor. Read Romans, chapter 13, to her and emphasize that she is a minister." The Lord also directed me to type the scriptures in a large font so I could easily read these verses to the mayor. Being obedient to the Lord, I followed these directions exactly as the Lord gave them.

When I met with the mayor around noon, I began reading Romans 13, just as the Lord had directed. While I was reading the scriptures, the Spirit began to move on her heart and the fear of the Lord fell upon her. She then asked if she could call me in a couple of hours after she spoke with the city council to discuss the matter. I left, and about two hours later she called my office and said that she could not locate any council members, but that she would approve our worship service there for one night. She would keep the police away. Though she said "for one night," I knew that God had opened a door for our church that no man could shut. We received "that day" a 24-hour breakthrough. It was the day of the Lord's vengeance!

There was no need for me to get emotional and say or do something that could cause more problems later. I followed the Lord's instructions and allowed Him to fight our battle. As a result, we held our New Year's Eve service in the mall that night, and have been praising God there ever since. God is a master strategist. Once the door opened, the village ordinances were changed to permit our church to have permanent residence on the mall campus.

This is a clear example of why the priest must hear from God and have the integrity, faith, and fortitude to confront and say, *"thus saith the Lord."* This also illustrates how kings and priests work together to fulfill God's plan. Realize, it wasn't people but the devil attempting to block our progress, and he came up against an "unbeatable team"—kings and priests and Almighty God—and was defeated. This unbeatable team and the vengeance of the Lord are why God's people can live with confidence in these last days. I declare that whoever or whatever has been resisting God's plan for your life is stopped today, in Jesus Name!

Now you don't need to be afraid of the dark any-more, nor fear the dangers of the day; nor dread the plagues of darkness, nor disasters in the morning. Though a thousand fall at my side, though ten thousand are dying around me, the evil will not touch me. I will see how the wicked are punished, but I will not share it. For Jehovah is my refuge! I choose the God above all gods to shelter me. How then can evil overtake me or any plague come near? For he orders his angels to protect you wherever you go. They will steady you with their hands to keep you from stumbling against the rocks on the trail. You can safely meet a lion or step on poisonous snakes, yes, even trample them beneath your feet! For the Lord says, "Because he loves me, I will rescue him; I will make him great because he trusts in my name. When he calls on me, I will answer; I will be with him in trouble and rescue him and honor him. I will satisfy him with a full life and give him my salvation" (Psalm 91:5–16 TLB).

PART 4
THE "ROI" OF PERSONAL ACCOUNTABILITY

CHAPTER 10

CHARACTER & INTEGRITY

"Character is power."[1] Booker T. Washington

When I was in the eighth grade, I told my dad a lie. I was supposed to sing in the choir one Friday afternoon, but I played hooky from choir practice (meaning I skipped it without permission) and went to play football instead. The music teacher got angry about it and called my dad at work. I was at home and happened to be passing by the phone when my dad called. I answered the phone, "Hello." "Son, how was choir today?" That was my chance to be honest and repent, but I didn't. I said, "Oh, Dad, it was great. It was just tremendous." "Son, your music teacher, Mrs. Nicholson, called me at work and said you were not there." "She did?" "Son, you have a punishment coming. I'll see you when I get home." When my daddy came home he did not spare the rod. When it was over, my dad simply said, "Son, don't ever lie to me again."

From that point on, I learned not to tell a lie. During my early home training is when I first began to understand the word *integrity*. If possible, children should first learn lessons about character and integrity, and the consequences of not being honest, in the home. Unfortunately, many people have never received proper home training and have had to learn about character and integrity in the church or, God forbid, through the legal system.

CLIMBING WITHOUT COMPROMISE

As I have shared throughout this book, God depends on us to advance His kingdom wherever He assigns us. Once we are born again into His kingdom, God trains us up and sends us into the world to represent Him. Jesus prayed, *"... as my Father hath sent me, even so send I you"* (John 20:21). We become *"ambassadors for Christ"* (2 Corinthians 5:20). Your influence on others, therefore, is critical to your success and theirs.

The best leaders are those who lead by example and influence. Because of their character, authenticity, and performance, people willingly want to follow them. As I've mentioned before, we are not invading the world as dominators, but deployed as liberators, with proper motives focused on demonstrating God's love. When people trust and respect you, they will listen to what you have to say and often want to be like you.

This is what happened to me at IBM when I began experiencing business success. Because of the results I was achieving and the positive changes in my life, people wanted to know if God could do for them what He was doing for me. This is also what happened in the life of Joseph. Because he saved Egypt from the famine through the wisdom of God, he was promoted to rulership over all of Egypt, being second in command only to Pharaoh. Joseph's promotion happened even though the Egyptians of his day thought it was an abomination to even eat with Hebrews (Genesis 43:32).

No matter the "mountain" or sphere of social influence in which you serve, God's plan is for you to go to the top. He knows that whoever occupies the top of the mountain will direct and influence the entire mountain. God wants you to be so successful that you will stand out, not for vainglory but for the glory of God. A key to your success, however, is not to compromise your integrity when faced with temptations. I call it "climbing without compromise." We must remember that whatever beliefs, values, and truth we compromise on the way up the mountain will rule us at the top of the mountain. As one man said, what you compromise to get, you must compromise to keep, and will eventually lose.

TIMES OF GREAT PRESSURE

In 2 Timothy 3:1 AMP, the apostle Paul writes, *"But understand this, that in the last days will come...perilous times of great stress and trouble [hard to deal with and hard to bear]."* The *Merriam-Webster Dictionary* defines *stress* as "something that causes strong feelings of worry or anxiety; a physical force or pressure."[2] Paul warns us that in these times great pressures would come.

The pressure or temptation to cheat, lie, dishonor commitments, or break vows attack people from the pulpit to the pew. The lures of fame and fortune, and the seduction of taking the "fast track" or shortcuts to the top, have caused even strong Christians to stumble. Satan has custom-made temptations for those ascending to the top, which no one can overcome with only human strength.

However, God promises you that *"There hath no temptation taken you but such as is common to man: but God is faithful, who will not suffer you to be tempted above that ye are able; but will with the temptation also make a way to escape, that ye may be able to bear it"* (1 Corinthians 10:13). Simply put, you will not face anything that you cannot overcome, for *"with God all things are possible."*

As we are rising in position and influence, the deception is..."I can do it alone or my way." This too is a carefully crafted temptation. The tendency is to stop putting God's work first and to put your own house first. Now there's the problem. It's like the rich man in Luke 12:16–18 whose *"ground brought forth plentifully...and he said, this will I do: I will pull down my barns and build greater."* To overcome temptation, you must trust in God and make Him your only Source and Sustainer. To win the battles God is leading you to fight, you must *"be strong in the Lord, and in the power of his might"* (Ephesians 6:10) for *"if you faint in the day of* (trouble) *adversity, your strength is small"* (Proverbs 24:10 AMP).

INTEGRITY IN THE KINGDOM OF GOD

Integrity is one of the most important things in the kingdom of God. How does a person act when no one is looking? What do we really do or say when no one is monitoring our every action? *Integrity* is defined as "a firm adherence to a code of especially moral or artistic values: incorruptibility...the state of being complete or undivided."[3] In other words, maintaining righteous standards when there's no one around to see what we're doing; that's integrity.

One 19th century British historian said, "The measure of a man's character is what he would do if he knew he would never be found out."[4] This can be a problem for someone who possesses only situational righteousness. Situational righteousness is akin to situational ethics; this is when a person's ethics change according to the situation or circumstance. No consistent standard is maintained. Therein is the problem.

A lack of integrity leads a person to conform to the world's standards. True integrity is like the foundation of a huge skyscraper—though we cannot see it, there is a foundation that causes the building to stand upright. Integrity emanates from deep within the heart. It is something that causes us to resist things that we shouldn't take part in, even though nobody else is watching.

> **MAINTAINING RIGHTEOUS STANDARDS WHEN THERE'S NO ONE AROUND...THAT'S INTEGRITY.**

For example, Peter told Jesus (in so many words), "Even though the others leave you, I will never leave you" (Matthew 26:33). Yet, after the Lord had been arrested, Peter displayed a lack of integrity when they confronted him saying, "Aren't you one of those who was with Jesus?" Peter lied and said, "No, I was not." This wasn't long after the Lord had told him that he would deny Him three times (verse 34). They asked Peter again, "Excuse me. Aren't you a Galilean? Weren't you with Jesus?" He said, "See that man over there? I just told him I wasn't with the Man." Then someone else came by and asked him again, and the Bible says Peter started cursing and swearing (see verses 69–74).

The question one might ask is what caused Peter to respond this way? The answer is that at this point in his life, Peter lacked integrity. He didn't have inside what he thought he had. You see, pressure has a way of bringing to the surface the things that are deep inside of us. Jeremiah 17:9 says, *"The heart is deceitful above all things, and desperately wicked: who can know it?"*

One man describes integrity as an individual's greatest asset. It means that we will get to the job on time. We are going to punch out when we are actually supposed to. We are going to fill out our expense reports accurately. We will not cheat on our income tax returns. Tax avoidance is legal; tax evasion is not.

Maintaining your integrity shields you against baseless accusation. It won't stop someone from accusing you, but if they do, they'll find no fault in you. While you were unsaved, you were on the devil's side and he didn't care if you cheated on your taxes. But now that you're in the kingdom, he's the accuser of the brethren (Revelation 12:10). He could be down at the IRS (the tax office) pointing you out right now. Therefore, you must maintain integrity in all areas of your life.

Psalm 15 gives an excellent description of integrity, *"In whose eyes a vile person is contemned; but he honoureth them that fear the LORD. He that sweareth to his own hurt, and changeth not. He that putteth not out his money to usury, nor taketh reward against the innocent. He that doeth these things shall never be moved"* (verses 4–5). As we can see here, a person of integrity keeps a promise, even if that promise causes him a great deal of pain. In many situations in life, keeping your word can be costly. But if you promise something, you are to keep that promise.

In Acts 5, we see that strength and integrity returned to Peter when the high priest and rulers of the temple questioned him about preaching in the name of Jesus. Because of the miracles, they had commanded Peter and the other apostles to stop preaching in that name. This time Peter basically tells them, "I don't care what you do to me. I'm not going to deny my Lord, and neither will I stop preaching the gospel in His Name. I ought to obey God than man" (verse 29).

TESTING INTEGRITY

The Bible tells us that when salt loses its savor, it is not good for anything but to be trampled underfoot of men (Matthew 5:13). That's what has been happening to many Christians; we have become ineffective. We haven't known or have forgotten the mission that we have in the world. We have forgotten that we are the Church; the Church is not a building. The world is not our enemy but our mission field, and we are to go out to rescue the lost and to establish God's kingdom.

The unsaved are going to see us, and God will set up a circumstance for us to be a witness. Someone may have a migraine headache and come to us for prayer. We must be ready to say, "I can go to God on your behalf." However, the unsaved won't be coming to us if we give people cause to question our integrity.

THE WORLD IS NOT OUR ENEMY BUT OUR MISSION FIELD.

This is the very reason the enemy is after our integrity—to compromise our witness. In Job, chapter 2, we see that the devil was after Job's integrity. In Genesis, chapter 20, he was after Abraham's integrity. In Genesis, chapter 39, he tried to seize Joseph's integrity. And, in Genesis 31:38–41, he was after Jacob's integrity. Read what Jacob said to Laban:

> This twenty years have I been with thee; thy ewes and thy she goats have not cast their young, and the rams of thy flock have I not eaten. That which was torn of beasts I brought not unto thee; I bare the loss of it; of my hand didst thou require it, whether stolen by day, or stolen by night. Thus I was; in the day the drought consumed me, and the frost by night; and my sleep departed from mine eyes. Thus have I been twenty years in thy house; I served thee fourteen years for thy two daughters, and six years for thy cattle: and thou hast changed my wages ten times.

Jacob had served Laban faithfully. He even made up the difference when a wild beast came in and took one of the sheep. However, Laban had changed Jacob's wages 10 times. This was unfair and scandalous treatment. Clearly, this was a case of the enemy setting Jacob up to cheat. The devil knows that if he gets us to compromise our integrity, we cannot get to our destiny and complete our mission.

Here are several important points to remember about integrity. First, a healthy fear or reverence of God is absolutely necessary to maintain integrity. God is not like men. He sees and knows everything. He is omniscient.

Second, when we maintain our integrity, the Lord stays with us. Our fellowship remains intact. As a result of Joseph's continued fellowship with the Lord, Joseph continued prospering, even while in prison (Genesis 39:20–22).

Third, small acts of integrity, or lack of integrity, do matter. Job 8:7 gives an important piece of wisdom. *"Though thy beginning was small, yet thy latter end should greatly increase."* The *New Living Translation* says it this way, *"Though you started with little, you will end with much."* People have the tendency to treat small things as insignificant and small beginnings as inconsequential. This is a serious mistake. As the parable of the mustard seed teaches, most things in the kingdom start out small. When things appear small, not much importance is often attached to them. Some feel that maintaining integrity under these circumstances is not important. But this is seriously flawed reasoning. A lack of integrity in the beginning stages will short-circuit THE BLESSING and our effectiveness in the kingdom of God.

CHARACTER MUST BE DEVELOPED

To change the world, we must have a superior position and superior principles. These principles include love, peace, goodness, justice, and integrity. Galatians 5:22 calls them the fruit of the Spirit. However, people are not naturally born as good, moral beings. Integrity and character are virtues that have to be developed, which anyone who has ever raised a child can tell you. David said he was born in sin and shaped in iniquity (Psalm 51:5), which is why we need to be born again. The nature that people are born with is sinful.

We all come into this world with a fallen nature. Even though the enemy exploits this fallen nature, it's still our nature and we are still responsible for *our* behaviors. When we come into the kingdom of God, we are born again with God's nature. The problem is that we still wrestle with the flesh, which carries the influence of our fallen nature. The nature that dominates our lives is determined by the one we feed or yield to the most. This is why we must renew our minds to the Word of God (Romans 12:1).

Earlier in this chapter, I defined *integrity* as who we are when no one is looking. Some people may say, "Well, if nobody sees me why does it matter? That's my private moment." My response is that with God we don't have any private moments. God sees everything. Furthermore, we need to understand that our private moments will eventually define our public moments.

The word *character* means "the particular qualities impressed by nature or habit on a person which distinguish him or her from other people."[5] Character is made up of the good qualities of an individual—particularly those that are esteemed and respected. When we come into difficulties—especially unexpected situations—that is when our character manifests.

For example, we can train ourselves how to respond to an emergency, like a fire drill, so that when the situation actually happens, we will be able to draw from our training to respond with wisdom. However, when we are hit with a circumstance for which we are not prepared, what comes out of us is often unexpected. Who we really are comes out when the pressure is on.

God has prepared for us "The Promised Land" (a symbol of God's best), and He wants us to enter into it; however, He is not going to overlook our lack of integrity. This is an area where teaching is seriously needed in the Body of Christ. Our desire for God's blessing is good, but it is vitally important that we first get an understanding of integrity so we can develop properly. One of the worst things that can happen to a person is to become wealthy without having the character and integrity to match.

OUR CHARACTER MANIFESTS WHEN WE ARE FACED WITH DIFFICULT OR UNEXPECTED CIRCUMSTANCES.

We never want to be elevated to a place where our character can't keep us. We can be sure that with each level, there is a new temptation waiting to exploit the weaknesses in our character. Having wealth is a great responsibility that will end up crushing us if we lack the integrity and character to help withstand the pressure. The good news is, like Peter, our integrity can grow stronger, and God is with us to help us overcome every temptation if we trust and rely on Him.

THERMOSTATS OR THERMOMETERS

Years ago, a young immigration officer had to escort a Colombian citizen to the Colombian consulate on Michigan Avenue in downtown Chicago. This Colombian citizen was being deported. Since the person being escorted was a criminal, the officer handcuffed him, as was normal procedure. However, when they walked into the consulate office, the consul ordered the immigration officer to take off the man's handcuffs. At first the officer said no, emphasizing his authority as a U.S. immigration officer. The officer also stated that he was responsible for this man while he was in his custody. The Colombian official looked at the officer and said, "You are no longer in the United States. You are in Colombia, and you are not in authority here—I am. Now, uncuff him." After hearing that, the officer had to submit and do as he was told.

The point is, even though the immigration officer and the Colombian prisoner were physically in Chicago, Illinois, in the United States of America, the second they walked through the doors of that consulate, they were under the authority of another government—Colombia. As ambassadors for the kingdom of God, wherever God plants us, that place now becomes kingdom territory; kingdom values, laws, and power are in authority because of our presence.

Wherever we go, we are to change the environment to a kingdom culture. In order to do that, we have to see ourselves as thermostats. A thermostat is an instrument that dictates whether the atmosphere will be hot or cold. It is different from a thermometer. A thermometer only reflects the current atmosphere. Whatever the temperature is, the thermometer only comes up to that level. So if it's 65 degrees in a room, the thermometer is regulated by that temperature. It can't change the temperature or have any effect on it. It only reflects the current temperature.

A thermostat, on the other hand, regulates its atmosphere. If you want it hotter in the room, you need a thermostat to change the temperature. Thermostats don't reflect; they change the atmosphere to what is desired. This is how we are supposed to be. We are to go into the earth and be world changers. We are supposed to go in and impose heaven in this society, by heating it up, and then society, as the thermometer, is supposed to reflect that change in temperature and come to the Church, where they can catch on fire.

Unfortunately, the Church has had a diminishing influence. We have been more of a thermometer than a thermostat. I believe this has happened because of the lack of integrity that has permeated the Church. Because we have not been practicing, demonstrating, or developing integrity, we lost our position of influence. We have not been the change agents we have been called to be. **I decree that the Church is climbing to a new level of integrity and that we become the world changers God made us to be.**

The Word of God is the source of integrity. The only way that we become kingdom thermostats to regulate our environment is through the Word of God. Second Timothy 2:13 says that even when we are faithless, God is still faithful. No matter where He sends us, His Word will work, but we've got to work His Word. We have to have enough integrity that when the storms come, we will remain steadfast. When we do, the Word of God is so powerful that it will change the atmosphere and environment around us—just like raising the temperature on the thermostat.

WHEREVER WE GO, WE ARE THE ONES WHO CHANGE THE ENVIRONMENT.

The key is that we have to trust in God's Word and be willing to stand on the integrity of His Word until we see manifestation. The enemy's job is to make us double-minded because he knows that a double-minded person cannot receive anything from God. Therefore, it's imperative that we believe God's Word. If we don't believe God's Word, we do not believe God. Remember that John 1:1 says, *"In the beginning was the Word, and the Word was with God, and the Word was God."* We cannot separate God's Word from God

Himself. That is why when you don't believe the Word it is equivalent to not believing God.

God's Word is truth, and *"His truth shall be thy shield and buckler* [or protection]*"* (Psalm 91:4). When a believer lies or is being dishonest, the person weakens their spirit and compromises their supernatural ability. Now, when the trials that are sure to come do come, the person doesn't have enough strength to stand.

SITUATIONAL AWARENESS

I have been flying airplanes for years now, and one of the first steps in safe flying is learning that we have something called "situational awareness." We should know where we are at all times. This same concept is true for the Christian walk. We can't ignore our spiritual guidance system and think, "This doesn't apply to me." That kind of thinking will only take us off course. We have to let our situational awareness kick in.

Look around and ask, "Why am I not doing well yet? After all these years, why am I still struggling with these same problems? Why aren't these promises working for me?" The answer could be that you're off course. You are not aware of what your true position is. You are not paying attention to your GPS, God's Positioning Spirit, which is designed to lead and guide you into all truth. Many of us want to skip some crucial steps, like building integrity and character. It is our responsibility to keep ourselves unspotted from the world

THE WORD OF GOD IS THE SOURCE OF INTEGRITY.

(James 1:27). That's why we see some ministries and companies imploding. One of the jobs of the priest is to teach lessons that will help keep a moral compass among those in the Body of Christ.

The enemy uses situational "unawareness" as a primary weapon against the believer. When we are unaware, the devil can cause us to stumble by transgression, doubting or disobeying God. Then it's God who delays us at that point, because He is not going to compromise His holiness and overlook sin or the lack of integrity. In the world, man promotes mostly on gifts, such as a gifted singer or a gifted basketball player. But God waits on our integrity and character so that as His representatives, we will not impugn His name. The only way some people will ever know what God is like is to look at us.

An example of this truth is found in Daniel, chapter 3. This is when King Nebuchadnezzar had been manipulated into making a golden image and decreeing that everyone should worship it under the threat of death. The ancient Babylonian system was a "type and shadow" of today's world system, a society trying to meet its needs without God. An ungodly law was activated, but as far as the three Hebrew men were concerned, they were not going to bow to any other god, because they were bound to a superior law—God's law.

Verses 16 through 18 say:

> Shadrach, Meshach, and Abednego, answered and said to the king, O Nebuchadnezzar, we are not careful to answer thee in this matter. If it be so, our God whom we serve is able to deliver us from the burning fiery furnace, and he will deliver us out of thine hand, O king. But if not, be it known unto thee, O king, that we will not serve thy gods, nor worship the golden image which thou hast set up.

They were told, in so many words, "If you don't bow and obey the law, you will burn." They said, "Wait a minute, king. We don't have to think about how to answer you in this matter. The God whom we serve is able to deliver us, and He will deliver us out of your hand. We will not serve your gods."

These men had integrity. They were unwavering in their honor and reverence of God, in whom they had absolute trust. Their situational awareness had not been thrown off by their circumstances, even the threat of death. They knew where they were; they knew where God was; and they knew, without a doubt, that He was going to deliver them. They trusted God's Word, which is full of integrity. It cannot fail, and God cannot lie (Titus 1:2).

When the three Hebrew men said *"If it be so,"* many people have interpreted this to mean, "If our God decides to deliver us, He will, and if He doesn't decide to deliver us, we will burn." If you study that scripture you will discover how that interpretation does not harmonize with the covenant. Think about it. If God doesn't deliver them, they are not going to serve anybody's god. They would be burned to a crisp in about two minutes. They were saying, "If you change your mind, king, if you tell us you are not going to throw us in the furnace, we still want you to know that we are not going to serve your god." The Hebrew men were not being double-minded. Their integrity and situational awareness had kicked into high gear. They simply were not afraid of the furnace or the fire.

INTEGRITY PRESERVES AND PROTECTS

God knows that He is sending us into some places that have fiery temptations. But integrity will preserve us—not one time, but every time (Psalm 25:21). Holding fast to God's Word is the only thing to do. If we don't have integrity, we won't hold fast to His Word. Liars don't believe anyone else's words because they don't believe their own.

Titus 1:15 says, *"Unto the pure all things are pure: but unto them that are defiled and unbelieving is nothing pure; but even their mind and conscience is defiled."* It is impossible to lie all day long, then turn around and believe God's Word that night—it won't work! Dishonesty weakens a person's spirit.

With no integrity, the devil gets us to operate in the flesh, trusting in natural skill, competence, and ability. Then, after he has elevated a person, he then exploits their weaknesses, and everything blows up in the person's face. That is not the way God intended for it to be. He intended for your name not to be shamed. He intended for you to be successful coming in and going out. **And I declare from this day forward, you will be!**

Integrity acts as a boundary, and boundaries are good, because you don't want to allow everything to enter your mind or spirit. God gave Adam a boundary in the garden of Eden when He said, *"Don't eat of that tree."* When Adam crossed that boundary through disobedience, he lost more than the garden. I have boundaries set up for my life so I can see things coming afar off. We have boundaries in our household. There are no arguments or strife in our home. We don't allow them.

When that kind of resolve is in your spirit, you can speak things and they will come to pass. It puts you in the driver's seat of your life. You are not a thermometer, you are a thermostat. You came to Earth to change the atmosphere of this Earth. You are an atmospheric regulator!

When we have integrity, we can stand up to those fiery trials that come to try us. We can come through those flames with a praise on our lips. First Peter 1:6–7 gives us this encouragement:

> Wherein ye greatly rejoice, though now for a season, if need be, ye are in heaviness through manifold temptations: that the trial of your faith, being much more precious than of gold that perisheth, though it be tried with fire, might be found unto praise and honour and glory at the appearing of Jesus Christ.

THE FIERY TRIAL OF THE FIRST SHOPPING MALL

When our church was in the process of purchasing our first shopping mall, I knew things were going to heat up. It seemed like the closer we got to the closing, the hotter it got. We didn't have all the money. The lawyers were calling and asking me, "Pastor Winston, where is the rest of the money?" With authority I replied, "I believe I receive it." They said, "Believe you receive? What is that? We need money! Show us the money!"

Then the developers started lining up when they thought that we would not be able to close on the deal. They were saying the same thing as the lawyers: "Where is the money?" So I went to the Lord and said, "Lord, where is the money?" He said, "Wait until Monday. If the money is not there, go to the bank." This is what I called a divinely arranged loan because I had already been to three of the largest banks in Chicago, and none of them would loan us the $2.5 million needed. We had $3 million already saved.

I waited until Monday, and the money still had not manifested. We had sown a significant financial seed, and now we were waiting on our financial miracle. I made one call, and the next day by 11:00 a.m., I had all the money from one of the smallest, minority-owned banks in the city. It's best not to borrow at all. However, because of the level of our faith, this was the way God provided the money we needed. That was a miracle. God had a ram in the bush all the time. Since that time, as I have shared, thousands of souls have been saved at our worship center at this same mall, which has also provided hundreds of jobs through its retail shops.

Proverbs 24:16 AMP says that *"a righteous man falls seven times, and rises again."* If you have a misstep in your walk of faith, get back up because faith is working on your behalf to perfect integrity and character. If you have made Jesus the Lord of your life, God chose you and this is all part of the process. God knows what you have in you, and He knows the work He must do through you. Therefore, do not be too hard on yourself. There is a big difference between the actions of Judas and those of Peter. Judas missed it and hanged himself. Peter missed it, repented and rebounded.

When I worked at IBM, I remember my boss teaching me a very valuable lesson about integrity. He was evaluating me and asked me about a particular customer.

"That man is crazy," I said sarcastically.

My boss responded, "What?"

"Yeah, he's an idiot. He doesn't know what he's talking about," I said.

"Don't ever say that," my boss replied. "The man may not act like you want him to act, but if you call him that, you'll begin to see him that way. And that will lead you into disrespecting our customers."

I have never forgotten those words. In essence, he was saying that your private life will eventually affect your public life. Even your thoughts about someone will eventually manifest in how you treat them.

BEWARE OF NEGATIVE ASSOCIATIONS

One of the biggest temptations the people of God encounter when becoming successful is negative associations. In Proverbs 22:24–25, we are warned *"Make no friendship*

with an angry man; and with a furious man thou shalt not go:
lest thou learn his ways, and get a snare to thy soul."

Simply put, the people you associate with can rub off on
you. If you look at your present behavior, you can probably
track it back to someone you knew. If you hang around angry people too much, you are going to become angry. If you
hang around with people who criticize too much, you will end
up with a critical spirit as well.

Evil communications do corrupt good manners (1 Corinthians 15:33). This is why we have to watch who our children
and loved ones associate with, because somebody else's bad
habits will become theirs. Proverbs 14:12 says, *"There is a*
way which seemeth right unto a man, but the end thereof are
the ways of death." In Proverbs 13, verse 20, we are also
cautioned that *"He that walketh with wise men shall be wise:*
but a companion of fools shall be destroyed." The Bible describes a fool as somebody who will not take instructions. I
don't care how much sense they may claim to possess, if they
won't take God's instruction that is a foolish person, and you
have to watch your association with them.

Folks who are angry, critical, and always talking negatively about someone can affect your vision. As one man rec-
ommended, "You might consider letting go of some friends,
if you know the relationship is toxic. Hanging around them
could affect your ability to see, and could diminish the effectiveness and purpose that God has for your life."[6] For you to
reach your destiny, you must have vision.

The enemy tries to blur your vision. Anytime the vision is
blurred, then you decelerate from moving toward your goal.
Anytime the vision is clear, you accelerate toward your goal.
Distractions and wrong associations can blur vision. Anger,
hatred, jealousy, envy, strife, and division are distractions
that ultimately will affect your (spiritual) sight. The Bible
calls these *"works of the flesh"* (Galatians 5:19–20). There is
no way we can restore the earth by yielding to the flesh and
using the principles of darkness. If the flesh is manifesting
itself in ways it shouldn't, you have spiritual love forces to
subdue it.

STAY ON THE LOVE LINE

Love is essential to reaching our destiny and completing our mission, because it keeps us from compromising. When Potiphar's wife tempted Joseph to "lie with her," his love for God kept him walking in integrity and moral uprightness. Joseph said to her, *"there is none greater in this house than I; neither hath he kept back any thing from me but thee, because thou art his wife: how then can I do this great wickedness, and sin against God?"* (Genesis 39:9). Satan tries to pull you off the "love line" through temptations and offenses to stop you from rising to the top.

Jesus said the greatest commandment is, *"Thou shalt love the Lord thy God with all thy heart, and with all thy soul, and with all thy mind...And the second is like unto it, Thou shalt love thy neighbour as thyself. On these two commandments hang all the law and the prophets"* (Matthew 22:37, 39–40).

Love embodies the kingdom nature. When we walk in honesty, truth, joy, peace, and holiness, we demonstrate the kingdom of God for all to see (Matthew 5:16). First John 4:8 says that *"God is love,"* so when we walk in love, we walk in God and He is with us to help us overcome temptation and to win every battle. Love is a spiritual force that helps us maintain integrity, because the love of God constrains us.

CHAPTER 11

STEWARDSHIP

A steward during biblical times was a manager or overseer to whom the head of the house entrusted the management of household affairs. These affairs could be handling business matters; keeping track of financial expenditures and receipts; or supervising servants, slaves, and even underage children.

A steward today is defined as someone who manages another's property or financial affairs, and administers any personal matter as the agent of another. The main point is that a steward cares for another's possessions as if they were his own.

So what is stewardship in the kingdom of God? Contrary to what many Christians may think, stewardship is not just about money or about how much money you can save. It is also about how we raise our children, how we help our employer achieve company goals, and how we help renew and revitalize our communities and cities. God told Adam to *"Be fruitful, and multiply, and replenish the earth..."* (Genesis 1:28) because he had stewardship responsibilities over the earth.

In the kingdom of God, stewardship is about doing God's work, God's way. For example, in 1 Chronicles 22:14, King David had amassed the equivalent in today's money of over $100 billion[1] in gold to hire the best craftsmen and to buy the finest materials for the construction of the temple. He spared no cost. David was committed to doing God's work, God's way, because he was a *"man after God's own heart."* David's attitude is a long way from taking a building project out to bid and choosing the lowest bidder because they are the cheapest. The lowest bidder could have the worst workmanship and the poorest quality building materials for the vision that God has given you. Again, stewardship is not about how much money you can save God, but about doing God's work, God's way.

Another aspect of stewardship is working to bring increase and solutions to the earth. Again, Adam had the stewardship responsibility of replenishing the earth. *Replenish* means "to stock with abundance, to complete, to recover to former fullness, and to perpetually renew and supply."[2] This mandate still exists today as far as the Church is concerned. God is still expecting mankind to replenish this earth and bring it back to its Edenic glory.

THE THREE SERVANTS

In Matthew 25:14–15, we get an understanding of the type of stewards that God desires us to be, *"the kingdom of heaven is as a man travelling into a far country, who called his own servants...unto one he gave five talents, to another two, and to another one; to every man according to his several ability."* This passage tells us that the talents were distributed to the servants according to their ability. I define *ability* as "level of intelligence, competence, skill, capacity, and giftedness." Based on these factors, God determines what to entrust to you. Initially everyone does not receive the same level of responsibility as it relates to their stewardship; however, God is an "equal opportunity employer." And as we are faithful over that which He gives us, only then does He give us more. In this parable, one servant received five talents. The second received two talents, and the third received one talent.

> **GOD DETERMINES WHAT TO ENTRUST TO YOU.**

Many people interpret these "talents" as being skills or intangible gifts like singing or playing a musical instrument. And that may well be; however, I believe this teaching of Jesus has a double reference, and that the talents mentioned here are also talents of gold. In my research, I discovered the ancient measure of a single talent of gold is worth as much as $2 million (U.S. currency) in today's money.[3] Imagine the Lord entrusting you with $2 million, another person with $4 million, and another person with $10 million.

Verses 16–17 then say, *"Then he that had received the five talents went and traded with the same, and made them other five talents. And likewise he that had received two, he also gained other two."* Their master or Lord then said to both of them, *"Well done, thou good and faithful servant: thou hast been faithful over a few things, I will make thee ruler over many things: enter thou into the joy of thy lord"* (verse 21).

THE GOOD AND PROFITABLE SERVANTS

In these verses, we get a picture of good and profitable servants. These servants obviously took good care of the master's money. They managed it skillfully and were resourceful. Put in today's context, they read their *Wall Street Journals*, did the company research to check the profit margins and company earnings, and then made the decision that led to sound investments. As a result, the first two stewards doubled the master's money. The master was pleased and said to them, *"Well done, thou good and faithful servant."*

Good means "beneficial" in Greek. There are few things more joyous to a boss than to entrust his affairs to an employee who handles them competently and increases his or her bottom line. As a result, promotion usually follows good stewardship. The scriptures speak about promotion for a believer, *"For promotion cometh neither from the east, nor from the west, nor from the south. But God is the judge: he putteth down one, and setteth up another"* (Psalm 75:6–7).

I recall when I was a computer salesman. I started off slow meeting my sales quota. I had been to the computer training that the company offered but things just weren't happening. After some major changes in my personal life, I began to see the light. My sales skills developed to the degree that I could predict months in advance when I would close new business for the company. My boss was well pleased with my performance and put me next in line for promotion. The company taught me the mechanics of selling, but the number one success book in the world, the Bible, gave me the knowledge and faith that put me over the top. I was awarded "Top Salesman" in my office in downtown Chicago.

So, what I am saying is, as a believer, your promotion doesn't really come from your supervisor; it comes from God. Through their God-given gifts and talents, and above all their faithfulness, these servants doubled their master's money and brought increase into the master's house. In Proverbs he writes: *"If you care for your orchard, you'll enjoy its fruit; if you honor your boss, you'll be honored"* (Proverbs 27:18 *Message Translation*). It's interesting how we can't get around the spiritual law that says..."A *man's harvest in life will depend entirely on what he sows"* (Galatians 6:7 *PHILLIPS Translation*).

THE WICKED AND UNPROFITABLE SERVANT

In Matthew 25:24–30, however, we read something very different about the third servant who was given one talent. Notice this servant's attitude toward his master and about his responsibility.

> He which had received the one talent came and said, Lord, I knew thee that thou art an hard man,... and I was afraid, and went and hid thy talent in the earth:...His lord answered...*Thou* wicked and sloth-ful servant...thou oughtest therefore to have put my money to the exchangers, and *then*...I should have received mine own with usury.

This third servant was called "wicked" because of a number of reasons, which made him "unprofitable" (verse 30). Let's look and hopefully learn from some of the critical mistakes this servant made. First, this servant was full of excuses, which are often the reasons a person gives for inaction and incompetence. Oddly, people who don't do anything often have the most elaborate reasons for doing nothing, and it's always about them.

Second, self-centered people always have the wrong perspective about the people in leadership over them, because they see the world through their own selfish (twisted) lens. The master calls him "wicked," which refers to someone or something evil or twisted or deviating from divine law. Faith is not making God or someone else responsible for the outcome. I call that "religion." **Real faith is sharing responsibility with God.** Notice, this servant tried to shift the blame and all the responsibility for his inaction onto his master's shrewd temperament. No. When our part is done, then God's part is guaranteed.

In today's vernacular, he was really saying, "Since I know you are basically unfair and unpredictable, I was scared to take a chance with your money." The servant blames his laziness and lack of trust on his master. I've found that when God gives you something to do or say, He seems to always take you past your comfort zone...beyond your own natural ability. And He seems to always leave you with a choice, one of faith and the other of human reason or logic usually based on fear. Remember, the enemy's goal is to keep us within the limits of reason, like he did to Eve in the garden of Eden; thus keeping us confined to our own ability and not tapping into the ability of our invisible partner, God.

> **REAL FAITH IS SHARING RESPONSIBILITY WITH GOD.**

Third, this servant wasn't interested in increasing or profits. However, bosses are usually always interested in increasing and improving their "bottom line." The only thing they do not want to increase is non-productivity or loss. Here's a revelation: In the kingdom of God, there is no such thing as "nonprofit," even though local churches in the United States and in some other nations are established this way because of government laws. There is no "nonprofit" in the kingdom. Everything done related to the kingdom is for the profit and advancement of the kingdom. One book defines *profit* as "a legitimate measurement of the value on (your) effort."[4]

Finally, the servant who was given one talent hindered it from increasing by burying it. He didn't use it as seed for bearing fruit in the kingdom of God. As a result, his master took away all that he had. To say it plainly, he was fired! And his master gave his talent to the one who had the most increase. I call it "putting money where money is made." I believe this is what's going on in the local Church today.

Because the Lord really cares for people, He is leading them from one ministry to another where they can be fed and fruitful. One where there is a focus on preparing, teaching, disciplining, and delivering value to people to send out into a hurting world and fulfill their destinies. Remember, it's all about advancing the kingdom.

By burying the talent, he didn't lose it, but he created a loss for the kingdom. Can you see that? Why? Because he didn't use it to generate increase. It's amazing how success can be sometimes perceived as evil. I've heard ministers say, "Oh, he's taking all my members." Or, "The people are leaving our denomination and going to those non-denominational churches." Well, maybe God is just reallocating His resources for profit. He's "putting money where money can be made."

In business or in the marketplace, "religion" has told us...you are expected to make a profit, but not expected to feel good about it for fear of becoming too materialistic. Well, here's the right way to look at it: Profit to a businessperson should be like winning to an athlete. It should be almost second nature. I heard someone say, "God designed both of them (sex and profit) for an honorable purpose...either can be abused."[5] Proverbs 28:20 says: *"A faithful man shall abound with blessings: but he that maketh haste to be rich shall not be innocent."* The faithful man in this passage is the "good steward," and God promises that he shall abound or have abundant blessings. But those *"...who makes haste to be rich [at any cost] shall not go unpunished"* (AMP).

THE SEED OF FAITHFULNESS

Webster's New World College Dictionary defines *faithfulness* or *faithful* as "maintaining an allegiance to someone or something: to be constant, loyal, having or showing a strong sense of duty or responsibility."[6]

Faithful is reliable, trusted, or believed. The idea is to have freedom from fickleness in affections or loyalties. The opposite of faithful is failure to adhere to an oath, duty, or obligation, being dishonest, disloyal, unreliable, or undependable. In Proverbs 25:19 it says: *"Confidence in an unfaithful man in time of trouble is like a broken tooth, and a foot out of joint."* People who are not dependable can be detrimental to an organization or team that depends on them. A faithful person, however, can always be trusted.

In the parable of the talents, the lord said to each servant who dutifully attended to the lord's business, *"Well done, thou good and faithful servant: thou hast been faithful over a few things, I will make thee ruler over many things."* He promoted them. So, promotion not only comes from being a good steward, but is also one of the benefits of faithfulness. In looking back to the book of Genesis at the life of Joseph, in each situation or environment where he was placed, Joseph kept getting promoted and having more influence. Like Joseph, we all have to develop faithfulness, learn to keep our Word, and how to withstand tough circumstances and let patience have her perfect work. In doing so, you are actually sowing a sacrifice seed of faith in God's faithfulness. In Hebrews it says, *"he is faithful that promised,"* which means He keeps His Word. Promotion for Joseph came *through* the Egyptians, but it didn't come *from* the Egyptians. God is not going to overlook our faithfulness or the lack of it.

When my family came to Chicago to start our ministry, we only had $200 to our name, but we were obedient and faithful to what the Lord had called us to. We started having services at our first location, a small store-front church at Lake and Pulaski Streets on Chicago's West Side. One night, someone stole our car. We now had to take public transportation, as the money we received from the insurance claim was hardly enough to purchase another vehicle. By faith, we sowed that insurance money—all of it—counting on the faithfulness of God. For almost eight months, we walked and rode the "L," Chicago's elevated rapid train system, because we didn't want to go into debt. It was important for us to be examples for our church members. We often had to wait for a train on a freezing platform in a brutal Chicago winter. But through it all, we remained

PROMOTION IS ONE OF THE BENEFITS OF FAITHFULNESS.

faithful standing on God's Word. Veronica had her guitar in one hand and our son, David, in the other (He is now married and the youth pastor at our church). Each night while we were out there, we were divinely positioned, and with divine positioning come divine protection and divine provision. Today, we have more than enough transportation, even bringing others to church services.

ETERNAL BENEFITS OF FAITHFULNESS

Faithfulness also has eternal benefits. With the average person, there is a tendency to live like there is no afterlife. However, the reality is that everyone is going to live on eternally somewhere, whether it is in heaven or hell. When the faithful servants in Matthew 25 were told, *"I will make thee ruler over many things: enter thou into the joy of thy lord,"* that was not just a "right now" joy but an everlasting joy. Faithful servants will be honored for their faithfulness throughout eternity. This places urgency on preaching the gospel and leading people to Christ. God places a desire in our hearts to go out and persuade men and women about the kingdom and we will receive eternal rewards for our witness.

As stewards, we will all give account before the all-knowing, all-seeing Lord, who will judge us according to our abilities, gifts, service, faithfulness, righteousness, attitudes, and motivations—in everything whether good or bad. Everything will be laid out before the Lord for judgment, and we shall receive rewards according to our own labor in the kingdom (1 Corinthians 3:7, 14). May these same words be spoken about your life at the end: **"Well done, my good and faithful servant."**

Being good and faithful stewards involves our witness to the world. This is why living righteous lives, being effective witnesses and maintaining integrity are so important. We are ambassadors for the kingdom of light, and we are the only "Jesus" some people are going to see until He returns. Until then, we are all the world has to point them to Christ. We must be the beacons of light and the salt of the earth the world needs. Wherever we are assigned, on the mission field or in the marketplace, *"Let your light so shine that men may see your good works and glorify your Father which is in heaven"* (Matthew 5:16).

STEWARDSHIP AND EXCELLENCE

As stewards, we want to be like Daniel. King Darius appointed 120 kingdom protectors over the Medo-Persian Empire and over the three presidents, of which Daniel was first. The Bible says in Daniel 6 that Daniel was preferred above the other leaders around him because he had an excellent spirit, and *"the king thought to set him over the whole realm... he was faithful, neither was there any error or fault found in him"* (verses 3–4). The *Good News Bible Translation* says, *"Daniel was reliable and did not do anything wrong or dishonest."* The *New International Version* says, *"They could find no corruption in him, because he was trustworthy and neither corrupt nor negligent."*

King Darius was so pleased with Daniel that he placed Daniel in a position above all the other presidents and princes. This is something that every steward should strive for—to be known for honesty, excellence and placed in a position of influence. *Excellence* is defined as "attention to detail that gives rise to superior performance that leads to promotion in life." This Daniel was unsurpassed in handling the king's business.

On the surface, Daniel was at a disadvantage, being a Jew taken captive to serve in the Medo-Persian government. Daniel was surrounded by jealousy, hate, and prejudiced people who didn't like him—yet he was getting promoted. That's what I call, "The Lord preparing a table before me in the presence of my (his) enemies." As stewards, when we are divinely positioned, we are divinely protected as well.

Even when Daniel's enemies set up a cunning trap to destroy him, his faithful stewardship delivered him. They persuaded the king to pass a decree that anyone caught praying to any other god or man but the king for the next 30 days would be thrown into the lion's den. Even though Daniel was faithful to the king,

GOD'S HEAVENLY LAWS ARE HIGHER THAN ANY EARTHLY LAWS.

he refused to dishonor or be unfaithful to God. Anytime our faithfulness to a king or government violates our faithfulness to the King of kings, we are to follow Daniel's example and stay on the Lord's side.

God's heavenly laws are higher than any earthly laws. The kingdom of God rules over all! Daniel was thrown into the lions' den because of an unjust law. But, like Daniel, if we stand on God's Word and remain faithful to Him, God will be faithful to us. He will do for us what He did for Daniel: protect, preserve, promote, and distinguish us.

The United States Marines have a saying in Latin, *Semper Fidelis* (Semper Fi), which means "always faithful." In the face of hard circumstances, remember to stay faithful. Don't give up. **"Endure hardness as a good soldier,"** for there is a due season coming for you. The dividend must surely answer to the investment someday. As Galatians 6:9 says, *"And let us not be weary in well doing: for in due season we shall reap, if we faint not."*

PART 5
ADVANCING THE KINGDOM OF GOD

CHAPTER 12

THE WEALTH TRANSFER

For almost a year, I ministered on the topic of the "Supernatural Wealth Transfer." I shared that it is God's plan to periodically hand over the wealth of the wicked to the just, the people of God. I'm talking about hard assets. This is His divine plan. Like other operations in the kingdom of God, they cannot be scientifically analyzed. God said, *"For my thoughts are not your thoughts, neither are your ways my ways"* (Isaiah 55:8).

He plans for every good man to leave an inheritance for his children's children (grandchildren). God is not timid about His opinion. Proverbs 13:22 says, *"A good man leaveth an inheritance to his children's children: and the wealth of the sinner is laid up for the just."* He clearly states that He expects you to provide for your spouse, children, and your grandchildren. Obviously, God does not expect His people to be poor.

Today, the Lord is allowing those who the Bible describes as wicked to stack up great sums of wealth for the sons and daughters of God. *"This is the portion of a wicked man with God...Though he heap up silver as the dust, and prepare raiment as the clay; he may prepare it, but the just shall put it on, and the innocent shall divide the silver"* (Job 27:13, 16–17). We are the just or righteous.

In short, God has given the wicked a ministry. He has commissioned them to heap up riches. Why? To transfer it into the hands of the righteous. Don't for a moment think scarcity or shortage. There is enough wealth here on Earth to establish a worldwide kingdom that will alleviate every physical need known to mankind. The problem is, it's been hidden and in the wrong hands.

All the money of cheats, loan sharks, embezzlers, racketeers, and lending establishments that charge unreasonable interest rates—all stolen wealth—will be given over to those who will pity the poor. Understand this is Bible, not God hating on people. The scripture says, *"God so loved the world..."* that includes wicked folk. However, He has declared that *"He that by usury and unjust gain increaseth his substance, he shall gather it for him that will pity the poor"* (Proverbs 28:8). If you will examine the situation closely concerning the gospel, you will see that failure to evangelize is not a people problem, but mostly a financial problem, along with effective prayer. To move the kingdom forward takes spiritual power and financial abundance.

Because of Adam's sin, mankind was lost and the earth was no longer in the hands to whom God had given dominion. However, because of Jesus' coming and His work of redemption, God is working His plan of salvation, which includes material wealth. One of the major things coming in this hour, which has occurred several times in biblical history, is a supernatural transfer of wealth from the ungodly into the hands of the righteous, God's people. Someone once told me, "Redemption is not complete without divine provision."

Through platforms, such as divine favor, for instance, over four hundred years of labor was paid for in arrears in one day (Exodus 3:21). Before the children of Israel departed Egypt, they became extremely wealthy overnight carrying with them money (gold and silver) in sacks. One of satan's deceptions is to get a person who is born again to think that healing and riches don't come in the same package. No! Health and riches are in the same redemption package. *"He brought them forth also with silver and gold: and there was not one feeble person among their tribes"* (Psalm 105:37).

This wealth transfer was the result of a prophetic agenda planned by God and it happened on a national or corporate scale. God spoke this prophetic word to Abraham concerning the seed of Abraham hundreds of years earlier saying, *"And also that nation, whom they shall serve, will I judge: and afterward shall they come out with great substance* (wealth)" (Genesis 15:14). And it happened right on time, just as God spoke it. He gave the children of Israel favor, and as one friend of mine says, "one act of favor can be worth years of labor."

Wealth transfers can also happen in the lives of individuals, or on a personal level. When a person obeys the kingdom principles that govern increase, money, and wealth, God can supernaturally transfer property, patents, assets, and even entire businesses into his or her possession.

For you to excel in whatever area God has placed you, you need wisdom. Through the wisdom of God, problems can be solved and we can get all kinds of ideas, concepts, and insights. The Scriptures tell us that in these last days ingenious waves of creativity will come through the Church (Ephesians 3:10). This wisdom will reveal better ways of doing things, and a "ten times better" approach to solving problems. Just as Joseph, through godly wisdom, was raised up to prominence and took over the government of Egypt, God is raising up His people with godly wisdom, which always brings wealth (Proverbs 3:16).

Many people believe, "If I can just work hard and long enough I'll get rich!" I'm certainly not against a good day's work, but how many have died trying to just make enough to retire on? It is not working alone that makes one rich. It is creative work that guarantees productivity and, in turn, wealth. In most cases, the missing link in labor is wisdom, whether that labor involves a nation or an individual. The economy of a country is never the problem. It is the mentality or lack of godly wisdom that can cause the economy of a country to suffer. A country, a company, or an individual will prosper and be in health even as their soul (mind, will, and emotions) prospers (see 3 John 2).

As the Bible teaches, all the wealth in the universe came out of wisdom (Psalm 104:24). Remember, most of the time wisdom does not find a path, it creates a new one. This wisdom is our heritage according to Revelation 5:12, and it's time to rise up and take delivery of what belongs to us. Our ministry was able to take possession of our 33-acre retail shopping mall through the principles of wisdom, divine favor, and sowing and reaping. Here is another account of how it happened.

In the earlier years of our ministry in Chicago we used to hold our services in a banquet hall that we were renting on Sundays and Wednesdays. One Sunday after our third service, I came out of the front door of the facility and looked across the street at a large shopping mall. It was almost vacant and had been in decline for several years.

As I looked at it, the Lord spoke to my heart and said, "Buy that mall." At that time, it was not officially for sale and two previous owners were unsuccessful in making it profitable. The mall was huge, larger than anything I could see myself believing for. I was going to have to completely renew my mind to thinking like God. Remember, the beginning step to creating abundance is to align our thoughts to God's.

When I decided to obey God, only then did He give me "word seed" to meditate from the Bible to transform my thinking. God does nothing without a seed. Luke 8:11 says, *"The seed is the word of God"* and it's the platform for all increase in the kingdom of God. Sowing and reaping is the cardinal law that controls everything in the kingdom of God. Once I began meditating the scripture He gave me, which was Joshua 1:3, the light of revelation broke through in my thinking. My capacity to receive was immediately expanded, and the understanding of how I could do what God was asking me to do came to me. *"The entrance of thy words giveth light; it giveth understanding unto the simple"* (Psalm 119:130).

As a part of His instructions, the Lord directed me to sow a financial seed from the ministry, part of what I was saving to someday buy our own worship center building. And when I obeyed God, miracles began to happen. We had favor with the sellers and they dropped the asking price down to something unheard of. We ended up purchasing the property for millions less than initially proposed. I'm almost tempted to say, "We got it at a steal." Since our purchase of the mall, we have restored the entire property, created more than 400 jobs, and through our construction of a worship center,

SOWING AND REAPING IS THE CARDINAL LAW THAT CONTROLS EVERYTHING IN THE KINGDOM OF GOD.

thousands have given their lives to Christ. Our mall's success has significantly upgraded the economy of the entire
local community.

I believe that we, the children of God, are at the season
of the greatest "end-time" transfer of wealth in the history
of this planet. Millions and billions in money, assets, and
ideas are coming into the Body of Christ. I can see in a vision
inventions are coming through the people of God that will
astound the world and make today's technology seem like
child's play. Understand that the covenant of God promises
to bless us so that we can be a blessing.

Jesus took personal responsibility for the darkness over
this earth saying, *"I am the light of the world,"* and as His
representatives, we are mandated to do the same. We should
see the drug problem, not as the world's problem, but as the
Church's problem. Poverty and sicknesses in the nations,
illiteracy and every other form of social disease should be
viewed as something the Church is responsible to eradicate.
We should be continuing in the covenant God made with
Abraham, *"...in thee shall all families of the earth be blessed"*
(Genesis 12:3). Here are some biblical reasons based on
scripture for the transfer of wealth.

Reason No. 1: To Advance the Kingdom of God

The first reason is for funding and advancing the kingdom and to **rapidly** evangelize the world, bringing in the end-
time harvest of souls; in short, to carry out the Great Commission given to the Body of Christ by our Lord. *"Go ye into
all the world, and preach the gospel to every creature"* (Mark
16:15). God needs the wealth in our hands to fulfill the call
that is on our lives for this generation, and to reclaim what
Jesus redeemed. There are billions of souls who need to be
reached with the gospel today.

Reason No. 2: To Build His Temple

A second reason is to *"prepare him an habitation"* (Exodus 25:8). There was only one thing the children of Israel
could use all that wealth for in the middle of *"the wilderness
of Sinai"*—to build Him a tabernacle or temple. The Bible

says, *"we are the temple of God"* (2 Corinthians 6:16). The Church is the true (spiritual) temple of the Living God and the wealth of the wicked is for us to build Him a temple. We are to make disciples of all nations, and to transform their lives into productive, mature sons of God, teaching and bringing them from living and struggling under the curse to living under THE BLESSING.

Tens of thousands of churches must be started, buildings and training centers must be built, and the debts in the Church and on churches must be paid off. The pastors and missionaries and other members of the five-fold ministry need proper equipment and facilities to help them bring the saving message of Jesus Christ to hundreds of souls. David paid for the building of the first temple at Jerusalem with the wealth they took as spoils in their battles against the heathen nations, which, by the way, was billions. Solomon, who actually built the first temple, didn't have to borrow a dime. To be rich is your birthright (Revelation 5:12); the saving of every soul is your responsibility. This goes all the way back to the words God released over Adam and Eve, *"And God blessed them, and said unto them, Be fruitful, and multiply and replenish the earth, and subdue it"* (Genesis 1:28).

Reason No. 3: To Restore Communities, Cities, and Nations

A third reason is to *"replenish and subdue the earth."* Again, the word *replenish* means "to stock with abundance, to recover former fullness or to perpetually renew and resupply." In the book of Ezekiel, it describes the cities and communities where the people of God will be, not employed, but deployed, *"And they shall say, This land that was desolate is become like the garden of Eden"* (Ezekiel 36:35). It takes financial resources to subdue and rebuild, and we are supposed to have more than enough to finish the job.

In Isaiah 61:4 it says, *"And they shall build the old wastes, they shall raise up the former desolations, and they shall repair the*

> TO BE RICH IS YOUR BIRTHRIGHT AND THE SAVING OF EVERY SOUL IS YOUR RESPONSIBILITY.

waste cities, the desolations of many generations." Again, wealth is to come from the sinner (kingdom of darkness) who God is allowing to stack up billions and trillions worth of wealth for the righteous. *"For God giveth to a man that is good in his sight wisdom, and knowledge, and joy: but to the sinner he giveth travail, to gather and to heap up, that he may give to him that is good before God. This also is vanity and vexation of spirit"* (Ecclesiastes 2:26).

These scriptures make clear God's plan to enable the Church to walk in financial dominion, not redistribution; that's a socialist concept, but "wealth transfer," that's a kingdom concept. As we meet the needs of others, God said He will give us more resources so that we can give again.

Here are some scriptures that validate this claim: *"He that hath pity upon the poor lendeth unto the LORD; and that which he hath given will he pay him again"* (Proverbs 19:17). *"Give, and it shall be given unto you; good measure, pressed down, and shaken together, and running over, shall men give into your bosom"* (Luke 6:38). *"God is able to make it up to you by giving you everything you need and more so that there will not only be enough for your own needs but plenty left over to give joyfully to others"* (2 Corinthians 9:8 TLB).

A loud and clear call that I passionately repeat throughout this book is that we—through the divine partnership of kings and priests—are sent to lift the curse off nations that would otherwise have no hope. The same way some nations around the world honor and look to the United States for aid and leadership, these nations will honor the kingdom of God when it is properly preached and demonstrated.

YOUR INEXHAUSTIBLE SUPPLY

Finally, as a kingdom citizen, you have a heavenly account, a "supernatural supply." Just like you may have an earthly bank account, you now have a "Heavenly Account." The main difference is that this heavenly account is inexhaustible. This storehouse for all God's people is referred to in some nations as a commonwealth (see the definition of *commonwealth* in chapter 2, "Kings & Priests: The Kingdom"), except this storehouse cannot be exhausted.

The world and all the wealth in it belongs to God. He gave it to Jesus and we are joint heirs with Him. There is no limit to the wealth that you have inherited. And everyone who makes God their Source automatically becomes as rich as God. He's not a trillionaire and makes you only a millionaire. NO! God makes you as rich as He is… *"And all that I have is thine"* (Luke 15:31; Genesis 25:5).

This is the way a true covenant works. It makes you one. Even if He wants to change His mind of His covenant…He can't. *"My covenant will I not break, nor alter the thing that is gone out of my lips. Once have I sworn by my holiness that I will not lie to David"* (Psalm 89:34–35). So, if there is ever a shortage on Earth, then there is an enormous supply in God's great invisible warehouse, which by faith can be accessed, materializing much more than this world could ever need or desire.

CHAPTER 13

MIRACLES IN THE MARKETPLACE

The divine partnership of kings and priests is critical for the Body of Christ, the Church, to complete its number one mission, which is to advance the kingdom of God and establish heaven's government wherever we are sent. The Lord God is restoring this "partnership" revelation, which will move the Church into a place of distinction and unquestionable dominion over all the earth. Jesus came preaching, *"The time is fulfilled, and the kingdom of God is at hand: 'Repent'..."* which means to "change your mind and your belief system...return to the original state." Through Christ, God was restoring things back to the way things were in Eden, the garden of God.

When God restores, He never just brings it back to its original state. Observe what was written about Job: *"And the LORD turned the captivity of Job...the LORD gave Job twice as much as he had before"* (Job 42:10). So, the Lord blessed the latter end of Job more than his beginning (Job 42:12). We have not seen anything compared to what God is now going to do. There will not only be healing and deliverance, but also financial miracles of phenomenal proportions.

I have often said that Christianity was never meant to be dictated but demonstrated. Most of Jesus' miracles were performed in the marketplace not in the temple. The same was true of His disciples. The miracles were performed where crowds of people could witness the love and power of God and His kingdom that was being preached.

Miracles are not just healings, casting out demons, or opening of blind eyes. Miracles also include: Jesus turning

CHRISTIANITY WAS NEVER MEANT TO BE DICTATED BUT DEMONSTRATED.

water to wine, not so they could just drink it all, but to be a wedding gift of 180 gallons of the best-aged wine in the world, probably valued at millions in today's dollars; or Jesus turning a few fish into a meal to feed the crowds; or Peter's miraculous catch of fish (which today would be like a stockbroker's tip that in one day returned millions in profit). When you command signs and wonders, you operate above what's going on in the world. You are in perfect control of life's situations.

Miracles are also in the form of witty inventions; solutions to seemingly unsolvable problems in society, such as gang violence and teenage murders; as well as supernatural economic advancements that bring new jobs and opportunities to the poor and disenfranchised in our cities and nations around the world. We are partakers of God's wisdom and power.

Miracles in the marketplace are a kingdom strategy to ultimately point people to the one true God. If you will recall, Pharaoh didn't ask about Joseph's family and father until Joseph solved Pharaoh's problems. Today, wherever believers

MIRACLES IN THE MARKETPLACE ARE A KINGDOM STRATEGY TO ULTIMATELY POINT PEOPLE TO THE ONE TRUE GOD.

are being sent, the supernatural is no longer an option, it is a requirement. We are designed to operate above the very best the world has to offer. When we begin to demonstrate our Christianity and the power of the government we represent, we will create a platform that will cause people to begin inquiring about our Father and His family.

Rather than complaining about the problems and what is wrong with our society, this divine "dream team" will provide solutions, alternatives, and most importantly, godly leadership in these challenging and exceptional times, as Joseph did when partnering with Pharaoh in Egypt. Instead of grumbling about what's coming out of Hollywood, the Church will raise up screenwriters, producers, directors, and actors. No sphere of influence will be untouched by marketplace ministers as they invade every high place or mountain of influence in our society.

We're coming into a time when the decisions of people who have a large footprint are more critical than ever. When they put their foot down it causes a rippling effect throughout their entire industry because their influence is so great. Without the wisdom of God, many people could be put in harm's way because of the weight of the ideas and the decisions made by these influencers. In the end, society should reflect the Church's influence. *"And they shall say, This land that was desolate is become like the garden of Eden"* (Ezekiel 36:35).

Over the decades, the Church has seen its influence diminished, especially in Western cultures, mainly because we have not taught and demonstrated the power of the "Word of the kingdom." We have become more like the world, rather than the world becoming more like us, resulting in the obscuring of vision or purpose and a dissipation of power and influence. We replaced revelation with only information, power with entertainment, faith with logic, and love with the law, all resulting in a decrease of the anointing or miracle-working power. This is the same thing that happened to Samson, who was stronger than any other man through God's anointing, when he was taken into captivity by the Philistines. He lost his strength and his eyesight, resulting in his inability to function as a judge over the nations. Consequently, the Church has been unable to bring transformation to our communities and the nations we live in.

But here's the good news! God has saved the best for last. As kings and priests, and ambassadors appointed by our King through the revelation of our callings and this end-time relationship, we shall reclaim and recover all that Jesus redeemed. We are on the move! *"Whereas thou has been forsaken and hated...I will make thee an eternal excellency, a joy of many generations"* (Isaiah 60:15). The *Good News Translation* says, *"...I will make you great and beautiful, a place of joy for ever and ever."* Everything contrary to the rule, justice and laws of heaven shall be brought under subjection.

A CALL FOR THE MIRACULOUS

People are hungry for the supernatural, and I believe a love for the miraculous is in every man and woman. The heart craves the supernatural, whether young or old, rich or poor, intellectual or non-academic; the call for the miraculous is deep-seated in mankind. Denial of the supernatural makes Christianity simply an ethical religion. And by the way, the supernatural does not always have to be spectacular or the "Big Bang."

An example of the supernatural is demonstrated when our church purchased its first shopping mall in the Chicago area, a story I share thoughout the book. We had great opposition from the local government and other "onlookers" who just didn't think a church group could do that, at least not something that large.

> **DENIAL OF THE SUPERNATURAL MAKES CHRISTIANITY SIMPLY AN ETHICAL RELIGION.**

I believe the local government's objection came out of the traditional mindset of its leadership regarding religion (i.e., the separation of church and state), along with the thinking that a black pastor, with largely African American congregants, would probably bring the poor and those with low income into a predominantly white community.

I also believe a bigger issue was the reputation of the "Church" as a "nonprofit" organization that would take a large amount of taxable income property off the village's tax rolls. Overall, I believe they saw us as not providing solutions, but as being part of the problem.

The outcome was that through a series of miracles (see chapter 18, "Taking Possession") we took possession of the mall property, providing the city government with retail shopping and restaurants, along with millions of dollars of sales tax revenues. In addition, the mall is the location of our Joseph Business School and the home of our worship center. In short, the mall has become a miracle in the marketplace.

A subsequent mayor of the village where the mall is located later shared that the village did not have to lay off a single employee during the economic crisis of 2008, unlike the surrounding villages. I'd like to think that our church and the mall's retail businesses had a hand in this great testimony. It is important that we, the Church, bring something of value to the community and the world. The psalmist David writes about what we, as believers, are to expect regarding our businesses and our personal lives: *"They will not suffer when times are bad; They will have enough in time of famine"* (Psalm 37:19 *Good News Bible*).

> **IT'S IMPORTANT THAT THE CHURCH BRING VALUE TO THE COMMUNITY.**

THE DEEP CALLS TO THE DEEP

Every human being comes into the earth with a purpose. God decided our purpose before we were born. He predestined the "why we were born" and the "what we were born to do."

Someone might be born to be a farmer, a physician, to work in construction, to care for children or to be a school teacher; another person is perhaps born to be a dental hygienist, or maybe a judge, policeman, or a plumber. One might ask, "Why on earth would someone want to be a plumber?" Well, if your sink is stopped up, I'm sure your question would be easily answered. We are all born for a purpose and with a gift to serve humanity.

The purpose of every individual weighs on him or her whether he or she is 12 or 92 years old. In Ecclesiastes 3 it says, *"I have seen the burden God has laid on the human race"* (verse 10 NIV). The word *burden* in the Hebrew is translated "employment, occupation or responsibility."[1] There is a longing or feeling (burden) that comes from God. It's something you feel responsible to do. Why? Because of His purpose in you. The *"Deep calleth unto* (the) *deep"* (Psalm 42:7) meaning that what God placed in your own heart is in His heart.

The Bible says He knew us before our members were formed in our mother's womb. God's order is purpose first. Then He creates something or someone with the gifting or talent to fulfill that purpose. Every human being was created to accomplish something no one else can accomplish.

He then stimulates your imagination based on your gifting and His plan for your accomplishment.

Ecclesiastes 3:1 tells us, *"To every thing there is a season, and a time to every purpose under heaven."* So, you and I were meant to be born at this time in history. If we were born centuries ago, we would be most unhappy because we would have been living in the wrong time. We were meant to be born... *"For such a time as this."*

What is inside you—your potential, your purpose, and your gifting—is for today...for this time, not for centuries ago. It makes no difference how you came into the world or where you are in life today. Successful or in the most deplorable condition, you have a purpose for being here and your time is now.

I once read a story where an artist set up his canvas in the park intending to paint a picture of the trees and landscape on a beautiful spring day. All of a sudden he saw a homeless man, unshaven and in need of a bath, lying over against a wall, with clothes torn, eating what someone had obviously thrown away.

The artist decided to paint a picture of the man. After some time had passed, the homeless man decided to inquire, "What are you painting?" The artist replied, "I'm painting a picture of you." The homeless man said further, "Is it okay if I see it?" The artist responded, "Sure, I just finished it."

When the man looked at the picture of himself, to his amazement what he saw was a businessman, smartly dressed, well-groomed, obviously successful and prosperous in life. He said, "Is that me?" The artist replied, "That's the 'you' I see." The homeless man then replied with courage and resolve, "Then that's the man I'll be!"

In biblical history, God had a purpose, or plan, and created a young man named Joseph to fulfill it. Esther, a Hebrew girl, ended up at the right place, at the right time, a queen in a heathen kingdom. Her strategic, divine positioning caused the children of Israel to be saved from being totally destroyed through an enemy of the Jews named Haman.

So, not doing what we are supposed to do, or not going where we're supposed to go, could have a profound ripple effect. In fact, I believe this is one of the things that plagues humanity. We've got a bunch of people doing something other than what they have been called to do.

I remember when I was called into the five-fold ministry. I was working in the marketplace at IBM making more money than I had ever made. There was a "call" I heard every morning when I woke up, one that came from outside this world. It was *deep calling unto* (the) *deep.*

One day I finally opened my Bible and read Isaiah 6:8, *"Then said I, Here am I; send me."* When I repeated these words out loud, it seemed like the world lifted off my shoulders. I had said yes to what I was now called to do from the foundation of the world. Think about those who are incarcerated, put in prison for selling drugs in their community. One can only reflect on how much better their communities would be if these individuals, with entrepreneurial talents, had been trained and directed to the right legal businesses and professions, building the economy and improving the standard of living of their neighborhoods.

YOUR CALLING IS FROM GOD

Whether king or priest, you must know that you have a calling from God to do something great. The Bible says God chose you: *"Ye have not chosen me, but I have chosen you, and ordained you, that ye should go and bring forth fruit, and that your fruit should remain"* (John 15:16). Think of it like this. Before He started, God had a finished plan for your life. In other words, God predetermined for you to be a success.

The phrase "to be called" is often used when someone decides to go into the pulpit as an apostle, prophet, evangelist, pastor, or teacher, or to the mission field. Interestingly, the phrase is less often used when someone decides to be an entrepreneur, media executive, a diplomat or enter a marketplace profession. Why? Many people, including some clergy and religious leaders, still reject the spiritual aspect of enterprise and view those in the marketplace who command great sums of money as "greedy, immoral and (sometimes worldly)."[2]

> **YOU MUST KNOW THAT YOU HAVE A CALLING FROM GOD TO DO SOMETHING GREAT.**

People whose professions involve the creation of wealth are often judged more harshly, especially when moral failings or lapses in ethical judgment occur (Sirico 2010).

This critical attitude and prejudice against those in business have often caused detrimental tension and distrust between kings and priests. When pastors fail to recognize the divine nature of "the entrepreneurs' creative ability to imagine new possibilities and to cultivate the earth to harness its potential,"[3] the entrepreneur's gifts and contributions are not celebrated, and worse, are not employed for kingdom purposes.

Every vocation, including entrepreneurship, is a calling. The Holy Spirit calls kings to certain works just as He calls priests. Romans 11:29 applies just as much to ministers in the marketplace as it does to ministers in the pulpit: *"For the gifts and calling of God are without repentance."*

CHAPTER 14

CALLING ALL KINGS

The invasion of Normandy, France, during World War II on June 6, 1944, changed the course of world history. Allied Forces heroically stormed and took the strategic beachfront that was designated Omaha Beach. Though the price in casualties was very high, the Allied Forces' eventual success can partly be attributed to the state-of-the-art equipment and machinery used by the courageous soldiers.

Much of the equipment was built by R. G. LeTourneau, who was discussed in an earlier chapter. LeTourneau, sometimes referred to as "God's Businessman," was raised by devoted Christian parents who prayed earnestly for his salvation.[1] After leaving home at the age of 14, LeTourneau worked in many jobs, acquiring considerable knowledge of the manual trades.

By the time he was 30 years old, LeTourneau had been a partner in a failing garage business that left him unemployed and $5,000 in debt. In the wake of this failure, LeTourneau landed a job with a farm equipment dealer and became involved in the "earth-moving business." Though he was very successful in his newfound career, he was still spiritually unfulfilled.

Everything changed for him one night after attending a week of revival meetings. Feeling that God had a calling on his life, he knelt in prayer and asked God if he was being called to be a preacher or missionary. Still unsure as to his purpose and destiny, he met with his pastor the next day. During his meeting Pastor Devol spoke these inspiring words: "God

needs businessmen as well as preachers and missionaries."
Of these life-changing words, LeTourneau would later write:
"Those were the words that have guided my life ever since....
I have discovered that many men have the same mistaken
idea I had of what it means to serve the Lord...I didn't realize
that a layman could serve the Lord as well as a preacher."[2]

Within the powerful prophetic words spoken into the life
of LeTourneau through Pastor Devol were the seeds of inspiration and faith that caused him to pursue his destiny. He
designed and built innovative excavating machinery that was
years ahead of its time, built his own factory, and pioneered
time-saving techniques in the construction business.[3]

Walking in his king's anointing and the favor of God,
LeTourneau weathered the Great Depression and credit
crunches. He faithfully stood his ground when he was challenged about his "No Sunday Work" rule that came from his
commitment to God and to honoring the Sabbath.[4]

Through faith in Christ, LeTourneau's business obsta-
cles actually became stepping stones to his success. A king who knows his or her purpose or calling is a force to be reckoned with and is one of the most powerful individuals in the marketplace. If a believer is kingdom-minded and is determined to work diligently in their area of gifting to advance the kingdom of God, they will succeed no matter what barriers or obstacles they might face.

> A KING WHO KNOWS HIS OR HER PURPOSE OR CALLING IS A FORCE TO BE RECKONED WITH AND IS ONE OF THE MOST POWERFUL INDIVIDUALS IN THE MARKETPLACE.

In sharing the keys to his success, LeTourneau often said, "If you are not serv-
ing the Lord, it proves you don't love Him; if you don't love Him, it proves you don't know Him. Because to know Him is to love Him, and to love Him is to serve Him."[5]

In LeTourneau's story, we can see some very important
kings and priests principles. First, he had a pastor who spoke
words of faith instead of condemnation into his life. This is
how it is supposed to be. The gospel is good news! The only
purpose condemnation serves is to weigh people down with
guilt and shame. It is God's desire for His people to walk in

righteousness and in the things that He has prepared in advance for them to do.

It is difficult for people who are called to the marketplace, who are creative and innovative, to flourish in an atmosphere of condemnation, feeling a sense of inferiority. People who are conflicted or remain in the wrong calling are missing an opportunity to become a blessing to their local church, or become successful marketplace leaders used by God to advance His kingdom, as was the case with LeTourneau. LeTourneau was well known for his philanthropic endeavors to advance the kingdom, which included establishing the LeTourneau University in Longview, Texas, and supporting numerous Christian causes.[6]

Second, Pastor Devol, through godly counsel, empowered LeTourneau to pursue his destiny as a successful businessman and history maker. Kings, like LeTourneau, are leaders who must be empowered by faith to release and develop their gift for maximum performance in the marketplace. Oftentimes, pastors want people to bow to them in unquestioning subservience, which can lead to bondage. It's like parents who manipulate their children into staying under their control and never letting go. When this happens, it can spoil creativity, hurt one's ability to think critically, and diminish the desire to achieve one's highest potential in Christ. A church that promotes an atmosphere of freedom will be teeming with people who are inventive, energetic, and successful, like LeTourneau.

> A CHURCH THAT PROMOTES AN ATMOSPHERE OF FREEDOM WILL BE TEEMING WITH PEOPLE WHO ARE INVENTIVE, ENERGETIC, AND SUCCESSFUL.

Third, Pastor Devol was not preoccupied with convincing LeTourneau to serve on the mission field or to become a pulpit minister. If LeTourneau had become a preacher instead of a marketplace minister, the invasion of Normandy may have turned out differently.

Last, LeTourneau's earth-moving machines would not have been there to make projects like the Hoover Dam and the Boulder Highway possible, nor would his nearly 300 patents that revolutionized the construction industry have been realized.[7] All of this hinged on the one defining moment in LeTourneau's life when his pastor said, "God needs businessmen as well as preachers and missionaries."

It is my desire that this book will help religious leaders and the Church begin to value all marketplace ministries, especially "the entrepreneurial profession...and the tangible contributions that entrepreneurs make to society."[8] As one insightful religious author writes, "The time has come for religious institutions and leaders to treat entrepreneurship as a worthy vocation, indeed, a sacred calling."[9]

He goes on to say, "Religious leaders generally display very little understanding of the entrepreneurial vocation, of what it requires, and of what it contributes to society. Unfortunately, ignorance of the facts has not kept them from moralizing on economic matters and causing great harm to the spiritual development of business people."[10]

THE BILLION FLOW

In 1 Chronicles 22:14 NKJV, King David says to his son Solomon, who will be succeeding him, *"Indeed I have taken much trouble to prepare for the house of the* LORD *one hundred thousand talents of gold and one million talents of silver, and bronze and iron beyond measure, for it is so abundant. I have prepared timber and stone also, and you may add to them."*

King David is saying that he went through a lot to secure the wealth for the temple-building project. This included spoils from war, taxes, investments, and other "capital gains" ventures. The king made sure there was plenty of money, materials, architects, and every skilled and unskilled worker available to guarantee that Solomon would have everything he needed to build a glorious temple for the Lord.

In a conservative estimation, based on the *Strong's Table of Monies and Weights,*[11] David stored up, just in gold, the equivalent in today's money of more than $100 billion. King David was operating in what I call "the billion flow." We're not even counting the one million talents of silver and the other metals that he stored up without measure.

King David was wise enough to store up billions, and not spend it on things that God had not laid on his heart, even if it looked like a legitimate need. An undisciplined son might have spent this money in some other way. King David said, *"Solomon my son is young and inexperienced"* (1 Chronicles 22:5 NKJV). Or, if the priest who has the ministry of mercy had control of it, he may have given it away to the poor.

Again, as I shared in an earlier chapter, kings and priests are different members of the same body, and they bring different strengths and gifting to accomplish the mission of advancing God's kingdom. This is why kings and priests must be on one accord. Kings may not always be as benevolent as priests. Priests may not be as financially savvy as certain kings in handling vast amounts of wealth. The eye has the vision, the hand brings the provision. The apostle Paul writes, *"And the eye cannot say unto the hand, I have no need of thee..."* (1 Corinthians 12:21).

A WORD ABOUT CAPITALISM

In a chapter that specifically addresses those called to the marketplace (kings), some discussion about capitalism is appropriate. *Capitalism* is defined as "an economic or political system that encourages private investment, ownership (of both assets and wealth), and the motivation of profit."[12] Capitalism, like money, is amoral (not immoral); it's neither good nor evil of itself, nor does it have a conscience of its own. I believe capitalism provides a structure and the means for creative entrepreneurship to generate wealth and to thrive. Its core value or priority is not to heal social ills or to improve the plight of the oppressed (Silvoso 2007). The Church (the Body of Christ) must supply that.

It is important to realize that capitalism is not an anti-Judeo-Christian principle. In the New Testament we see an illustration of capitalism in Luke 19:11–27. The master gave different amounts of money to his servants, and they were to increase primarily by trading, which I discussed in the chapter on stewardship. As we see here, as well as other places in the Scriptures, this fits our definition of capitalism. So, capitalism is a just and biblically based system. The problem comes when people pervert the purpose of profit, which often takes the form of greed, especially in Western culture, and brings resentment toward capitalism and those companies that are honestly profitable (Silvoso 2007).

The growth of capitalism, void of any social conscience, places us on a dangerous course. If we withdraw our faith or "the Judeo-Christian culture from where [capitalism first] drew its ethical compass, [we will] end up abdicating social responsibility...and doing what is legal while missing the higher moral standard."[13]

In today's world, capitalism, more than any other economic system, encourages private investment, ownership, and profit. In this system, entrepreneurs and others in the marketplace are freely allowed to grow and increase, benefitting themselves and the people in the communities and nations they are called to serve.

In this chapter, you can see how the "dream team" flows: The priests being guided by the Holy Spirit can speak a word into the lives of kings that leads to abundant blessings, not just for them, but for countless others. This was illustrated in the life of R. G. LeTourneau, when his pastor told him that "God needs businessmen as well as preachers and missionaries." LeTourneau's obedience to his marketplace calling affected the course of world history. His company's goods and services were needed and available to the Allied Forces during World War II, and they were later used in peacetime for important construction projects.

A CLOSING THOUGHT

Take my word for it; your life is a lot more fabulous than you have the mental capacity to receive right now. However, **I decree that before you are finished reading this book, you will have a greater capacity for conceiving what God might accomplish in and through your life.** If God is calling you to the marketplace, I pray that you will be obedient to His call and, like LeTourneau, position yourself to have a life you may have never thought possible, not only affecting the world, but through your gift lift the burden of the curse off humanity.

PART 6
A NEW GENERATION OF KINGDOM LEADERS

CHAPTER 15

LEADERSHIP BEGINS
WITH VISION

Every human being was created to lead in the area of their gift and to fulfill a specific purpose and assignment in their lifetime. Their assignment is directly related to their area of leadership, and every leader must be developed. Leadership is not exclusive or reserved for some special group.

The leadership spirit is a natural desire of all mankind, and every person has the "instinct" for leadership and the potential to lead. The problem is that most have not been in the calling or area they are designed to lead, or they have not cultivated their leadership or have had their leadership ability developed. The result is that they have settled for the role of lifelong followers.

This book on *Faith and the Marketplace* would not be complete without some discussion of leadership. Leadership in any sphere of influence begins with vision. Vision is a snapshot of your future or a picture of circumstances that do not presently exist. It is a strong mental image of something beyond what you can see right now.

Merriam-Webster Dictionary defines *vision* as "something seen in a dream...especially a supernatural appearance that conveys a revelation; a thought, concept, or object formed by the imagination; the act or power of imagination, mode of seeing or conceiving; unusual discernment or foresight (a person of vision).[1] *The Webster's 1828 Dictionary* gives the following as a definition of *vision*: "In scripture, a revelation from God; an appearance or exhibition of something

> **VISION IS A PICTURE OF CIRCUMSTANCES THAT DO NOT PRESENTLY EXIST.**

supernaturally presented to the minds of the prophets, by which they were informed of future events. Such were the visions of Isaiah, Amos, and Ezekiel."[2]

Vision is vital to leadership because it produces a certain mental picture of the future. It determines destinies and affects attitudes, it attracts opportunities and promotes persistence, and, last but not least, it separates the visionaries from others.

Having vision creates a sense of value that affects self-worth or self-esteem. Many times one's attitude is affected by who they think they are and the value they have among the masses. Leadership is more than a position; it is a mindset. Leaders think differently about themselves. They have to in order to inspire and motivate others. This mindset distances them and distinguishes them from followers. As a follower, what you think about your purpose in the world influences your attitudes and actions that, in time, will move you into leadership, sometimes without being physically promoted.

Whether in a classroom, or on a football team, or leading a nation or a sanitation crew, there is something a leader

> **TRUE LEADERSHIP IS MORE THAN A POSITION; IT IS A MINDSET.**

can see that creates strong, positive, and confident beliefs that distinguishes them and causes others to want to follow. Again, we were all created to be leaders and will lead at some point in our lives.

Proverbs 29:18 says, *"Where there is no vision, the people perish: but he that keepeth the law, happy is he."* The *Amplified Bible* says, *"Where there is... [no redemptive revelation of God], the people perish...."* Vision is something that every leader needs to be successful. To lead, the leader must see or have a mental picture of conditions that do not currently exist, mainly because of their responsibility for the welfare of others who are following.

Jesus remarked about the religious leaders of His day, *"Let them alone: they be blind leaders of the blind. And if the blind lead the blind, both shall fall into the ditch"* (Matthew

15:14). He was talking about leaders who had natural sight, but didn't have vision or spiritual sight. They couldn't see what God had planned or who God had placed in their midst, meaning the Messiah, the Son of the living God. The scriptures tell us, *"He came unto his own, and his own received him not."* As a result, they were unable to move forward in the plan and purpose God had for their lives. They were the "blind leading the blind."

Imagine **two blind men**, and the one being led by the other thinks the one **who is leading** can see, because he's in the position of the leader. Just because a person is in the position of leadership does not guarantee sight. Again, true leadership is more than a position. It requires a person to have both insight and courage, whether leading a family, a company, or a nation. To successfully navigate through crises or challenges, especially these of today, visionary leadership is not an option, it is a requirement.

Albert Einstein once said, "We cannot solve our problems with the same level of thinking that created them." In other words, "Level One" problems will require "Level Two" solutions, mainly because there is a spiritual component called "the curse" that is behind much of it. What used to be simple in our lives and society is now much more complex and even chaotic. Any time a person can use a simple laptop computer to hack into a country's confidential database or the database of a major retail chain and steal customers' credit card and personal information, we are truly in what the Bible calls "perilous times." This calls for a new generation of leaders, which God foresaw and prepared for a new day of challenges. Sometimes it takes a crisis for someone to step up and reveal his or her own leadership potential.

God is training up the Church with what He refers to as *"the manifold wisdom of God,"* to be the anointed problem solvers in every pillar of influence in these final days. These are visionary leaders who are graced to see beyond current circumstance, foreseeing developments prior to their occurrence and able to guide society safely through these challenging and difficult times.

In the United States, fifty years ago, Detroit, Michigan, was a great economic hub. It was a city of culture and had

manufacturing jobs galore! It was home to some of the largest companies in the world, supplying products worldwide.
And Detroit, at that time, was the fourth largest city in the
nation with the largest per capita income in the nation.[3] Today, there are pockets of decay and despair with an unemployment rate of about 18 percent.[4] The culture has shifted,
and those high-paying jobs have disappeared, most of them
replaced by technology, resulting in a collapse of their economy. One man said, "Detroit went broke long before it went
bust."

This is the importance of visionary leadership, or leaders who can see beyond current circumstances and guide
society safely into its destiny. Now, with national economies
and the welfare or safety of the citizenry becoming a major
challenge, visionary leadership is needed to lead society out.
Some might think these problems can't be fixed. Probably
not with man...*"but with God all things are possible"!* You
and I are born for this hour and uniquely designed to lead
this generation out of every impossible situation. God will
give us answers to problems we have never had and give us
strategies to win battles we have never been trained to fight
...ask King David.

JOSEPH WAS A VISIONARY

Joseph was an example of a true visionary leader—a
man used by God to lead the world through the greatest crisis of that time. It was a great famine that would normally
have wiped out most of humanity. This is one reason I believe the Lord gave me the Joseph Business School as the
name for our ministry's business school. As shared earlier
in the book, the mission of this school is to train up entrepreneurs and business leaders, using biblical and practical
business principles, to lead successful companies that will
generate wealth to eradicate poverty globally, to rebuild and
transform communities, and to finance the spreading of the
gospel to a lost generation, which will establish His kingdom
bringing heaven to Earth.

The two main areas of Joseph's influence were the areas
or mountains of economics and government; that is, where

both money and laws are made. Joseph had a dream and told his brothers how they were binding sheaves in the field and his sheaf arose, stood upright and their sheaves bowed down to his sheaf. His brothers became envious and outraged.

Then Joseph dreamed another dream. He basically said, "The eleven stars and the moon all bowed down to me and then you bowed down to me too" (Genesis 37:9 paraphrased). Now, Joseph should have learned something from his brothers' reactions to his first dream. However, when a dream or vision is big enough on the inside, it often spills over to the outside. A lesson here is that sometimes you're better off not telling everyone your dream because it could provoke envy or even anger. An evil, envious spirit could arise to either talk you out of the dream or, as in the case of Dr. Martin Luther King, Jr., destroy the dreamer. Understand, the agent behind all this persecution is satan. He knows that your dream or vision has the potential to take you to a place of leadership that can impact the lives of millions.

YOUR DREAM OR VISION CAN IMPACT THE LIVES OF MILLIONS.

Joseph's dream was prophetic, meaning that when he first mentioned it, it was for some time in the future. Well, a few years later it was fulfilled. God had given him a snapshot of the future—his future and the future of the world—that a great dearth was coming. While he worked Potiphar's land, because of THE BLESSING of the Lord upon him, he prospered the house of his Egyptian slave master. Being developed in leadership or management, he soon rose to a place of prominence...the one in charge over the entire estate, and fulfilling his leadership potential.

Your leadership ability inside of you is waiting to be discovered. Remember, the secret to greatness in the kingdom is in serving not bossing everyone else. Each one of us is created to be distinguished in a specific area of gifting. We don't need to be envious or jealous of someone else's gift, we just need to serve in the area of our

THE SECRET TO GREATNESS IN THE KINGDOM IS IN SERVING.

unique talents. Through false accusation Joseph found himself in prison but even there he became a leader. After some time God gave Pharaoh a dream and Joseph was sought to interpret it. This gifting made room for him taking him from obscurity to prime minister over Egypt. He was promoted from the worst place in his life to the best place in his life. He became second in command to Pharaoh, king of Egypt.

My observation has been that most people in the earth are living without a vision or a dream and have settled for barrenness and defeat, contrary to God's plan for them. Within that missing vision are their purpose, potential, and power (anointing). So, if people are not functioning with a vision, they are living a purposeless life and because of this will never reach their God-planned destiny. Hear what the scriptures reveal about God's plan for all our lives:

> For we are God's [own] handiwork (His workman-ship), recreated in Christ Jesus, [born anew] that we may do those good works which God predestined (planned beforehand) for us [taking paths which He prepared ahead of time], that we should walk in them [living the good life which He prearranged and made ready for us to live]. Ephesians 2:10 AMP

God never intended for you and me to live without a purpose and without discovering our leadership potential. People are looking for purpose, the reason for their being on this planet. This is why *The Purpose Driven Life* became the second best-selling hardback book in American history.[5] People hunger for significance and purpose. God designed us that way.

Again, God has uniquely designed and chosen you to fulfill a specific assignment in your lifetime, and this assignment points to your area of gifting, leadership, and influence. The highest purpose for all godly leadership in these last days is to lead people, or point the way, to Christ. In whatever sphere of influence God places you, remember that your leadership there is predetermined, and not according to your preference, but according to His sovereign plan. God's gifts and callings are for you to serve humanity. As God did with Moses or Esther, He will also do with you. He will show you that your desire to lead is natural and that you have been equipped and uniquely gifted to make a vital contribution to the world.

Jesus knew exactly why He came into the earth. First John 3:8 says, *"...For this purpose the Son of God was manifested, that he might destroy the works of the devil."* This was Jesus' kingdom assignment. My hope and prayer is that this book will help you discover the purpose God has for your life and that you reach a level of influence and leadership that you never thought possible.

CHAPTER 16

THE RIGHTEOUS
ARE RISING

He raiseth up the poor out of the dust, *and* lifteth
the needy out of the dunghill; that he may set *him*
with princes, even with the princes of his people.
Psalm 113:7–8

A s I have said before, God deliberately plants the
righteous among the ungodly, mainly for the purpose of shifting the culture and dismantling a system leading
to self-destruction. Remember, Adam's original assignment
was to produce a culture like Eden but Adam sinned and
introduced another culture, one that would produce outside
of God. Our job, as the righteous, is to bring the government
of God to bear upon the earth wherever we are sent (Luke
22:29), releasing creation from the curse. Jesus said, *"the
gates of hell shall not prevail against it* (the Church)*"* (Matthew 16:18).

For instance, a Christian might be planted inside a company as an assistant manager, displaying talent and bringing solutions to help grow the company. Yet, because he
or she will not conform to a corporate requirement that is
against Christian conscience and values, he or she does not
rise beyond a certain corporate level. For centuries satan has
been giving "high-place" access to whomever he wills (Luke
4:6). He is well aware that the believer who refuses to bow or
compromise while rising in an organization or industry is the
only one capable of shifting the climate or culture at the top
of that mountain (i.e., company or industry). And, whoever is
at the top of that mountain controls what is in the mountain.

You see, the system of Babylon works to make sure that the righteous do not occupy strategic positions of authority, especially in strategic institutions. It wants Christians to occupy the lower, non-decision-making positions in the corporate hierarchy so they have limited influence. For example, it is a great blessing for the secretary to the chief justice of the U.S. Supreme Court to be a dedicated Christian, but for the chief justice himself (or herself) to be an unwavering and committed Christian that gets the attention of all of hell.

FROM OBSCURITY TO PROMINENCE, FROM PRISON TO PRIME MINISTER

God strategically positioned both Joseph and Esther for leadership and set up the conditions for them to rise. Likewise, you and I have been divinely positioned for leadership. Esther, whose father or mother had died, was adopted and mentored by her uncle, Mordecai. Because of certain events that happened in the palace between the King and Queen Vashti, he sought another queen. Because of divinely arranged circumstances, a Jew ended up becoming the new queen and, as Mordecai said, she has *"come to the kingdom for such a time as this"* to save all the Jews. The Bible clearly states that *"she obtained kindness,"* meaning that God gave her favor with King Nebuchadnezzar who ended up offering her half of his kingdom.

YOU AND I HAVE BEEN DIVINELY POSITIONED FOR LEADERSHIP.

Joseph was sold as a slave by his brothers and eventually bought by Potiphar, an Egyptian captain, to serve in Potiphar's house and in the field. Because of God's blessing upon Joseph and his uncompromising integrity, Joseph rose to be overseer over all that Potiphar had. Joseph was later falsely accused of sexual misconduct by Potiphar's wife and ended up with a life sentence in prison. However, God was still with Joseph and all the prisoners were soon placed under his leadership. We soon see that God was positioning him to be promoted from the prison to prime minister in Pharaoh's Egyptian government...second in command to Pharaoh.

Understand, if you've been divinely positioned by the Holy Spirit, you are on your way to the top. Each one of us faces unique situations that try to make us victims, but in the kingdom of God, "A setback is always a set up." You're on your way to the top, so keep the faith. Your persecution could be racial or gender-based, political or religious, or just plain envy and hatred. Keep a good attitude. The Bible speaks about Jesus while He was on the cross, *"...who for the joy that was set before him endured the cross, despising the shame, and is set down at the right hand of the throne of God"* (Hebrews 12:2). He went from the lowest depths of hell to the highest place in heaven.

But remember, no one can reach their maximum leadership potential with a victim mentality...at least not in the kingdom. Victimization and righteousness do not go together. They are on opposite ends of the spectrum. One is about powerlessness and criticism while the other is about courage and dominion. One is fear-based and the other is faith-based.

I've found, never appeal to God on the basis of fairness because God is not fair. He's just. As I mentioned in an earlier chapter, the late Dr. Martin Luther King, Jr., quoted a passage of scripture in one of his speeches that the nonviolence movement for civil rights would continue until *"judgment* (justice) *run*(s) *down as waters and righteousness as a mighty stream"* (Amos 5:24). God responds on the basis of justice, not on what someone might think is fair.

Neither Joseph nor Esther nor Jesus, nor even Dr. King, took the bait of blaming others and becoming a victim. In fact, Jesus said, *"Father, forgive them; for they know not what they do"* (Luke 23:34). If Joseph had gotten into a "pity party," guaranteed, he would have stayed in that prison and served his full time. Daniel also maintained a righteous attitude when he was thrown in the lion's den because of an ungodly law that his haters persuaded the king to sign. When the next morning came, the king brought Daniel out untouched by the lions. Daniel was in great spirits and declared, "Long live the King."

There is always a way out of every dilemma, but we need faith to find it. Every godly leader must protect themselves against the temptations of a "victim mentality." Remember, you are in a hostile world and it requires faith and love, and plain old mental toughness. Jesus Himself even said, *"They hated me without a cause."*

The apostle Paul writes, *"There hast no temptation* (test or trial) *taken you but such as is common to man: but God is faithful, who will not suffer you to be tempted above that ye are able; but will with the temptation* (test or trial) *also make a way to escape, that ye may be able to bear it"* (1 Corinthians 10:13). Here's my simple translation of that verse, "You will never face anything you cannot overcome" and whatever you are going through now, heaven has already declared that you are the victor and not a victim.

THERE IS ALWAYS A WAY OUT OF EVERY DILEMMA, BUT WE NEED FAITH TO FIND IT.

I recall a time when a dear sister approached me to pray for her after one of our Sunday worship services. She explained that she had applied for a job at her company that would be a significant promotion. She explained that she had prayed to God, and by faith, believed she had received it.

She asked me to agree with her in prayer. Before I did, I asked her did she have the skill set for this new position and she quickly replied, "Yes!" So, I said the prayer of agreement with her and she turned and left. About two weeks later, she approached me again after one of our Sunday services with a sad look on her face. I asked her, "What's wrong?" She said that someone else got that job. Without allowing her to explain, I quickly replied, "You didn't let that job go did you?" It seemed that she immediately caught on to what I was getting at and she said, "Well, no...I haven't!" I said, "Let's cancel any negative words you might have spoken and declare that we are still in agreement for that position."

THE WORD OF GOD NEVER FAILS.

She came back about a week later, but this time with a smile on her face. I said, "Sister, what's happening?" She said, "The person who they gave the job to quit and they offered me the promotion and new position and I have it now." You see, that was meant to be her position, but, as I mentioned, the spiritual forces of the world system work to ensure that the righteous do not occupy strategic positions of influence.

Here are a few scriptures that have helped me to keep the right perspective about leadership in the world and to continue to increase in my upward journey.

> When the righteous are in authority, the people rejoice: but when the wicked beareth rule, the people mourn. Proverbs 29:2

> Though thy beginning was small, yet thy latter end should greatly increase. Job 8:7

> For promotion *cometh* neither from the east nor from the west, nor from the south. But God *is* the judge: he putteth down one, and setteth up another. Psalm 75:6–7

> But seek ye first the kingdom of God, and his righteousness; and all these things shall be added unto you. Matthew 6:33

> And I will make of thee a great nation, and I will bless thee, and make thy name great; and thou shalt be a blessing. Genesis 12:2

The Word of God never fails. Believe, speak, and act on God's Word, and guaranteed, you will overcome every spiritual force resisting your rise to higher leadership.

CHAPTER 17

THE MIRACLE IS IN YOUR STAFF

In Exodus, chapter 4, Moses, a prophet and vision-ary leader, is having a serious conversation with God. Moses is about to confront probably the most powerful world ruler of his day, and he is giving God excuses about why he is not quite the right man. *"And Moses answered and said, But, behold, they will not believe me, nor hearken unto my voice: for they will say, The LORD hath not appeared unto thee"* (verse 1).

But the Lord asks Moses, *"What is that in your hand?"* And he said, "A rod (or staff)." If you've read the story or seen *The Ten Commandments* movie about the exodus of the chil-dren of Israel from Egypt, you know what happens next. God tells Moses to drop the staff on the ground and it becomes a snake. Then Moses picks it up by the tail and the snake turns back into a staff.

What is God showing Moses? He is showing him that when He chooses someone as a leader, He is also the one who divinely equips, confirms, and authenticates that person's leadership. God showed Moses that he was representing Him. Moses was God's representative, just as every believer is an *"ambassador for Christ."*

God later goes on to say, *"And you shall take this* (staff) *in your hand, with which you shall do signs"* (verse 17). If you replace the word *signs* with *miracles,* God is basically saying, "With this staff you shall do miracles." Again, God is delib-erately planting the righteous among the ungodly and those marketplace achievements that seem humanly impossible to accomplish through your business or ministry, will mostly

GOD DIVINELY EQUIPS, CONFIRMS, AND AUTHENTICATES A PERSON'S LEADERSHIP.

MARKETPLACE ACHIEVEMENTS THAT SEEM HUMANLY IMPOSSIBLE TO ACCOMPLISH ARE DONE THROUGH YOUR STAFF.

be accomplished through you and your anointed staff.

Your staff is a key ingredient in helping you accomplish the mission God has given you; therefore, you have to select the right people. Jesus knew the importance of selecting the right team. Before Jesus chose the twelve disciples, He prayed all night. *"And it came to pass in those days, that he went out into a mountain to pray, and continued all night in prayer to God. And when it was day, he called unto him his disciples: and of them he chose twelve, whom also he named apostles"* (Luke 6:12–13).

My point is: He didn't choose just anyone who walked through the door. Whether a king or priest, we should take the time to commit the selection and hiring of our staff to prayer. And even when God sends you help, there are some you may still need to develop. Sometimes skilled people come in "seed form," particularly in the early years of a business or ministry. That's why we need to identify the right people and be prepared, if necessary, to develop their potential.

IT TAKES A TEAM

Booker T. Washington founded Tuskegee University with nothing. No buildings, no books, no students, and no teachers. He only started with a vision. He started having classes in a little wooden church with students he had to find by going from house to house in a horse-drawn buggy. At each house he would ask the parents if he could teach their young people how to read and write.

Keep in mind, most of these parents and young people were ex-slaves. Slavery had just ended in 1865, sixteen years before starting the school (Tuskegee Normal) in 1881. Booker T. Washington, a devout Christian, used his faith in the marketplace of education and achieved phenomenal success.

Washington brought his students into this one-room church and began to teach them. Because they didn't have any money, he would also give them work to offset the expenses of their education (work-study). They would farm, and then go study. They would chop down trees, and then go study. They would build the buildings, and then go study.

One book cites that in 1905, Booker T. Washington, turned out more "self-made" millionaires than Harvard, Yale, and Princeton combined—out of ex-slaves![1] By 1915, Washington had built 107 buildings mostly out of bricks, which they made themselves, including dormitories with cafeterias.

> **NO VISION IS IMPLEMENTED BY ONE PERSON. YOU NEED A TEAM.**

Booker T. Washington had a mission, and he attracted very talented and gifted people to be a part of his team, such as Dr. George Washington Carver. My point is this: No vision is implemented by one person. You need a team.

BUILDING AN A-TEAM

The "A" stands for "anointed." This team, empowered by God Himself, is not to be ordinary but extraordinary. One man said this about a team that worked together— "Teamwork: If you could get all the people of an organization flowing in the same direction, you could dominate any industry, in any market, against any competition, at any time." Let's look at what the Bible says are the traits of a good leader and how to select them.

*"Moreover thou shalt provide out of all the people **able men**, such as **fear God**, **men of truth**, **hating covetousness**; and place such over them, to be rulers of thousands, and rulers of hundreds, rulers of fifties, and rulers of tens"* (Exodus 18:21, emphasis mine). In this verse, Jethro, Moses' father-in-law and a Midian priest, told Moses to look for certain qualities in selecting the leaders who were to help him lead and govern the children of Israel. What were these qualities? Four simple but vital attributes that should be the standard for every generation of new leaders:

1. Able men (and women)

2. Who fear God

3. Men of truth

4. Who hate covetousness

1. Able Men

"Able men" means skillful, competent men and women. Surprisingly, competency can sometimes be a problem for the team. Why? Because some people feel they do not have to continue improving their skills to achieve greater proficiencies in their work or professional lives. Many have an expectation that the Lord will bless whatever they do regardless of its quality. Or worse, they feel excellence in their earthly life is unimportant because they are just waiting to die and go to heaven. They have no idea that performance is very important to God, and that excellence in any field of endeavor will promote you. The attitude of "just getting by" is unacceptable to God and to any real leader in today's environment. Those who feel this way are dismissing the scripture, *"Whatever you do, work at it with all your heart, as working for the Lord, not for human masters, since you know that you will receive an inheritance from the Lord as a reward. It is the Lord Christ you are serving"* (Colossians 3:23–24 NIV).

The Lord expects us to grow into our giftedness. Leaders should motivate their people to develop themselves so they can cultivate their gift(s) and raise their level of competency, and discover their personal value to the world. It also provokes the world to want to know your God when they see your excellence and superior performance.

2. Who Fear God

"Moreover thou shalt provide out of all the people able men, such as fear God, men of truth, hating covetousness" (Exodus 18:21, emphasis mine). Another way of saying this is "the fear of the Lord." The *"fear of the LORD is to hate evil"* (Proverbs 8:13). This fear of the Lord is synonymous with walking in God's ways. It means to obey God.

When leaders have the fear of the Lord, they hate what God hates. God does not hate people, He hates sin. God loves people, *"For God so loved the world"* (John 3:16). King Saul was chosen but he wasn't God's choice for king. The Bible says he stood head and shoulders above everyone else. He was a tall, good-looking guy, what I call, "the people's choice." They cried out for a king to judge them like all the other nations and go out before them and fight their battles. God gave the people their choice, and Saul turned out not to be a very good king. In fact, he disobeyed God and eventually went insane. *"And Saul said unto Samuel, I have sinned: for I have transgressed the commandment of the LORD, and thy words: because I feared the people, and obeyed their voice"* (1 Samuel 15:24).

Saul disobeyed God because he feared the people more than he feared God. Fearing people can lead a person into disobedience. Proverbs 29:25 AMP says, *"The fear of man brings a snare...."* Fearing God doesn't mean to be terrorized by God but to have a reverent respect for God and His Word. That's the fear of the Lord, and it brings wisdom and knowledge.

God can trust you when you revere and respect Him and His Word. Why do some of our political leaders place their hand on the Bible during the swearing-in ceremony, and then vote "yes" on issues that contradict the commandments of the very Book they swore by when taking their oath of office? I believe the reason is either a lack of knowledge of what's in the Book or an absence of the fear of the Lord. Any time you fear God, He gives you a place of distinction in the earth and a place with Him.

3. Men of Truth

"Men of truth" refers to people of integrity. The Bible says in Proverbs 25:19, *"Confidence in an unfaithful man in time of trouble is like a broken tooth, and a foot out of joint."* God looks for a person who is faithful, and when He chooses a leader, He looks on the heart of a man (character) and not at his appearance, his height, or how he dresses (see 1 Samuel 16:7). I believe that the main reason that many Christians have not experienced financial success in the kingdom is because of a lack of integrity regarding their tithes and offerings.

True leadership is often not seen until there is a crisis or during a time of extreme testing. It could be a father or mother who will stand firm through thick and thin to keep the family together in hard times, or a president who keeps hope alive during a national crisis such as a terrorist attack like 9/11.

Harriet Tubman, called the "Black Moses of her era," was a fearless leader. Slave owners had placed a $12,000 bounty on her head (a lot of money at that time) as a reward for her capture. She was transporting hundreds of slaves to freedom in the safe harbors of the North.[2]

Tubman knew that escaped slaves who were captured or returned would be beaten and tortured until they gave information about those who had helped them. She never allowed any of those she led out to give up. She would put a loaded pistol to his or her head saying, "Dead folks tell no tales. You go on or die."[3]

She calmly returned over and over saying, as quoted in William Lloyd Garrison's newspaper, *The Liberator*, "Let there be no mistake, for this I will not equivocate. I will not excuse nor will I retreat a single inch until the last slave breathes free."[4] She wasn't a very impressive looking woman—just a little over five-feet tall in her late thirties. She couldn't read or write. When she smiled people could see that her two front teeth were missing. Yet, there were some three hundred slaves who followed her to freedom out of the South. They respected and recognized her "true leadership."

In chapter 10, I covered the subject of character and integrity. I will only cover a few additional points here. First, God does not promote on skill alone nor does He promote on gifts. God also develops character, integrity, and competency. He will wait for a person's integrity to be developed before He promotes them. Thank God for skills and gifts, and usually that's all the world system requires, but not so in the kingdom. Remember, He is molding us, making us like Him.

Many people have "heart problems," meaning that their hearts are not right from a spiritual standpoint. Before you can delegate great responsibility to a person, you must know they are men of truth. This was Jethro's counsel to Moses. God has to be involved when you are choosing your leaders because a person may look good on the outside and say all the right things, but once the pressure gets on them, "A broken tooth will give way." *"The heart is deceitful above all things, and desperately wicked: who can know it"* (Jeremiah 17:9).

Real leadership can be clearly seen during a crisis based on how a person responds to the problems. Does the person break down, or do they continue to walk by faith, trusting in the integrity of God's Word? Peter thought he was developed in his heart when he told Jesus, *"Lord, all these people will leave you, but I will never leave you."* Jesus said, "Peter, before the cock crows you will deny me not once, not twice, but three times." Peter was an undeveloped leader in the Gospels, but by the book of Acts, Peter had become strong, full of integrity.

In Acts, chapter 5, Peter and the other apostles were put in jail because their preaching was producing miracles in the marketplace. The religious leaders were angered by these miracles, and demanded that they stop teaching and preaching in the Name of Jesus. Then Peter, who had before denied Jesus three times, became bold as a lion. *"Then Peter and the other apostles answered and said, We ought to obey God rather than men"* (verse 29).

Peter demonstrates that leadership and integrity can be developed. Don't ever think that because you missed an opportunity to stand up for what's right at a particular point in time, that God has given up on you. Just stay with God and He will stay with you. Repent like Peter did and start again. Remember, God is committed to our development. Let me repeat: God is committed to our development, and He will continue to develop those qualities of leadership, character, and integrity. Job's wife asked the question during the worst time in Job's life... *"Dost thou still retain thine integrity?"* (Job 2:9). It's all about what's in the heart. Job kept his integrity and everything satan stole, Job got back—twofold.

4. Who Hate Covetousness

Covetousness has to do with a strong or excessive eagerness to obtain and possess something or someone, usually for selfish or self-seeking gain. Therefore, "hating covetousness" has to do with being incorruptible by wealth, power, or gain.

During a trip to one of the African nations, the pastor of a very large church told me an interesting story. He had to battle for several years for his son who had been on drugs. The devil was trying to destroy his seed. But through years of prayer, his son came to the Lord, was totally delivered, and is now pastoring a second church location they started in the same city.

I asked him, "How did you decide to put your son over that church?" "You know, Dr. Winston, I had two other pastors there before my son went there," he replied. "Did you?" I said. "Yes, I raised both of these ministers up and I put them over the church at different times. But after they had been placed in these leadership positions, they both ran off with all of the people, on separate occasions," he said.

He continued, "I thought it may have just been something that happened with the first leader, so when the second person came along, I took him under my guidance, raised him up as a leader and rebuilt the church. Then soon after, he also ran off with all the people."

As this pastor unfortunately experienced, there are some people who should not be promoted into leadership because they are only looking for selfish gain. They will even go as far as to associate with well-known ministries to enhance their own popularity. By the way, covetousness is not restricted to the ministry. It affects people from all walks of life, from business and politics to sports and entertainment.

To change or improve the world, we must operate in the superior principles of the kingdom of God: love, peace, justice, honesty, holiness, unity, faithfulness, and compassion. These principles are very powerful and effective when employed against the principles of darkness, such as greed, selfishness, threats, envy, bribes, manipulation, and so on. God's kingdom rules over all.

THE ART OF DELEGATION

Once a leader has selected the right team to help carry out the vision, they need to train, trust, and delegate authority and responsibility to them.

Jethro helped Moses develop the art of delegation. Jethro saw that Moses was about to work himself into an early grave, *"So Moses' father-in-law said to him, 'The thing that you do is not good. Both you and these people who are with you will surely wear yourselves out. For this thing is too much for you; you are not able to perform it by yourself'"* (Exodus 18:17–18 NKJV).

Jethro continues, *"Listen now to my voice; I will give you counsel, and God will be with you: Stand before God for the people, so that you may bring the difficulties to God. And you shall teach them the statutes and the laws, and show them the way in which they must walk and the work they must do"* (verses 19–20).

Jethro tapped into the wisdom of God. He told Moses that if he keeps doing what he's doing, he is going to wear himself out. When my wife and I first started our ministry in Chicago, I would counsel everybody because we only had ten people. I also swept the floor, preached the sermon, and took the offering. I did almost everything...my wife helped too. As the church grew, I had to begin to think differently. I had to delegate to remain an effective leader and to ensure that the church kept growing.

I actually developed my skills in delegation and teamwork while still in the marketplace at IBM. When making sales calls, I would pull in the talents and special skills of others in the organization because I knew I couldn't do it all myself. I would invite my manager on certain field calls to help me market the product and to add credibility to the visit. Sometimes I'd ask the systems engineer (responsible for software) to come with me to ensure that the customer was buying the right product and I was selling him the right services. At other times, I would invite my customer engineer because he would focus on the correct hardware. My point is: I relied on all the resources the company offered to leverage the sale, and at the same time, ensure the greatest value to the customer.

Delegation is a leadership principle that every leader, whether in the marketplace or in ministry, must learn if they are to be successful. Delegation is an art, not a science, and comes with practice and experience and the guidance of the Holy Spirit.

Acts, chapter 6, gives guidance on the qualities to look for in delegating to others. The early Church was growing and the disciples were not able to meet the increasing demands of both serving and preaching. Then, *"there arose a complaint against the Hebrews...because their widows were neglected in the daily* (food) *distribution"* (verse 1 NKJV). The twelve disciples summoned the other disciples and told them, *"It is not desirable that we should leave the word of God and serve tables. Therefore, brethren, seek out from among you seven men of* **good reputation, full of the Holy Spirit and wisdom**, *whom we may appoint over this business; but we will give ourselves continually to prayer and to the ministry of the word"* (verses 2–4 NKJV, emphasis mine).

The disciples knew they now had to delegate to others if they were going to remain effective as spiritual leaders over the new converts. They wisely delegated to leaders who were honest, had a good reputation, and full of the Spirit of God and wisdom.

As you develop as a leader, guard against others trying to make you feel guilty about delegating tasks. In the famous story of David and Goliath, David's brothers tried to make him feel guilty when he left his sheep to go to the front lines as his father had commanded. *"So David rose early in the morning, left the sheep with a keeper, and took the things and went as Jesse had commanded him. And he came to the camp as the army was going out to the fight and shouting for the battle"* (1 Samuel 17:20 NKJV).

Notice, David left the sheep with a keeper. He delegated, but this made his oldest brother angry.

> Eliab's anger was aroused against David, and he said, "Why did you come down here? And with whom have you left those few sheep in the wilderness? I know your pride and the insolence of your heart, for you have come down to see the battle. verse 28

David's brother tried to make him feel guilt and shame about delegating his responsibilities. And there are people who will try to do the same thing to you. I encourage you to develop your confidence and skill in delegating work or tasks to others so that you won't fall victim to weariness and exhaustion, and your business or ministry will continue to flourish.

Every vision requires a team to bring it to pass, and choosing and building the right leadership team is critical to your success. With the guidance of the Holy Spirit and the principles shared in this chapter, you can have confidence in selecting the right leaders every time.

CHAPTER 18

TAKING POSSESSION

Psalm 115:16 says, *"The heaven, even the heavens, are the LORD's: but the earth hath he given to the children of men."* Possessing an ownership mentality is a requirement to properly govern this planet. God is not running the world. I know that statement might shock a lot of people, particularly Christians, but God is running the Church and the Church should be running the world. This is a vital revelation for both kings and priests to understand if they are going to possess and control their high places (spheres of influence) on Earth and carry out the Great Commission on the level God intended.

The Bible strongly supports this truth in Genesis 1:26, *"God said, Let us make man in our image, after our likeness: and **let them** have dominion over the fish of the sea, and over the fowl of the air, and over the cattle, and over all the earth, and over every creeping thing that creepeth upon the earth"* (emphasis mine).

As I've said earlier, God, from the very beginning, gave this Earth and the authority to manage it to mankind—Adam and Eve. Not long after, Adam lost control of the earth to the devil, but Jesus, the Son of man and the "Last Adam," got it back. Now the Church is to take up where the first man (Adam) left off before he sinned. Again, *"Let them have dominion."*

In the *Webster's 1828 Dictionary*, the word *dominion* means "sovereign or supreme authority; the power of governing and controlling; power to direct, control, use and dispose of at pleasure."[1] Words that further describe dominion include rulership, lordship, oversight, caretaker-ship (stewardship) and ownership.[2] God gave Adam ownership of the earth and made him responsible to govern it and generate increase (man and *Adam* are actually the same Hebrew word).[3]

Genesis 1:28 says,

> And God blessed them, and God said unto them, Be fruitful, and multiply, and replenish the earth, and subdue it: and have dominion over the fish of the sea, and over the fowl of the air, and over every living thing that moveth upon the earth.

From the beginning, it was part of God's plan for mankind to always live in heaven's atmosphere, Eden. Adam was to use the power of THE BLESSING to make the whole Earth like the garden of Eden (Genesis 1:28). Adam and Eve were to create or "cultivate" a garden everywhere they went, which means to "improve by labor." They were to establish the culture of the kingdom throughout Earth.

God had given Adam dominion over this Earth, but somewhere he failed to take it. Let's say it like this: He never took ownership. When he didn't, he lost his lordship, his right to caretakership or stewardship, and his position as the ruler over this planet. I see that same thing happening today. The scriptures tell us, *"...the heaven, even the heavens, are the LORD's: but the earth hath he given to the children of men"* (Psalm 115:16). This is ownership of the whole Earth.

GOD'S PLAN IS FOR MANKIND TO LIVE IN HEAVEN'S ATMOSPHERE, CREATING A GARDEN OF EDEN EVERYWHERE WE GO.

Because the Church has not seen herself as responsible for this entire planet (stewardship), satan, through lies and deception, has taken itself over and established his Babylonian culture in almost every place in our society. For example, through suggestion, the people of God thought that the only way they could serve God was to be a pastor, or if they really loved God, then they should be out on the mission field building and starting churches. Wrong! If they did this, they could potentially forfeit their calling to the marketplace in the field of business, education, arts and entertainment, media, and so on.

We are equipped and empowered to dominate every sphere of influence. God has already preplanned our purpose for being on this planet. And through biblical practice, we should display Bible power and train up the kingdom culture wherever we are planted.

Remember, all the power and authority that can be exercised in the earth has to be exercised through the Church or an anointed vessel. In short, problems exist because we permit them. The Church has not seen itself as the earth's rightful heirs and owners, and therefore responsible for all that happens here, from laws to education, from employment to social unrest. We've been waiting for someone else or the government to fix or manage it.

Let me further illustrate this by using the opening story in Mark, chapter 5, AMP, when Jesus and His disciples land at the coast of the Gadarenes and were met by an apparent mad man who had been terrorizing the region.

> And as soon as He got out of the boat, there met Him out of the tombs a man [under the power] of an unclean spirit. This man continually lived among the tombs, and no one could subdue him any more, even with a chain; For he had been bound often with shackles for the feet and handcuffs, but the handcuffs of [light] chains he wrenched apart, and the shackles he rubbed *and* ground together *and* broke in pieces; and no one had strength enough to restrain *or* tame him. Night and day among the tombs and on the mountains he was always shrieking *and* screaming and beating *and* bruising *and* cutting himself with stones. verses 2–5

Demons were actually controlling this man from within; that's "possession" or "ownership." Through this one man, they were controlling the entire economy and community. That is, they had a sphere or mountain sovereignty. I believe this was a shipping community for trade and commerce from the sea, but because *"no one had strength enough to restrain or tame him,"* (AMP) people were suffering and at the mercy of this man. Mark 3:27 says, *"No man can enter into a strong man's house, and spoil his goods, except he will first bind the strong man; and then he will spoil his house."* Jesus "entered in" and conquered the demons in this man, numbering about 2,000, and restored the man to his right mind.

This story in Mark 5 illustrates a few points: First, to take "the land," which can be symbolic for an industry or business or a sphere of influence, you must first enter the land and conquer it. This is why the Church was never meant to stay behind the four walls of a building or, as I said earlier in this book, confine the Church to the five-fold ministry (e.g., apostles, prophets, evangelists, pastors, and teachers). When we do, "we render 95% of the Church irrelevant." For example, the best way to change the R- and X-rated movies coming out of Hollywood is to raise up and send Christian screenwriters and producers to Hollywood, anointed to write, direct, finance, and make entertaining and commercially profitable movies. And this is starting happen.

Second, once you enter and conquer the land, you are to possess it, which means ownership and "controlling the land from within." Until you render satan helpless, you cannot possess your possessions. *"When the Lord your God brings you into the land you are entering to possess..."* (Deuteronomy 7:1 NIV).

Third, satan uses a man or woman to do his will; his demons entered the man in Mark 5 and controlled him from within. This man was possessed! The kingdom of God operates in a similar way—from within—but by willingly yielding to God's love, not by control and coercion. This is why Jesus said, in speaking about the kingdom, *"neither shall they say, Lo, here! or lo, there! for behold, the kingdom of God is within you"* (Luke 17:21). When we are born again, the kingdom is planted inside our hearts (spirits). When we willingly yield to its values, laws, authority, and power, then the kingdom begins to rule over all wherever we are sent or assigned. Satan knows that if one believer makes it to the top of the mountain, which could be various industries or spheres of influence he controls, that millions of lives will be affected. Yes, I said millions as in the lives of Joseph, or Moses, or Esther, or Peter, Paul, and Mary. Or like our Lord Jesus Christ. He made it to the top of His mountain without compromise and billions of lives were, and still are, being affected.

I decree, every harassing Goliath in your life shall be brought down. And you will make it to the top of your mountain.

COUNTERFEIT OWNERSHIP

Satan set up his counterfeit system and society (Babylon) mainly through fear, deception, and by convincing people to try to meet their own needs without God. As a result, he has been directing the resources and revenues of the earth. This present Babylonian system guarantees economic inequity to the entire world because it is based on an economic model that is void of THE BLESSING and any genuine intention to improve the lives of all those living under its control, both rich and poor.

Not surprisingly, satan's inferior, counterfeit system promotes counterfeit ownership. While visiting two separate countries, the host pastors shared with me a growing occurrence of fake, counterfeit title deeds. Because of corruption in the system and weaknesses in the governing institutions, unscrupulous people are bribing government officials to create and sell them fake titles to such things as land and property in exchange for money. Sadly, they know the property does not belong to them. One of the pastors who was a victim in this fraudulent scheme shared that it took him nearly three years and a great deal of money to get his property—that he legally and rightfully owned. It was eventually returned back to his possession. He took "dominion" over what was rightfully his. Ultimately, God, who is the judge, will execute vengeance or justice on those who abuse and defraud His people (see Isaiah 33:22).

HEIRS OF GOD AND JOINT HEIRS WITH CHRIST

Now, through Christ, we, the Church, are here on Earth to reclaim and repossess all that Jesus redeemed, from the people to the property, from ministry to the marketplace. The scriptures tell us

> And so we should not be like cringing, fearful slaves,
> but we should behave like God's very own children
> born into His family, and calling to Him, "Father,

Father." For the Holy Spirit speaks deep into our hearts, and tells us we are really God's children. And since we are His children we will share His treasures. Romans 8:15–17 TLB

Ask yourself, "How much does God have?" The answer is...everything! As His heirs, we inherited what God has and therefore have joint ownership. When the father told the disgruntled elder son to come and celebrate with them that his prodigal son had returned, he shared with the elder son... *"All that I have is thine"* (Luke 15:31). We are not just stewards. No! I say, we are owners with stewardship responsibility. There is a difference.

The *Webster's 1828 Dictionary* states, *owner* or *to own* means "to have the legal or rightful title to."[4] Owners have "controlling" interest. Stewards, as I shared in a previous chapter, are limited to managing another person's property or affairs. They are like agents—most of the time with limited decision-making power. As owners, God has given the Church the authority to decide what goes on in the earth. As stewards, we understand that we are accountable to God for our decisions and actions, and that He is holding us responsible to bring increase wherever He sends us in service of the kingdom. (Matthew 25:14–29.)

In 2008, many people in the United States of America thought they owned their own home until the mortgage crisis caused the economy to fail. They ended up losing their homes to foreclosure, and the properties went back to the "rightful owners"—the ones who had the "title deed." The same thing happened to those who had "car notes" and loans on buildings and businesses. They could not make their payments and, eventually, the item was repossessed, going back to the bank, the finance company, or whoever held the loan note. Don't confuse mortgages and car payments with ownership. It could cost you. As a kingdom citizen, all your stuff is bought and paid for and you receive them or acquire and access them by faith.

ALL THINGS ARE YOURS

Jesus died and rose again to restore back to mankind what one man calls "unquestionable dominion." He was our

"Jubilee." He made it so that the earth and everything in it could be returned into the hands of its rightful owners, God's people. God told Abraham, which is also for us to-day, *"For all the land which thou seest, to thee will I give it, and to thy seed for ever"* (Genesis 13:15). So, until we can see it, we are not entitled to possess it. He does not mean "seeing" with your natural eyes, but seeing with the eyes of your spirit—to see it by faith. Faith sees the invisible, and brings it to pass, *"Through faith we understand that the worlds were framed by the word of God, so that things which are seen were not made of things which do appear"* (Hebrews 11:3). Creation was not in view when God saw it. Then faith speaks and calls things that be not as though they were.

> AS OWNERS, GOD HAS GIVEN THE CHURCH THE AUTHORITY TO DECIDE WHAT GOES ON IN THE EARTH.

The Bible defines *faith* as *"the assurance (the confirmation, the title deed) of the things [we] hope for, being the proof of things [we] do not see and the conviction of their reality"* (Hebrews 11:1 AMP). Notice, **faith is the "title deed,"** or the "proof," that these things exists and that they belong to you. Once you show "proof" that things belong to you—from healing to houses or anything else in Christ—God gets involved in transferring what is rightfully yours into your hands.

The Lord said to Joshua before he marched around the city of Jericho, *"See, I have given into thy hand Jericho"* (Joshua 6:2). Because Joshua could see it, God got involved in transferring it. The same concept applies to blind Bartimaeus, who, in the gospel of Mark, was physically blind. But by faith, he saw his covenant promise of healing and cried out for it. God made the transfer through Jesus into his body. And he miraculously received his sight. Understand, we are not waiting on God...God is waiting on us—your miracle is already there from the foundation of the world.

God showed Abraham a land that someone else occupied. But, now, it's time for all that was stolen from God's first man, Adam, to be returned into the hands of God's "last Adam," Jesus Christ. Because of His obedience and the price Jesus paid for humanity, the Bible tells us that *"He has*

> ## FAITH IS THE TITLE DEED AND WITHOUT IT, WE CANNOT SEE WHAT RIGHTFULLY BELONGS TO US.

(been) *appointed heir of all things"* (Hebrews 1:2 NKJV). The *Charles B. Williams Translation* says, *"...Jesus is the lawful owner of everything."*

How does this apply to us as "joint heirs" with Christ? Well, we get what Jesus gets. Yes, He is preeminent, and He is Lord. But He is "Lord of lords" and we are joint heirs with Him, His body and His bride. Everything is owned together equally. Jesus gets one hundred percent and we get one hundred percent of everything bought and paid for by His precious blood. (Remember, my story at the end of chapter 8 that humorously illustrates the meaning of being a joint heir?)

I heard one man of God say this speaking about Adam and Eve in the garden of Eden, "If Adam didn't own it he had no seed to sow." Oh, I like that! The devil knew after Adam sinned in the garden that the authority of the earth now was turned over to him. This is why he said to Jesus in the temptation, *"I will give you all this power and all this wealth...It has been handed over to me, and I can give it to anyone I choose"* (Luke 4:6 *Good News Translation*). Thank God, Jesus came and recovered all.

OWNERSHIP HAS ITS REWARDS AND RESPONSIBILITY

God plans for us to live and enjoy a quality of life, far beyond what those living without the Lord could ever experience. As I like to say, what comes with "yours" is "The Good, the Bad, and the Ugly." The cities whose morals and economy are all broken down are ultimately the Church's problem, not the world's. Why? Because we are responsible for this planet and we're owners with stewardship responsibility. The Church is the only entity strong enough and wise enough to fix whatever is broken. Plus, we have THE BLESSING, which again is the scriptural name for the power that God used to create all matter. When we go to a place that needs transformation, through faith we are to superimpose heaven's reality over the current conditions. This is part of the operation of faith in THE BLESSING. What you believe and decree, God can create. Read what the prophet declares about the power of this blessing:

> And the desolate land shall be tilled, when as it lay desolate in the sight of all that pass by. And they shall say, This land that was desolate is become like the garden of Eden; and the waste and desolate and ruined cities *are become* fenced, (fortified) *and* are inhabited. Ezekiel 36:34–35

The Church is to actually make the desolate places a type of heaven right here on Earth. This is one of the rewards of being a joint heir. Our stewardship responsibility is to lift the curse wherever we are sent or deployed. THE BLESSING that is on our lives, along with the kingdom of God within us, can literally transform the worst places on Earth.

Here's one last thing about ownership. An ownership mentality carries an attitude of little or no tolerance for things not desired. I say it like this: "No ownership, no outrage." When one owns an apartment building there is little or no tolerance for destruction of their property by the tenants paying rent. A good example of this was when Rosa Parks, a black woman who refused to move to the back of the bus in the segregated South, took ownership and stood up for her rights as a U.S. citizen. When asked by the bus driver to move to the rear, she refused, which precipitated the Civil Rights movement headed by a "dreamer" and a "world changer" named Dr. Martin Luther King, Jr.

My point is that all this started with a mentality of "ownership." When the children of God take their ownership rights over this Earth, we will become intolerant of the injustice, terrorism, illiteracy, poverty, political corruption, joblessness, prison populations, media immorality, or anything else the devil has perpetrated. You and I are created to matter to our generation by bringing transformation and breaking the curse off of communities, cities, and nations. Whenever and wherever the Church takes ownership, the devil will be evicted and the culture of the kingdom will be established, fulfilling God's prophetic agenda that says, *"The kingdoms of this world are become the kingdoms of our Lord, and of his Christ; and he shall reign for ever and ever"* (Revelation 11:15).

It is time to shift our thinking. We're not passing through this Earth "just trying to make heaven our home." No! The "Owner's Manual" says, *"We are ambassadors for Christ"* sent from God into this world to make every place the soles of our feet shall tread upon a "heaven on earth."

TAPPING INTO GOD'S WISDOM

God is training up a new generation of leaders, both kings and priests, for a new day of challenges. As I discussed, He is moving His children into positions of leadership in business, ministry, entertainment, government, education, and all spheres of influence because we have been chosen to control the mountains from within. This new generation of leaders will not only need to be strong, uncompromising, and very courageous, but will also need to tap into the superior wisdom of God, as Joseph did for the government of Egypt, and Daniel did while serving under King Nebuchadnezzar. Their wisdom was far beyond anything taught at secular universities and colleges. The scriptures say, speaking about Daniel and the three Hebrew men: *"God gave them knowledge and skill in all learning and wisdom"* (Daniel 1:17). It was "divine wisdom," which came from God through His Holy Spirit, and it is your heritage.

As discussed in this book, there is also another kind of wisdom I refer to as "natural" or "human wisdom" that comes through the intellect, being taught in our secular universities, which is a product of the senses and mental deduction. Remember, without the Lord, we are left with only "dark" information. Darkness means ignorance or without a full perception of reality, usually resulting in experimentation or the process called "trial and error." As members of the Body of Christ, we are designed to operate on a much higher level, excelling in our work, even 10 times better. The apostle Paul writes in Ephesians 3:10 that we are to operate in *"the manifold wisdom of God,"* or on a mental frequency that far exceeds human wisdom. Operating in this higher dimension that Paul writes about places us in a position of prominence in the world.

As owners and heirs of God, we should be the problem solvers, running to problems, not running from problems. This was the mentality David had when he went up against the giant Goliath. David knew that while he couldn't match Goliath when it came to size, he could surpass him when it came to strategy flowing from the wisdom of God. You know the story. He took a slingshot and one small stone to slay a giant who had been a major problem for forty days for the entire army of Israel.

One reason we were born into this generation is that there are problems that we were specifically created to solve. How? Through God's wisdom. In the book of Proverbs it says, *"Wisdom is the principle thing, therefore get wisdom..."* (Proverbs 4:7). This means that wisdom has the solution to every challenge our society faces today. By exercising godly wisdom, all those challenges can be overcome.

Earlier, I mentioned how God gave Joseph the ability to interpret Pharaoh's dream, the results of which saved Egypt and the surrounding nations from starvation during a seven-year famine. After that happened, Pharaoh invited Joseph's entire family to relocate to Egypt. Again, Pharaoh showed no interest in Joseph's family until after Joseph had solved the king's problem. Suddenly, Joseph had gained great favor with Pharaoh—his name had become great! And his family reaped some of the benefit of that favor.

As you and I are sent to lift the curse off of humanity in the cities and nations of this world, God will do for us just as He did for Joseph. He will grant us favor and give us His wisdom to light the way and ultimately lead the world to Him.

Jesus teaches, *"But wisdom is justified of her children"* (Matthew 11:19). In other words, the proof of wisdom is results. Jesus changed the world because He used godly wisdom and got results. When the wisdom of God speaks no one can *"gainsay or resist"* (Luke 21:15). A priest can speak wisdom in counseling a king. A lawyer can speak wisdom in trying his or her case.

As heirs of God, covenant access to wisdom is our birthright. Pharaoh said, speaking about the wisdom of God spoken through Joseph, *"...Forasmuch as God hath shewed thee all this, there is none so discreet and wise as thou art"* (Genesis 41:39).

Guaranteed, there is a problem with your name on it. It's time for you to enjoy this all-important heritage and get results too. One man said, "You will only be remembered for the problems you solve or the ones you create."[5]

If you know how to tap into God's wisdom, you can find answers to every challenge or problem you will ever encounter, whether it's in operating your business or ministry; in running the local, state, or federal government; or in managing your personal life. No matter how bad the situation, wisdom will turn it around. Just remember to give God the glory. It helps to keep you connected to more wisdom (Proverbs 4:7; Daniel 2). It's important to know that most of the rewards in life will be directly related to the problems you solve for others.

One of my favorite examples of someone who used the wisdom of God to change a culture and an economy is Dr. George Washington Carver, who I spoke about in earlier chapters. Dr. Carver revolutionized the economy of the southern region of the United States through the introduction of hundreds of uses for the peanut, soybean, pecan, and sweet potato in the place of cotton. These crops replenished the soil and provided income for the South that grew to hundreds of millions of dollars.[6]

Dr. Carver was visited at Tuskegee by President Franklin D. Roosevelt and Vice President Calvin Coolidge, and became a confidante and advisor to leaders and scientists from all over the world, including Henry Ford and Thomas Edison.[7]

In 1921, Dr. Carver was invited to address the United States House Ways and Means Committee, and given 10 minutes to discuss potential uses of the peanut and other crops. However, upon hearing just a portion of what Carver had to say, the committee chairman spoke up and said, "Go ahead Brother. Your time is unlimited!" Carver addressed the committee for one hour and forty-five minutes.[8] When his talk concluded, the following dialogue took place between Carver and the committee chairman:

> "Dr. Carver, how did you learn all of these
> things?"

"From an old book," Carver answered.

"What book?" the chairman asked.

"The Bible."

"Does the Bible tell (us) about peanuts?"

"No, Sir. But it tells (us) about the God who made the peanut. I asked Him to show me what to do with the peanut, and He did."[9]

> **COVENANT ACCESS TO WISDOM IS OUR BIRTHRIGHT.**

Wherever God has placed you, it's your stewardship responsibility to break the curse off that place. No matter what assignment He has given you and no matter how difficult it may seem, THE BLESSING of God and the wisdom of God are sufficient to keep you moving forward.

CONCLUSION

YOUR GIFT IS FOR NATIONS

This is the most challenging time to be alive on planet Earth. And as nations experience more political, economic, and social distress, it will be the dedicated, godly men and women, kings and priests, who will come to the rescue with the right answers and practical ingenuity to solve the world's problems. Kings and priests should know that they have tremendous, God-given potential inside them, which is tied to their unique purpose on Earth to bless and benefit others.

Entrepreneurs, for example, are given gifts not just for themselves, but for the good of their neighborhood or nation. God calls business leaders and entrepreneurs, just like He calls pastors and preachers, and gives them the responsibility to drive the economy forward. Entrepreneurs must realize that their entrepreneurial gifts are to preserve and prosper entire nations, creating ways to expand the economic pie, rather than have people fight over the same slice (Sirico 2010). They have an obligation to expand business markets, identify new ways of organizing resources, create jobs, discover cures, or simply help dreams become reality. Their entrepreneurial gifts are mainly for the benefit of others. One of the greatest tragedies within the Church could be not applying our talents, gifts, and faith to achieve material success, when it can do so much in helping to lift the curse off humanity.

The promotion of entrepreneurship is becoming increasingly more important around the world, especially in areas that are most vulnerable to systemic and generational poverty. I firmly believe that the growth of entrepreneurship is one answer to the economic erosion happening in many U.S. cities and communities heavily populated by minorities. Research shows that there is a direct correlation between the number of entrepreneurs in a country and the standard of living that country enjoys.[1] Entrepreneurs, therefore, have the moral obligation to accept their call and to confront economic uncertainty by positively affecting the economic health of a nation.

Just as the gifts and genius of entrepreneurs are to move an economy forward, the God-given genius of all marketplace leaders is for the good of others. No matter the vocation—scientist, teacher, movie producer, actor, athlete, or homemaker—God calls each of us to influence and shape our culture with the superior principles and power of the kingdom of God. You were called for such a time as this.

Pastors (priests) or spiritual leaders, on the other hand, need to know that entrepreneurship and all marketplace callings are rooted in the spiritual realm, and that they have a spiritual responsibility to encourage everyone to answer their callings, and to use their gifts beyond the four walls of the church. Just as I was taught while working at IBM, pastors need to teach their congregations how to use their faith in the marketplace. Jesus performed most of His miracles not in the temple, but where people gathered to live everyday life.

God is deploying Christians into every sphere of influence in the marketplace to bring these spheres under kingdom control and jurisdiction, *"The kingdoms of this world are become the kingdoms of our Lord, and of his Christ; and he shall reign for ever and ever"* (Revelation 11:15). Just as Joseph's gift preserved Egypt during a time of extreme famine, so should the gifts of God's kingdom citizens—who are innovative and faithful to their calling—do today.

God treats a nation as He does an individual. He comes to its aid when in trouble. He blesses it (Psalm 33:12). He gives it a vision, and the provision—whether it's obvious or obscured—to manifest that vision, providing natural resources, commerce, potential for technology, and the seeds of ideas to increase productivity or output. He deposits gifts and talents for indispensable skills into its people.

Our job is to draw these resources out, and to develop them through education, training, and work opportunities. As I heard one man say, "There is nothing capricious about the nature of God. He doesn't give a vision without providing provision."[2] Provision, by the way, includes intellectual capital, manpower, skills, raw materials, tools, and strategies. God's heart is for nations, and so is your gift.

Scarcity and shortages are mainly tied to a lack of creativity, limited competency, or corrupt leadership. So, the problem is usually not a shortage of resources, but rather a shortage of creativity interacting with resources that are usually right within reach. God created abundance in this Earth and to this date, nothing has changed.

THE PROPER PERSPECTIVE

With any revelation or teaching, there is always a possibility for misinterpretation and misapplication. Therefore, let me be clear about what this teaching in this book is not. This is not a "get-rich-quick" scheme, where one group manipulates or gets ahead at the expense of the other. No, this book is about advancing the kingdom, where the kings and priests are flowing together as one unbeatable team. Without these two coming together, the enormous wealth or provision God has provided could be lost or wasted, and as a result, hundreds, thousands, and even millions of souls could be lost or never become part of the unbeatable team of kings and priests, and Almighty God.

APPENDIX

THE BUSINESS PROPHECY

This is a Word that was given to Dr. Bill Winston during his morning prayer on August 8, 1986, prompting him to establish the Joseph Business School, a new type of business school.

The Spirit of the Lord spoke to me about the businessman and businesses in this last hour. He is raising up ministries, which will be called companies in this last hour. In the past, we have made a distinction between the ministry and the company, and we thought of a ministry as a church or an evangelistic outreach or some type of traditional "religious" organization. God said to "Take the straps off." He is taking us to a higher truth. One that would allow us to see a ministry as any enterprise where Jesus is Lord. People will then recognize a ministry as a manufacturing company, or a publishing company, or "ABC Distribution Company." There will be godly men with great integrity managing these companies. They will be God's ministers. They will operate these businesses using the principles of faith along with their basic business skills. *"I am the LORD thy God which teacheth thee to profit..."* (Isaiah 48:17). Large sums of money will be planted by these businesses into the local churches and other associated work of the gospel.

These businesses will not be born out of the intellect or out of tradition, but will be born out of the SPIRIT. Some are even operating today. Their operations cannot be hindered by the forces of the world such as the economy, because they will function by faith in God's Word. As these ministers manage these businesses through the Godly principles and by the Spirit, they will allow the Lord to work through them to build His House *"Except the LORD build the house, they labour in vain that build it: except the LORD keep the city, the watchman waketh but in vain"* (Psalm 127:1); thus receiving credit for eternity, remembering that the Lord can only give credit to what He has done.

ENDNOTES

PREFACE

[1]Press article, "Supreme Court's 1963 school-prayer decision didn't ban school prayer," *First Amendment Center*, June 8, 2003, *http://www.firstamendmentcenter.org/ supreme-court% E2%80%99s-1963-school-prayer-decision-didn%E2%80%99t-ban-school-prayer.*

[2]The World Bank, "World Bank Forecasts Global Poverty to Fall Below 10% for First Time; Major Hurdles Remain in Goal to End Poverty by 2030," press release, October 4, 2015, *http:// www.worldbank.org/en/news/press-release/2015/10/04/ world-bank-forecasts-global-poverty-to-fall-below-10-for-first-time-major-hurdles-remain-in-goal-to-end-poverty-by-2030.*

[3]Os Hillman and Lance Wallnau for the definition of the term "seven pillars of society," or the seven spheres, or mountains of society that are the pillars of any society. These seven mountains are business, government, media, arts and entertainment, education, the family, and religion. *http:// www.7culturalmountains.org/.*

INTRODUCTION

[1]Kevin Miller, "Living the Entrepreneur's Dream," *Power to Change Ministries* website, February 18, 2016, *http:// powertochange.com/discover/faith/browne/.*

[2] Ibid.

[3]Dave Browne, "Dr. Townsend's Leadership Training and Institute Fellows: Building a High-Performance Culture, Part 1" (opening symposium of the Townsend Institute, Townsend Institute for Leadership & Counseling at Huntington University, Huntington, IN, October 23, 2015).

[4]Charles Nieman, audio CD *Kings & Priests: Partners for the* Kingdom for introducing the "divine partnership" term, *Charles Nieman Ministries*, El Paso, Texas, 2007, *http:// www.charlesnieman.com*.

[5]Sunday Adelaja, *Church Shift: Revolutionizing Your Faith, Church, and Life for the 21st Century* (Lake Mary, FL: Charisma House, 2008), page 33 (hereafter cited as Adelaja, *Church Shift*).

CHAPTER 1 – KINGS & PRIESTS: A REVELATION

[1]Janet Chismar, "Billy Graham: Pastor to Presidents: Short stories and a photo collection," *Billy Graham Evangelistic Association* website, *BGEA Features*, February 19, 2012, *http://www.billygraham.org/articlepage.asp?articleid=8495* (hereafter cited as Chismar, "Billy Graham").

[2]Ibid.

[3]Adelle Banks, "'Billy Graham & Me': Remembrances, Big and Small," *USA Today*, Religion News Service, February 13, 2013, *http://www.delawareonline.com/usatoday/article/1916297* (hereafter cited as Banks, "Billy Graham").

[4]General article, "The Persian Gulf War," special feature from the film *George H. W. Bush*, WGBH, American Experience. WGBH Educational Foundation, 2008. PBS, *http://www.pbs.org/wgbh/americanexperience/features/general-article/bush-gulf-war/?flavour=mobile* (hereafter cited as General article, "The Persian Gulf War").

[5]Ibid.

CHAPTER 2 – KINGS & PRIESTS: THE KINGDOM

[1]Myles Munroe, *Rediscovering the Kingdom: Ancient Hope for our 21st Century World* (Shippensburg, PA: Destiny Image Publishers, 2004), page 70.

[2]Nikhila Henry, "Stargazers on Cloud Nine" article in *Times of India*, India Times.com, TNN, November 21, 2008, *http://articles.timesofindia.indiatimes.com/keyword/Vedic-astrology/featured/3* (hereafter cited as Henry, "Stargazers").

[3]Mike TeSelle, "New Chief to Deploy First-of-Its-Kind Cops and Clergy Teams," KCRA.com, News, February 13, 2013, *http://www.kcra.com/news/New-chief-to-deploy-first-of-its-kind-cops-and-clergy-teams/-/11797728/18536338/-/ir1ukp/-/index.html*; and Kim Minugh, "Sam Somers Jr., Sacramento's New Police Chief, Focuses on Community Building," *The Sacramento Bee,* sacbee.com, Crime, Sacto911, April 4, 2013, http://*www.sacbee.com/2013/04/03/v-print/5315039/sam-somers-jr-sacramentos-new.html*.

[4] Hansi Lo Wang, "A New Baltimore Model? 'Officer On The Beat...Pastor On The Corner'," NPR.org, News, May 8, 2015, *http://www.npr.org/2015/05/08/405222336/a-new-baltimore-model-officer-on-the-beat-pastor-on-the-corner?utm_medium=RSS&utm_campaign=news*.

[5]Ibid.

CHAPTER 3 – KINGS & PRIESTS: A DIVINE PARTNERSHIP

[1]Rev. R. A. Sirico, "The Entrepreneurial Vocation." *Entrepreneurship: Values and Responsibility, Praxiology: The International Annual of Practical Philosophy and Methodology.* Vol. 17. Eds. W. W. Gasparski, L. V. Ryan, & S. Kwiatkowski (New Brunswick, NJ: Transaction Publishers, 2010), pages 154–155, (hereafter cited as R. A. Sirico, "The Entrepreneurial").

[2]Ibid., page 165, quoted form Michael Novak, *The Spirit of Democratic Capitalism* (New York, NY: Simon & Schuster, 1982), page 98.

[3]Ibid., page 156.

[4]Ibid., page 155.

[5]Henry, "Stargazers."

[6]James H. O'Neill, "The True Story of The Patton Prayer," *Review of the News,* October 6, 1971, Reprinted on the Patton Society website, *http://pattonhq.com/prayer.html* (hereafter cited as O'Neill, "Patton").

[7]Ibid.

[8]Ibid.

[9]Ibid.

[10]Banks, "Billy Graham."

[11]General article, "The Persian Gulf War."

[12]Chismar, "Billy Graham."

[13]Ibid.

[14]Ibid.

[15]Larry Gordon, *After the Due Order* (Sergeant Bluff, IA: The Name Ministries, 1990), page 31.

[16]Ibid., page 31.

[17]Ibid., page 16.

[18]Ibid., page 16.

[19]Ibid., page 31.

[20]Ibid., page 33.

CHAPTER 4 – A MENTAL REVERSAL

[1]James Lee Beall, *Laying the Foundation: Achieving Christian Maturity,* ReadHowYouWant ed. Containing the complete,

unabridged text of the original publisher's edition. (Accessible Publishing Systems PTY, Ltd., 2010; Alachua, FL: Bridge-Logos, 1976; Reprinted 1999, 2002, 2004, 2006, 2009), page 19. Citations refer to the ReadHowYouWant edition.

[2]Joseph Thayer and James Strong, *Thayer's Greek-English Lexicon of the New Testament: Coded with Strong's Concordance Numbers* (Peabody, MA: Hendrickson Publishers, 1995), "metamorphoo," G3339.

[3]James Strong, *Strong's Exhaustive Concordance of the Bible* "Greek Dictionary of the New Testament" (Nashville, TN: Thomas Nelson Publishers, 1990), ref. 3339.

[4]Ibid.

[5]Merriam-Webster.com. *Merriam-Webster,* s.v. "paradigm," accessed July 22, 2012, *http://www.merriam-webster.com/dictionary/paradigm.*

CHAPTER 5 – NO MORE TOIL

[1]*1828 Edition of Noah Webster's American Dictionary of the English Language* online, s.v. "toil," accessed August 16, 2013, *http://1828.mshaffer.com/d/search/word,toil.*

[2]Bishop David O. Oyedepo, *The Unlimited Power of Faith* (Lagos, Nigeria: Dominion Publishing House, 2011), page 109 (hereafter cited Oyedepo, *The Unlimited Power of Faith*).

[3]James Strong and W. E. Vine, *The New Strong's Concise Concordance & Vine's Concise Dictionary of the Bible* (Nashville, TN: Thomas Nelson Publishers, 1997, 1999), in *Strong's Concise Concordance,* ref. 4983, "soma," Greek translation for "body," page 36.

[4]J. Gunnar Olson, *Business Unlimited: Memories of the Coming Kingdom* (Orebro, Sweden: ICCC, International

Christian Chamber of Commerce, Hjalmarbergets Foretags-center, 2002), pages 71–73.

[5]William J. Federer, *George Washington Carver: His Life & Faith in His Own Words* (St. Louis, MO: Amerisearch, Inc., 2008), page 61, quoted from Carver, George Washington. November 19, 1924, in a speech before 500 people of the Women's Board of Domestic Missions in New York City's Marble Collegiate Church. Ethel Edwards, *Carver of Tuskegee* (Cincinnati, OH: Ethel Edwards & James T. Hardwick, a limited edition work compiled in part from over 300 personal letters written by Dr. Carver to James T. Hardwick between 1922–1937, from Carver Memorial, Locust Grove, Diamond, MO, 1971), pages 141–142.

[6]*1828 Edition of Noah Webster's American Dictionary of the English Language* online, s.v. "grope," accessed February 4, 2016, *http://1828.mshaffer.com/d/search/word,grope*.

[7]"Ergon." Greek translation for "work," accessed December 5, 2012, *Strong's Exhaustive Concordance of the Bible,* "Greek Dictionary of the New Testament," ref. 2041, *www.biblos.com*.

[8]Dr. Myles Munroe, *Releasing Your Potential* (Shippensburg, PA: Destiny Image Publishers, 1992, Revised 2002), page 188.

[9]Merriam-Webster.com. *Merriam-Webster,* s.v. "potential," accessed February 4, 2016, *http://www.merriam-webster.com/dictionary/potential*.

[10]William J. Federer, *America's God and Country: Encyclopedia of Quotations* rev. ed. (Coppell, TX: FAME Publishing Inc., 1994; St. Louis, MO: Amerisearch, Inc., 2000), page 94. Citations refer to the Amerisearch edition.

[11]Ibid.

[12]Ibid., page 96, quoted from Carver, George Washington. November 19, 1924, in a speech before 500 people of the

Women's Board of Domestic Missions in New York City's Marble Collegiate Church. Ethel Edwards, *Carver of Tuskegee* (Cincinnati, OH: Ethel Edwards & James T. Hardwick, a limited edition work compiled in part from over 300 personal letters written by Dr. Carver to James T. Hardwick between 1922–1937, from Carver Memorial, Locust Grove, Diamond, MO, 1971), pages 141–142.

[13]Shawn Bolz, *Keys To Heaven's Economy* (North Sutton, NH: Streams Publishing House, 1992), page 59.

CHAPTER 6 – LIVING IN THE KINGDOM

[1]David O. Oyedepo, *Understanding Financial Prosperity* (Lagos, Nigeria: Dominion Publishing House, 2005), pages 152–153 (hereafter cited as Oyedepo, *Understanding Financial Prosperity*).

[2]Ibid., pages 187, 189.

[3]Oral Roberts, *Seed-Faith 2000* (Tulsa, OK: Oral Roberts Ministries, 1999), page 50.

[4]Ibid., pages 50–51.

[5]Ibid., pages 53–54.

[6]Ibid., page 55.

[7]"Answering God's Call: Every Workplace, Every Nation. LeTourneau University," *The Vision of LeTourneau University*, accessed December 28, 2014, *http://www.letu.edu/_Other-Resources/presidents_office/vision/*.

[8]Ronald C. Jordan, "A Word to Build On," Believer's Voice of Victory, *Kenneth Copeland Ministries, Inc.,* December 12, 2012. Accessed October 20, 2015. *http://www.kcm.org/read/magazine*.

[9]Joseph Thayer and James Strong, *Thayer's Greek-English Lexicon of the New Testament: Coded with Strong's Concordance Numbers,* (Peabody, MA: Hendrickson Publishers, 1995), ref. 3670.

CHAPTER 7 — MANIFESTING KINGDOM ABUNDANCE

[1]"Eden." Hebrew translation for "live voluptuously, a place of pleasure, or place of delight," accessed February 5, 2016, *Strong's Exhaustive Concordance of the Bible,* "Hebrew Chaldee Dictionary," *http://biblehub.com/hebrew/5730.htm.*

[2]Kenneth Copeland, "Whatever He Says to You...," Believer's Voice of Victory, *Kenneth Copeland Ministries, Inc.,* April 4, 2015. Accessed October 21, 2015. *http://www.kcm.org/read/magazine.*

[3]Oyedepo, *Understanding Financial Prosperity,* page 24.

[4]Oyedepo, *The Unlimited Power of Faith,* page 196.

[5]James Strong and W. E. Vine, *The New Strong's Concise Concordance & Vine's Concise Dictionary of the Bible* (Nashville, TN: Thomas Nelson, Inc., 1997, 1999) in *Strong's Concise Concordance,* ref. 6680, "tsawah," Hebrew translation for "command," page 59.

CHAPTER 8 — STEPS TO MANIFESTING KINGDOM ABUNDANCE

[1]*1828 Edition of Noah Webster's American Dictionary of the English Language* online, s.v. "rich," accessed February 8, 2016, *http://1828.mshaffer.com/d/search/word,rich.*

[2]William J. Federer, *George Washington Carver: His Life & Faith in His Own Words* (St. Louis, MO: Amerisearch, Inc., 2008), page 44.

[3]Ibid., quoted from Carver, George Washington. January 21, 1921, in an address before the House Ways and Means

Committee. Charles E. Jones, *The Books You Read* (Harrisburg, PA: Executive Books, 1985), page 132.

[4]Ibid., page 44.

[5]Jesse Duplantis, guest speaker, "International Faith Conference" (IFC 2015), Living Word Christian Center, Forest Park, IL, September 2015.

[6]Debra Glanton Horn, guest on panel discussion held during the Joseph Business School Alumni Association meeting at the Joseph Business School, Forest Park, IL, December 12, 2013.

CHAPTER 9 – VENGEANCE & RECOMPENSE: THE JUSTICE SYSTEM OF GOD

[1]Dr. Martin Luther King, Jr., "I Have a Dream" (speech), transcript, *FOXNews* online; FOXNews.com, *http://www.foxnews.com/us/2013/08/27/transcript-martin-luther-king-jr-have-dream-speech/#ixzz2dIMiXW5s.*

[2]*1828 Edition of Noah Webster's American Dictionary of the English Language* online, s.v. "recompense," accessed October 15, 2015, *http://1828.mshaffer.com/d/search/word, recompense.*

[3]O'Neill, "Patton."

[4]James Strong, *Strong's Exhaustive Concordance of the Bible*, "Hebrew Chaldee Dictionary" (Nashville, TN: Thomas Nelson Publishers, 1990), ref. 892.

[5]Michael Galiga, guest speaker, "Economic Empowerment Summit" (EES 2010), Living Word Christian Center, Forest Park, IL, November 2010.

[6]Michael Galiga, *Win Every Battle* (Minneapolis, MN: Bronze Bow Publishing, 2009), pages 61–71.

[7]Ibid., page 71.

CHAPTER 10 – CHARACTER & INTEGRITY

[1]"Character is power." Quote from Booker T. Washington, accessed February 10, 2016, *http://www.goodreads.com/author/quotes/84278.Booker_T_Washington.*

[2]Merriam-Webster.com. *Merriam-Webster,* s.v. "stress," accessed October 9, 2015, *http://www.merriam-webster.com/dictionary/stress.*

[3]Merriam-Webster.com. *Merriam-Webster,* s.v. "integrity," accessed July 22, 2012, *http://www.merriam-webster.com/dictionary/integrity.*

[4]Baron Thomas Babington Macauley, British historian and statesman (1800–1859).

[5]"Character." *Random House Dictionary of the English Language College Edition* (New York, NY: Random House Publishers, 1960).

[6]Dr. Myles Munroe, *The Principles of Power and Vision: Keys to Achieving Personal and Corporate Destiny* (New Kensington, PA: Whitaker House Publishers, 2003, Reprint 2006).

CHAPTER 11 – STEWARDSHIP

[1]James Strong, *Strong's Exhaustive Concordance of the Bible* "Tables of Monies and Weights" (Nashville, TN: Thomas Nelson Publishers, 1990) (hereafter cited James Strong, "Tables of Monies and Weights").

[2]*1828 Edition of Noah Webster's American Dictionary of the English Language* online, s.v. "replenish," accessed October 22, 2012, *http://1828.mshaffer.com/d/search/word,replenish.*

[3]A standard talent is equal to 75 U.S. pounds. The price of gold on January 23, 2015, was $1,294.10 an ounce. There

are 14.583 troy ounces in a U.S. pound. That means a talent of gold would be worth $1,415,422 (one million, four hundred fifteen thousand, four hundred twenty-two dollars U.S.) Accessed July 13, 2015, *http://www.biblestudy.org/ beginner/bible-weights-and-measures.html; http://www.kitco. com/scripts/hist_charts/daily_graphs.cgi.*

[4]C. William Pollard, *The Soul of the Firm* (Grand Rapids, MI: Zondervan, 1996), page 20.

[5]Ed Silvoso, *Anointed for Business: How to Use Your Influence in the Marketplace to Change the World* (Ventura, CA: Regal Books, 2002 and 2006), page 57.

[6]*"Faithful." Webster's New World College Dictionary, Fourth Edition.* Eds. Michael Agnes, David B. Guralnik, (Foster City, CA: IDG Books Worldwide, Inc., 2001, 2000, 1999).

CHAPTER 13 – MIRACLES IN THE MARKETPLACE

[1]James Strong, *Strong's Exhaustive Concordance of the Bible* "Hebrew Chaldee Dictionary" (Nashville, TN: Thomas Nelson Publishers, 1990), ref. 6045.

[2]R. A. Sirico, "The Entrepreneurial," page 153.

[3]Ibid.

CHAPTER 14 – CALLING ALL KINGS

[1]Wikipedia, s.v. "Speaker Named for Lions Event" (Minden, LA: Minden Press, Dec. 17, 1962), page 1, *https://en.wikipedia. org/wiki/R._G._LeTourneau.*

[2]Rick Williams, with Jared C. Crooks, *Christian Business Legends* (Ashland, OH: Business Reform and The Business Reform Foundation, 2004), page 50 (hereafter cited as Williams with Crooks, *Christian Business Legends*).

[3]Ibid.

[4]Ibid.

[5]Ibid., page 51.

[6]Ibid.

[7]Dr. John H. Niemelä, *Celebrating the R.G. LeTourneau "Mountain Mover,"* brochure documenting the designation of the mountain mover as a historical landmark by the American Society of Mechanical Engineers, November 29, 2004, *https:// www.asme.org/about-asme/who-we-are/engineering-history/landmarks/231-letourneau-mountain-mover-scraper.*

[8]R. A. Sirico, "The Entrepreneurial," page 154.

[9]Ibid., page 155.

[10]Ibid., page 156.

[11]James Strong, "Tables of Monies and Weights."

[12]"Capitalism." *Oxford Dictionary of Finance and Banking.* Eds. Jonathan Law, John Smullen, (New York, NY: Oxford University Press, 2008).

[13]Ed Silvoso, *Transformation: Change the Marketplace and You Change the World* (Ventura, CA: Regal Books, 2007), pages 137–138.

CHAPTER 15 – LEADERSHIP BEGINS WITH VISION

[1]Merriam-Webster.com. *Merriam-Webster,* s.v. "vision," accessed June 17, 2013, *http://www.merriam-webster.com/dictionary/vision.*

[2]*1828 Edition of Noah Webster's American Dictionary of the English Language* online, s.v. "vision," accessed June 17, 2013, *http://1828.mshaffer.com/d/search/word,vision.*

[3]John Hope Bryant, *How the Poor Can Save Capitalism: Rebuilding the Path to the Middle Class* (San Francisco, CA: Berrett-Koehler Publishers, Inc., 2014), page 17.

[4]Ibid.

[5]Rick Warren, "What On Earth Am I Here For?" *Ministry-Today*, January/February 2013, page 16.

CHAPTER 17 – THE MIRACLE IS IN YOUR STAFF

[1]Williams with Crooks, *Christian Business Legends,* page 37, quoted from George Grant, Lecture on Booker T. Washington (Moscow, ID: Canon Press, 2000) Cassette tape.

[2]John C. Maxwell, *The 21 Irrefutable Laws of Leadership: Follow Them and People Will Follow You* (Nashville, TN: Thomas Nelson Publishers, 1998 and 2007), page 75.

[3]Ibid.

[4]Dennis P. Kimbro, *What Makes the Great Great* (New York, NY: Doubleday, 1998), page 93.

CHAPTER 18 – TAKING POSSESSION

[1]*1828 Edition of Noah Webster's American Dictionary of the English Language* online, s.v. "dominion," accessed July 26, 2013, *http://1828.mshaffer.com/d/search/word,dominion.*

[2]Dr. Frederick K. C. Price, *Name It and Claim It: The Power of Positive Confession* (Los Angeles, CA: Faith One Publishing, 1992), page 139.

[3]James Strong and W. E. Vine, *The New Strong's Concise Concordance & Vine's Concise Dictionary of the Bible* (Nashville, TN: Thomas Nelson, Inc., 1997, 1999) in *Vine's Dictionary,* ref. 120, "adam," pages 230–231.

[4] *1828 Edition of Noah Webster's American Dictionary of the English Language* online, s.v. "own," accessed July 26, 2013, http://1828.mshaffer.com/d/search/word,own.

[5] Mike Murdock, *The Law of Recognition* (Ft. Worth, TX: The Wisdom Center and Wisdom International, 2007), chapter 29, "Recognition of the Problem You Are Presently Assigned to Solve."

[6] William J. Federer, *George Washington Carver: His Life & Faith in His Own Words* (St. Louis, MO: Amerisearch, Inc., 2008), page 9.

[7] William J. Federer, *America's God and Country: Encyclopedia of Quotations* rev. ed. (Coppell, TX: FAME Publishing Inc., 1994; St. Louis, MO: Amerisearch, Inc., 2000), page 94. Citations refer to the Amerisearch edition.

[8] Ibid., page 95.

[9] Ibid., page 96, Carver, George Washington. January 21, 1921, in an address before the House Ways and Means Committee. Charles E. Jones, *The Books You Read* (Harrisburg, PA: Executive Books, 1985), page 132.

CONCLUSION

[1] Sangram Keshari Mohanty, *Fundamentals of Entrepreneurship* (Connaught Circus, New Delhi, India: Prentice Hall of India Private Limited, 2005), page 160.

[2] Peter J. Daniels, guest speaker, "Business and Leadership Conference" (BLC) Living Word Christian Center, Forest Park, IL, November 1995.

REFERENCES

Adelaja, Sunday. 2008. *ChurchShift: Revolutionizing Your Faith, Church, and Life for the 21st Century.* Lake Mary, FL: Charisma House.

Gordon, Larry. 1990. *After the Due Order.* Sergeant Bluff, IA: The Name Ministries.

Kachaje, Henry. May 29, 2014. "When Good People Commit Gross Crimes by Remaining Silent." *Afriem* (blog). Accessed February 17, 2016. *http://www.afriem.org/2014/05/good-people-commit-gross-crimes-remaining-silent/.*

Keesee, Gary O. 2011. *Fixing the Money Thing.* Shippensburg, PA: Destiny Image Publishers, Inc.

Oyedepo, David O. 2005. *Understanding Financial Prosperity.* Lagos, Nigeria: Dominion Publishing House.

Shepherd, Jeremy. 2004. In a working paper "Christian Enemy #1: Dualism Exposed & Destroyed." Pages 2–3. The Friday Symposium at Dallas Baptist University. Accessed February 17, 2016. *http://www3.dbu.edu/naugle/pdf/FridaySymposiumFa04/Christian_Enemy_1.pdf.*

Silvoso, Ed. 2007. *Transformation: Change the Marketplace and You Can Change the World.* Ventura, CA: Regal Books.

Sirico, Rev. R. A. 2010. "The Entrepreneurial Vocation." In *Entrepreneurship: Values and Responsibility, Praxiology: The International Annual of Practical Philosophy and Methodology.* Vol. 17, eds. Wojciech W. Gasparski, Leo V. Ryan, & Stefan Kwiatkowski, pages 153–175. New Brunswick, NJ: Transaction Publishers.

PRAYER OF SALVATION

Heavenly Father, I come to You, in the name of Your Son, Jesus Christ. You said in Your Word that whosoever shall call upon the Name of the Lord shall be saved (Romans 10:13). Father, I am calling on Jesus, right now. I believe He died on the Cross for my sins, and that He was raised from the dead on the third day, and He's alive right now. Lord Jesus, I am asking You now, come into my heart. Live Your life in me and through me. I repent of my sins, and surrender myself totally and completely to You. Heavenly Father, by faith, I now confess Jesus Christ as my new Lord and Savior. From this day forward, I dedicate my life to serving Him. Amen.

PRAYER FOR BUSINESS SUCCESS

Father, in Jesus' name, I thank You for Your wisdom, guidance, and peace in my business, and in every area of my life. You are the Source and Supplier of all I set my hands to and everything I do in business shall prosper and come to maturity. I am diligent in business, and I am a faithful steward over all God has entrusted to me.

Father, You said wisdom is the principal thing; therefore, I get wisdom, and with all my getting, I get understanding, discernment, comprehension, and interpretation. I operate my business above and beyond the systems of this world. In the evil time, I shall not be ashamed and in the days of famine, I shall be satisfied.

Thank You for the tremendous success that my associates and I experience in our business(es) and for the increase in profits and productivity that we will enjoy. All grace, every favor and earthly blessing comes to us in abundance, so that we always, in all circumstances, whatever the need, are self-sufficient, requiring no aid or support. Our team is furnished in abundance for every good work and charitable donation (2 Corinthians 9:8 AMP).

The favor of God is upon me and my team, and goes before us, producing supernatural increase, promotion, debt cancellation, restoration, honor, increased assets, greater victories, recognition, prominence, petitions granted, policies and rules changed, and battles won that we didn't have to fight, for God fights them for us! You have confirmed and established the work of my hands, and I give You all the glory, honor, and praise for it, in Jesus' name, amen.

ABOUT THE AUTHOR

Dr. Bill Winston was born in Tuskegee, Alabama, surrounded by an abundance of educators, scientists, and physicians, and by the famous Tuskegee Airmen who inspired and influenced him for leadership. He is a graduate of the internationally known Tuskegee Institute in Tuskegee, Alabama (now Tuskegee University), where Booker T. Washington's and George Washington Carver's legacies of leadership and invention permeated the environment.

Dr. Winston served for six years as a fighter pilot in the United States Air Force, where his extraordinary achievement in aerial flight earned him The Distinguished Flying Cross, The Air Medal for performance in combat, and the Squadron Top Gun Award. After completing his military service, Dr. Winston joined the IBM Corporation as a marketing representative. After rapidly earning several promotions, he resigned in 1985 to enter full-time ministry.

Today, Dr. Winston is the founder and senior pastor of Living Word Christian Center (LWCC), a multicultural, non-denominational church with more than 20,000 members located in Forest Park, Illinois; the founder and president of the nationally accredited Joseph Business School (JBS), with headquarters in Forest Park and partnership locations on five continents.

He is also the founder of Bill Winston Ministries (BWM), a partnership-based global outreach ministry, which produces the internationally televised *Believer's Walk of Faith* reaching over 800 million households worldwide. Through Faith Ministries Alliance (FMA), Dr. Winston also has 882 national and international churches and ministries under his spiritual covering.

Dr. Winston's ministry owns and operates two shopping malls, Forest Park Plaza, in Forest Park, and Washington Plaza in Tuskegee. He is also the founder and CEO of Golden Eagle Aviation, a fixed base operation (FBO) located at the historic Moton Field in Tuskegee.

Dr. Winston received his Honorary Doctorate of Humane Letters from Friends International Christian University and has received numerous awards and honors for his leadership in ministry, entrepreneurship, and community development. He is married to Veronica and is the father of three, Melody, Allegra and David, and the grandfather of eight.

BOOKS BY BILL WINSTON

- *Climbing Without Compromise*

- *Possessing Your Mountain*

- *The God Kind of Faith*

- *Born Again and Spirit Filled (English Version & Spanish Version)*

- *Divine Favor: A Gift from God, Expanded Edition*

- *Imitate God and Get Results (English Version & French Version)*

- *Power of the Tongue*

- *Seeding for the Billion Flow*

- *Supernatural Wealth Transfer: Restoring the Earth to Its Rightful Owners*

- *The Kingdom of God in You: Discover the Greatness of God's Power Within*

- *Tapping the Wisdom of God*

- *The Power of Grace*

- *The Power of the Tithe*

- *The Law of Confession: Revolutionize Your Life and Rewrite Your Future with the Power of Words*

- *Training for Reigning: Releasing the Power of Your Potential*

- *Transform Your Thinking, Transform Your Life: Radically Change Your Thoughts, Your World, and Your Destiny*

BILL WINSTON MINISTRIES

We'd like to hear from you!
Please send us your prayer request or praise
report. For more information about Bill Winston
Ministries and a free product catalog, please
write to us or visit us at:

BILL WINSTON MINISTRIES

P.O. Box 974
Oak Park, Illinois 60303-0947
(708) 697-5100
(800) 711-9327
www.billwinston.org
Prayer Call Center
(877) 543-9443

CONNECT WITH US!

www.iTunes.com/billwinston

www.facebook.com/billwinstonministries

www.twitter.com/drbillwinston

www.youtube.com/drbillwinston

pinterest.com/drbillwinston

instagram.com/drbillwinston

www.facebook.com/josephbusinessschool

www.twitter.com/JBSedu

www.jbs.edu